Mismanaging America

STUDIES IN GOVERNMENT
AND PUBLIC POLICY

Mismanaging America

The Rise of the Anti-Analytic Presidency

Walter Williams

 University Press of Kansas

© 1990 by the University Press of Kansas
All rights reserved

Published by the University Press of Kansas (Lawrence, Kansas 66045), which was
organized by the Kansas Board of Regents and is operated and funded by Emporia
State University, Fort Hays State University, Kansas State University, Pittsburg State
University, the University of Kansas, and Wichita State University

Library of Congress Cataloging-in-Publication Data

Williams, Walter.
    Mismanaging America : the rise of the anti-analytic presidency /
Walter Williams.
        p.   cm. — (Studies in government and public policy)
    Includes bibliographical references and index.
    ISBN 0-7006-0446-4 (alk. paper)
    1. Administrative agencies—United States.   2. Executive
departments—United States.   3. Political planning—United States.
4. Policy sciences.   5. United States—Politics and
government—1945-   I. Title.   II. Series.
JK421.W475   1990
353.07'2—dc20   90-38704
                                                                        CIP

British Library Cataloguing in Publication Data is available.

Printed in the United States of America

10 9 8 7 6 5 4 3 2 1

The paper used in this publication meets the minimum requirements of the
American National Standard for Permanence of Paper for Printed
Library Materials. Z39.48-1984.

In memory of the
Office of Economic Opportunity
May America begin again its quest for the Great Society.

Contents

Preface

My basic concern in this book is how to organize and staff the executive branch to increase the availability to the president of sound policy information and analysis, to strengthen presidential governance, and to increase the capacity of government agencies to manage the president's policies. Three factors are of particular significance. First is the increasing importance of expert policy information, analysis, and advice for public decisionmaking and the ensuing analytic revolution. Second is the decline of institutional analytic capacity throughout the executive branch. Finally, there is the deterioration in executive branch policy management capability that reached crisis proportions in the Reagan years. The stage is set by the deleterious outcomes of Reagan policies that have left the nation with massive budget and trade deficits, public sector underinvestment in physical and human capital that threatens the status of the United States as the world's economic superpower, and a widening gap between rich and poor that can tear apart the nation's social fabric. My most critical argument is the causal linkage between cutbacks in expert policy information and analytic capacity, the poor policies and inept presidential governance that followed, and the policy outcomes that put the United States on a declining path as an economic superpower. Both the gravity of the economic and social problems and the severe restrictions on presidential policy choices, because of the two deficits and the unwillingness to raise federal income taxes, place a heavy burden on future presidents. Future presidents must have an Executive Office of the President (EOP) producing sound policy information, analysis, and advice if they are to govern effectively. Reagan was the first explicitly anti-analytic president, launching a war on information and policy analysis. However, earlier presidents, who were anti-bureaucratic, anti-government, or both, reduced the value of sound policy information and analysis by diminishing the managerial capacity of the executive branch to use analytic products. The bitter legacy is an executive branch institutional structure in an advanced state of disrepair — a hollow, incompetent executive government.

This is the second book from a project begun in 1980 to look at policymaking at the top of the American and British governments. The first, *Washington, Westminster and Whitehall* (Cambridge: Cambridge University Press, 1988), treated British government from the perspective of my involvement in Washington policy analysis and management efforts during the Johnson years and subsequent research that focused on these issues. The institutional focus continues as I trace the development of executive branch analytic processes and explore the importance of the inherent structural interconnection of White House policy information, analysis, and advice with agency policy management. At the same time the role of White House policy analysts should not be overemphasized. The key players are the top generalist policy advisers, who seldom are policy analysts. These advisers often have failed to develop the White House policymaking structure sufficiently to produce sound policy information and analysis and to synthesize policy and political factors so that policy analysis would be useful to the president and his inner circle. I argue that the executive branch analytic and managerial structure is broken and badly needs a major institutional fix. But institutional magic alone cannot set things right; the leadership imperative remains. The study of White House policy analysis must be far-ranging and ultimately needs to treat the presidency in its policy and political dimensions, particularly the indelible interrelationships between politics and policy.

One point driven home to me over nearly a decade of study is how much individual political leaders matter. Reagan, central to the study, was the first truly charismatic president since Franklin Roosevelt. Despite innumerable misstatements, gross mismanagement, and significant policy failures that would have destroyed other presidents, Reagan thrived. Even the Iran-Contra scandal held down his popularity rating for only a few months. He left office with the highest ending approval ratings in history. Such charismatic political power was critical in the case of policy analysis and advice. Ronald Reagan launched an eight-year war on policy information and analysis and more broadly on the institutional capacity of the executive branch; he won. The most ideological president in memory, certain of the rightness of his policies without needing facts and figures, became the first modern anti-analytic president. His unconcern with or distaste for expert policy information, analysis and advice led to the destruction of much of the institutional analytic capacity built up in the executive branch in the postwar period as Reagan cut deeply into the personnel, budgets, and influence of analytic and evaluation units. Just as he stood astride the American political scene for much of his two terms, Reagan dominated the institutional process in the executive branch.

Presidents shape the EOP institutional structure, not the other way around. Effective presidential governance demands both political and organizational mastery. The former derives from the president's capacity to exercise influence on his party, the Congress, interest groups, and the people. Organizational mastery involves command of the institutions of government. Political mastery is the first critical need, the fundamental requirement for a successful elected official. Politics alone can win the presidency. As the Reagan years have made so clear, political mastery can create a favorable presidential image in the face of failing policies. Moreover, a strong political base is a necessary element of organizational mastery. Competent presidential governance also depends, however, on the president's mastery of the machinery of government. A basic argument in the book is that in the last three decades, organizational mastery has been the critical missing link of effective presidential governance.

Although structural reform of the presidency is the central focus of the book, it travels a long route from the EOP policy units to the ballot boxes where presidents are selected. The trip is not a line between two distant points, however, but more of a circle. The voters' presidential choice becomes the central person determining the quantity and quality of policy information, analysis, and advice in the executive branch and the capacity of the federal agencies to implement and manage the nation's policies. Ultimately, we must confront the fundamental assumption by the Founding Fathers that U.S. democracy depends on citizens' willingness to exercise the effort needed to choose a president wisely. That effort in the era of expert policy information and the analytic revolution has become far more difficult than the men of the eighteenth century could have imagined. Nevertheless, the critical obligatory choice remains in the voters' hands. Their picking a president who lacks analytic and strategic capabilities and organizational wisdom can blight executive branch analytic and managerial efforts and yield inept governance and undesirable policy outcomes. No amount of institutional change is likely to camouflage such a president's organizational incompetence.

Effective presidential governance demands a president who can balance policy, organization, and politics. Students of structural reform of the presidency cannot slight politics; nor can students of presidential political leadership spurn organizational factors. There is a real danger that EOP institutional reformers will ignore politics and make a sound organizational and analytic structure an end in itself, not a means. This tendency to downplay politics is likely to be more pronounced if the focus is on the analytic structure, where hard-edged policy analysis is a dominant issue. The policy analyst is often cast as objective and nonpartisan, turning out unobjectionable numbers and analyses. I reject such an approach. Top policy analysts must be partisans both in seeking ways to fulfill the goals of their political masters and in selling their policy advice in the political-bureaucratic arena. But partisanship does not absolve policy analysts of the need to produce credible information and analysis. Credible data are the stock-in-trade of policy analysts. Nor does politics overturn basic organizational imperatives. Those who seek institutional reforms in the White House policymaking structure must range far and wide, lest they trap themselves in strictly organizational or political concerns. They must understand that structural reforms to undergird a managerial presidency are necessary to serve political objectives and are not themselves a final goal.

The themes of interconnectedness and balance dominate the book. Policy and politics, politics and management, policy analysis and management – all are interrelated. Indeed, from a policy perspective, these factors are not only interconnected, but inseparable. Most often the interconnection demands trade-offs. The critical need is for balance. A primary argument of the book is that politics and policy have been out of kilter in the presidential policy equation during the last quarter century and that this imbalance increased significantly in the eight years of the Reagan administration. Government, as it became fashionable to say in the Reagan era, is the problem. But that is only half the story. Government is also the solution. The need is for corrective action toward greater organizational mastery by presidents and sounder White House structure and staffing. The most critical aspect of organizational reform is not structural, but political, in the choice of a president who first and foremost must be a political master. At the margin, however, he needs enough organizational ability to balance politics and policy and to lead the structural and staffing reforms required to put the two in good working balance. At issue is not whether those of us who write on the presidency recognize that politics and policy are interrelated – obviously they are – but whether presidents and their top staff can see the interconnection and better balance them in the heat of White House policymaking.

I write in anger and frustration, with a sense of urgency. I came to the Office of Economic Opportunity – Lyndon Johnson's flagship for his War on Poverty – at the apex of the United States' power as the world's economic hegemon and of its confidence in its ability to combat poverty and other problems. Government was the solution. America moved over two decades from the high hopes of the early Great Society years with its concern for the plight of the poor and the disadvantaged, to the Reagan era that fostered greed, consumerism, and overt rejection of federal responsibility for the needy. Not only did the Reagan administration cut domestic aid funds, it grossly mismanaged them, as in the case of the Department of Housing and Urban Development (HUD), by using the diminished funds to benefit the wealthy more than the poor. Even more damaging may be the policies that led to massive foreign debt and economic weakness. All these problems cry out for immediate action. I am not simply focusing on structure and staffing for its own sake. My ultimate concern is sound presidential domestic policies and better presidential performance. Tempting as it is, however, I forgo offering specific prescriptions for new domestic policy initiatives; I believe inept presidential governance is the critical barrier blocking the effective pursuit of sound policies. Federal domestic policies cannot be successful unless the government is competent, and that requires major structural reforms in the executive branch. The ultimate need is for people at the top with sufficient integrity and analytic and managerial competence to develop and implement effective policies.

Acknowledgments

My greatest debt is to a number of unnamed interviewees, particularly those who graciously agreed to lengthy interviews on several occasions over a ten-year period. A number of people read part or all of the manuscript: Richard Brandon, Brewster Denny, Fred Greenstein, Harry Havens, Robert Levine, Peter May, William Morrill, and Joseph Pika. The German Marshall Fund and the Graduate School of Public Affairs, University of Washington, provided financial support for the study. However, I am solely responsible for the final product. Finally, I am especially indebted to the staff of the University Press of Kansas, who did a masterly job of cutting and tightening the manuscript and eliminating my purple prose, and to Karen McLaughlin, who typed and retyped the manuscript.

1

Expert Information, the Analytic Revolution, and Presidential Governance

The United States is *the* information society. Washington, more than any other capital in the world, has incredible numbers of people developing, procuring, selling, trading, analyzing, and often hiding information. Increasingly, the most valuable information in the government is the "expert policy information" that requires specialized knowledge to develop and analyze. The thick computer printout or the slick report from a think tank are the apt images. Expert policy information fuels the vast government organizations. Expert information fuels the presidency.

Of particular concern are those experts who use their specialized knowledge and techniques to aid generalist policymakers in the decisionmaking process. These policy experts — the economist is the prototypical example — do not just produce the numbers, they analyze and interpret data in support of policymaking. And they are a fairly recent addition to the Washington policy circle. In his 1980 update of *Presidential Power*, written in 1960, Richard Neustadt observed: "Two big things in Washington that, relatively speaking, were but small things twenty years ago are television news and the professional crowd."[1] Television news is the average person's main source of information and analysis about politics and public policy. The professional crowd increasingly is made up of policy specialists who develop expert information and policy analysis and of sophisticated users of their products. Much like television, data and statistics (although many may not apply this nomenclature) are now so commonplace that little thought is given to how the plethora of information is developed and analyzed or how it is verified for accuracy or for soundness of interpretation. And that is a crucial problem. The information explosion has outrun the nation's competence to make sense of the deluge of data in forms ranging from the offerings of the mass media to the esoteric products of universities and think tanks. Nowhere is the information explosion problem more critical than in the White House.

The numbers — particularly expert information — have overwhelmed American policymaking, creating a profound dilemma. Policy problems grow more and more complex, so that expert information and the policy analyses required to cope with them are needed increasingly by policymakers and the public. The information explosion begat an analytic revolution. At the same time the distrust of policy experts and their products has increased dramatically. Moreover, few developments of the last decade have been more discouraging than the extent to which citizens have come to distrust their government. And many of the problems centered on expert information and how it is controlled. Information is there to be used wisely or unwisely. Or it is not available because a government chooses not to get it or to hide it; or it is used with evil intent. As Elliot Richardson observed of Watergate: "In a sense, all abuses of Watergate have been abuses of information: its theft, distortion, fabrication, misuse, misrepresentation, concealment, and suppression."[2]

Overt abuse is not the only danger. At the heart of the American brand of democracy has always been the notion of a responsible citizenry willing and able to obtain the information needed to choose competent representatives. Those who framed American government saw an informed public as crucial to the hard scrutiny of those who govern. To cut citizens off from information or to cast it in terms that are difficult to understand is to bar them from significant involvement in critical public governance decisions that affect the tenor and quality of their lives. But how are the people to deal with the deluge of expert information and policy analysis? Frank Fischer has written: "In the 'knowledge society' expertise has become a key commodity essential for political power. . . . As a system of decisionmaking geared toward expert knowledge, technocracy . . . necessarily blocks meaningful participation for the average citizen. Ultimately only those who can interpret the complex technical languages that increasingly frame economic and social issues have access to the play of power."[3] In this modern world, no one can imagine sound governance without expert information and analytic frameworks for developing and interpreting it. But if expert information and knowledge increase the power to cope, they also increase the power to obscure or to avoid judgment and commitment. The paraphernalia of modern science offers the finest smoke screen yet invented for hiding from responsibility behind the high principle that more information is needed before interpretation is warranted.

Two critical questions predominate. First, can we find a workable means of using expert information and policy analysis that is compatible with democratic principles in the current complexity of American society? Second, can the federal government in general — and the presidency in particular — use this information to cope successfully with the economic and social problems that confront the United States? Drawing partly on his own service in several administrations, Bradley Patterson wrote of White House staffs: "In government, as in every institution, information is blood. Clamp it off from any part and the member cannot function."[4] Not only must information flow, it must be interpreted. The demand is for a new breed of presidential policy adviser.

THE RISE OF INSTITUTIONAL DOMESTIC POLICY ANALYSIS

As the War on Poverty burgeoned in the 1960s, President Lyndon Johnson sought to deal with the growing quantity of expert policy information flowing from the just-initiated social programs through a new set of institutions — policy analysis offices in federal agencies. The analytic revolution started in earnest. Based on work done in the 1950s by the Rand Corporation, the military think tank, Secretary Robert McNamara in 1961 had started the first full-blown analytic office at the Department of Defense (DOD) under Charles Hitch, a Rand alumnus. Following suit, the Office of Economic Opportunity (OEO) at its inception in mid-1964 set up the first analytic office in the domestic policy arena, but that office did not become fully operational for nearly a year. Impressed by the DOD office, Johnson in October 1965 initiated the Planning, Programming, Budgeting System (PPBS) in the federal government by requiring all major executive branch agencies to "establish an adequate central staff or staffs for analysis [with] . . . the head of the . . . analytic staff . . . directly responsible to the head of the agency or his deputy." The basic tasks of the analytic offices were to develop information, policy analysis, and advice in support of decisionmaking by agency heads and other key policymakers. The charge to these offices was to scrutinize programs and policies and hence be skeptical of them. Rigorous evaluations of how well agency programs were working became a critical activity. A few of the agency domestic policy analysis offices, particularly the ones at OEO and the (then) Department of Health, Education, and Welfare (HEW), flowered in the remainder of the Johnson years. Policy analysis gained momentum in the Nixon administration; indeed, the Johnson/Nixon years in retrospect were the golden period for executive branch policy analysis. Although it did subsequently level off, policy analysis continued to have an important place in executive branch policymaking up to the start of the Reagan administration.

Beginning the discussion of the institutionalizing of policy analysis in the federal government with PPBS does not mean there were no precursor offices, such as the Department of State's highly influential Policy Planning Staff started in 1947 and first directed by George F. Kennan. Laurence Lynn, who headed analytic offices in several domestic agencies in the Nixon/Ford years, wrote in 1989 to explicate this starting point:

> But what was new? Certainly it was not the use of information created in the spirit of scientific inquiry to inform policy. . . . What seemed to

be new a quarter of a century ago was the self-conscious incorporation of policy analysis and policy analysts as a matter of principle into the central direction of large, complex government organizations. A new group of staff officers — policy analysts — answerable only to the organization's senior executive, were given privileged access to that executive and were empowered to speak for that executive in a variety of forums. Almost overnight, the views of young, professionally trained analysts came to matter, and to matter visibly and decisively, in important matters of state. Henceforth the result of bureaucratic politics would reflect the influence of these policy analysts — the influence of their ideas and of their access to power.[5]

The typical early policy analysts at the top were Ph.D. economists out of academia or, more likely, think tanks — in the Johnson era three of the four heads of the OEO and HEW analytic offices had been at Rand, and the fourth came from the Brookings Institution, then the dominant domestic policy think tank. What made these policy advisers different from earlier advisers such as lawyers, people with accounting or public administration training, or broad generalists was their mode of thinking. Policy analysis emphasizes trade-offs and choices among alternative policy options after the systematic development and rigorous examination of these alternatives. It is a policy problem-solving approach using a collection of quantitative and qualitative techniques derived from various scientific disciplines — statistical decision theory, operations research, economics — to synthesize relevant information, including research results, to inform policy deliberations and decisionmaking.

To be successful, the policy analyst, like other key agency advisers, must be a skilled practitioner of bureaucratic politics. Giandomenico Majone has observed that the policy analyst's "basic skills are not algorithmical but argumentative."[6] However, the scientific base is the analyst's comparative advantage in the decisionmaking process, a key factor distinguishing the policy analyst's advice from that of other policy advisers. The scientific base also should constrain how far the analyst will go in using techniques and information. The apt analogy is to boxing under Marquis of Queensbury rules instead of a back-alley fight with no holds barred. Analytic advocacy is bounded by the rules of acceptable practice but is still partisan. At the top it is clear that the analyst is more the advocate than the scientist as he or she engages in bureaucratic politics. The analytic product most often must be argued and sold in a highly charged political setting.

Critical to the success of agency central analytic offices was support from the agency head, who had to provide high status for the top analyst and the organizational resources needed to establish and maintain a strong analytic presence. In the decade and a half between the PPBS directive establishing the agency analytic offices and the start of the Reagan administration, a number of agency offices were granted the needed top-level support and gained sufficient power and competence to provide a useful flow of expert information and policy analyses in support of agency decisionmaking.

Strong analytic staffs developed in the EOP. The Office of Management and Budget (OMB), with its large component of career civil servants near the top of its structure, was the place the president and his senior advisers could get hard analysis without partisan political spin on it. The National Security Council (NSC) staff, too, developed a reputation for solid analysis. The Council of Economic Advisers (CEA), created by the 1946 Full Employment Act, has on occasion had a major domestic policy advisory role beyond its economic advice, particularly in the 1960s in the development of the War on Poverty. While the White House domestic policy units under various names — Carter's Domestic Policy Staff (DPS) and Reagan's Office of Policy Development (OPD) — did not have such a strong reputation for critical analysis, they too became a major supplier of policy advice for the president. In addition, the top policy and political advisers generally are in the West Wing, which is part of the White House Office.[7] *Hereafter the terms Executive Office of the President (EOP) and White House will be used interchangeably.* After all, the EOP is the president's office mainly to do with as he likes.[8]

Congressional policy analysis began to flourish after passage of the 1974 Budget Act, which established a new budget process, Senate and House Budget Committees and staffs, and the Congressional Budget Office (CBO). CBO had as its first director and deputy director Alice Rivlin and Robert Levine, who in the 1960s headed the strong central analytic offices at the Department of Health, Education and Welfare and the Office of Economic Opportunity respectively. The CBO leaders saw as the first need a critical mass of capable, experienced policy analysts such as those found in the federal executive branch. Once CBO began to gain a reputation for analytic competence and to win influence, other offices, such as the Congressional Research Service (CRS) and the Office of Technology Assessment (OTA), followed suit in developing analytic capability. The General Accounting Office (GAO), which had started earlier to shed its image as an audit agency, strengthened its policy analysis capability. GAO was the first congressional agency to move into hard analysis and evaluation. This experience led GAO to begin the continuing process of diversifying its staff; formerly composed mainly of accountants, it began to include more people with advanced degrees in various disciplines. In addition, congressional committees increased their staff analytic competence, which not only carried out independent analysis but facilitated using the analytic work of GAO, CBO, CRS, and OTA.[9]

The story in the executive branch is quite different. Peter May indicates that between 1980 and 1988 eight agency analytic offices for which he could develop data suffered a 43 percent decline in staff while three congressional offices stayed constant.[10] These numbers tell only half the story. The qualitative changes involving declining competence and influence in agency analytic offices and the EOP were more drastic yet.

Despite significant reductions in policy analysis capacity in the executive branch during the Reagan years, policy analysis has been a growth industry since the 1960s, developing not only at the national level but in both the executive and legislative branches of state and local government.[11] Perhaps the most important change at all levels of government has been the diffusion of policy analysts into staffs that are not separate analytic units. Budget staffs are a clear case in point, but policy analysts also serve on agency operational staffs and legislative committee staffs. As a result, analytic thinking has spread deeply in the executive and legislative processes at all levels of government. The message of the roughly two decades of analytic experience of the 1960s and 1970s is that policy analysis is most useful when it is institutionalized in a continuing process of analysis and evaluation that informs decision-making in the White House, the agencies, and Congress. Over time the analytic process in the executive branch should yield both prospective estimates of how well programs are likely to work and retrospective evaluations of how well programs actually did work. Credible analyses and evaluations should be a key element in policy debates in the executive branch and between that branch and Congress. Indeed, in the era of expert information, sound analysis and evaluation over time should be the mark of credible government.

POLICY ADVISERS AND PRESIDENTIAL GOVERNANCE

The label "policy adviser" covers a broad band of people from the highly quantitative, model-building policy economists to the "generalist generalists" who lack any particular policy analysis skills or experience. In the latter case it is anyone the president chooses to listen to or designate as policy adviser, be it a presidential campaign loyalist, a spouse, or a political crony. Furthermore, policy units that use policy information and analyses to develop policy advice range from those dominated by and staffed exclusively by policy analysts to those staffed by persons without policy analysis skills. Moreover, what has been a policy analysis unit may cease to be one. All presidents have policy advisers, but whether the advisers will be policy analysts depends on many circumstances. For example, a president may not know what distinguishes the product of policy analysis from policy advice based on other frameworks, such as legal thinking. The Carter administration is a case in point. Both the president and his top domestic policy adviser, Stuart Eizenstat, were unclear about what differentiated policy analysis, and Eizenstat's DPS had few competent policy analysts. Though Carter and Eizenstat were both bright and "analytic," the former drew on an engineering framework and the latter on a legal one.

Policy Analysts and Other Policy Advisers

The label "policy analyst" itself applies to a fairly wide range of people. The prototypical image of the policy analyst remains that of the "hard-edged" type with a doctorate in economics and an economic model to fit any situation. Some of these analysts think that they are doing rigorous, neutral, objective studies without any taint of political partisanship or ideology. These purists have their role outside the government policy office or inside it, if supervised by more realistic policy analysts who recognize the importance of political feasibility and organizational imperatives.[12] Far more important are policy analysts who also have Ph.D.s in economics but who combine technical analysis and advocacy. Here is one place to find the generalist policy adviser who knows policy substance and analytic techniques and can also think in terms of the big picture. Another important type of policy analyst is more program oriented, with a technical background probably from public administration, accounting, or budgeting; with experience that includes extensive government service, probably in a staff, as opposed to a line position; and with a policy problem-solving approach that may have been acquired on the job. These program examiner policy analysts may lack the research tools of the Ph.D. economist policy analysts, but they can bring to a policy issue a sound analytic focus. They compensate for this lack of technical research capability by having a greater understanding of the bureaucracy and its peculiarities. A third type of policy analyst, more similar to the economists than to the program examiners, are policy-oriented people from academic disciplines other than economics. There is also a growing number of people with masters' degrees or doctorates from public policy schools that prepare their graduates specifically to do policy analysis. The critical need is for a balancing and blending of skills so that policy analysis benefits not just from hard-edged economic rigor but from political and bureaucratic thinking and from the work in other academic disciplines.

Policy analysts, if they are to be effective in government, must work and confront other policy advisers and political advisers. As we move to the top in the executive branch agencies and the White House, partisan politics becomes an integral element. Nothing could be more wrong than a technocratic approach by presidential policy analysts or policy analysis units that try to be above partisanship, above ideology, above the fray, turning out allegedly "objective" data on which all can agree. Such an approach fails to recognize the inadequacies of the available policy analysis tools and techniques. The competent policy analyst must be neither a pure politician nor a pure scientist, but a person who can successfully balance policy and bureaucratic politics.

The most critical presidential policy need is for generalist advisers who are competent users of the analytic product. The actions of these top policy advisers determine the degree to which a president will be linked to the analytic process of the executive branch. A failure to make this key linkage or to insure the reliability, relevance, and timeliness of the analytic process means a president does not have an adequate basis for policymaking. Policy analysis capacity is essential for top policy advisers, but it is not enough. Competent policy adviser generalists must be able to move beyond narrow, technical analysis to integrate broad policies and synthesize across policy and politics so as to link the White House institutional analytic process to presidential policymaking. That the policy analysis units' stock-in-trade should be sound information, analysis, and advice is not a normative judgment but a reading of the evidence that policy analysts need credibility to work and advocate effectively in the policy/political process.

A Model Linking Policy Analysis,
Presidential Governance, and Desired Outcomes

It is useful for discussion purposes to set out a model that indicates the relationship of policy advice and analysis to presidential domestic policy governance and ties the president to desired societal outcomes. The model assumes that there are grants-in-aid to states and localities for complex domestic programs that are funded in whole or in part by the federal government but operated in the field by subnational governments. The seven factors in the model are: (1) a sound EOP structural process and competent analytic staff that will yield (2) relevant, timely, reliable policy information, analysis, and advice that provide a base to develop (3) well-formulated policies that support (4) effective presidential governance that leads to (5) well-implemented and well-managed federal policy efforts by the executive branch agencies that produce (6) well-implemented and well-managed subnational government programs that produce (7) desired societal outcomes.

Several points are important. First, the requirements for a sound EOP structural process must be spelled out. The Tower Commission expressed one critical aspect of soundness in its charge to the national security adviser: "It is his responsibility to ensure that matters submitted for consideration by the [National Security] Council cover the full range of issues on which review is required; that those issues are fully analyzed; that a full range of options is considered; that the prospects and risks of each are examined; that all relevant intelligence and other information is available to the principals . . . that difficulties in implementation are confronted."[13] A sound institutional process in action will thoroughly air an issue, including the hearing of opposing views by advocates. Furthermore, it will ensure an adequate flow of advice, information, and analysis over time in the White House and executive agencies. These demands, of course, require competent analytic staff. Second, presidential domestic policy governance in the model is used broadly with the responsibility for leading and managing the executive branch, resting with the president and his political appointees. Such a statement denies neither the role of Congress nor the roles of the career civil servants. Nor does it aggrandize the president and downplay the agencies. The statement, however, does affirm the president's responsibility to govern. Third, an EOP structure will be sound only if it ties the White House to the agencies, since the latter bear responsibility both for the executive branch in-depth analyses, which EOP policy staffs will draw on, and for the implementation of the president's policies. This institutional link between the White House and the federal agencies is critical.

Fourth, the decision was made to have presidential governance precede executive branch implementation and management efforts (factor 5) in order to emphasize that a president has dominant direct control over the first three factors, in contrast to sharing direct control with the agencies and Congress over agency implementation and management efforts. Like first three factors, however, the latter is a critical aspect of presidential governance. Serving both the president and the Congress in a setting of interest group politics makes it difficult, if not impossible, to establish a rational agency design driven mainly or exclusively by outcome performance criteria. As Terry Moe put it, "American public bureaucracy [the executive branch agencies] is not designed to be effective. The bureaucracy arises out of politics, and its design reflects the interests, strategies and compromises of those who exercise political power. . . . The problem is inherent in our democratic system as a whole, and it is our basic framework of political institutions, not the bureaucracy, that must be reformed if solutions are to be found. That is a big job, and perhaps an impossible one."[14] But the underlying government structure of the United States is the hand dealt the president.

Fifth, the critical feature of the model is the interconnectedness of the factors. Each is related to the others, so that failure early in the causal chain— e.g., an unsound EOP structural process and incompetent analytic staff— portends failure later on. Even the president in most policy settings is still rather far back in the chain. In federal grants-in-aid to states and localities, the federal agencies may provide the funds to states, which in turn grant them to localities. Not only will Congress, here as elsewhere, be a key actor, at times as central or more central than the president, but both Congress and the president may be far removed from the real action. In complex domestic programs, it is not necessarily the major decisions made by the president or Congress or the top federal agency people, but the management and delivery capacity of local organizations providing services directly that will determine the degree to which those served receive significant benefits. Here is the field implementation problem in the complexity of shared governance as it manifests itself in fifty states and hundreds of communities. American federalism makes management from the center far more difficult in the United States than in other advanced democracies.[15]

Finally, and this is critical, each factor cited is likely to be only one of several. For example, not included are "deep" structural factors such as those set out in the Constitution, over which a president has little or no control. Both politics generally and congressional politics specifically are left out of the model for expository purposes. Politics, and its interrelationship with policy, however, is discussed extensively. Moreover, as we move toward the final desired outcomes, factors outside the model loom larger and larger. Such factors as the international economy, technology, socioeconomic class, and income and wealth distributions are likely to have far more impact on final outcomes than anything the government does explicitly to treat the policy problems in question. One of the most vexing aspects of public policy is that by far the most significant factors are either totally outside the policymaker's control (exogenous factors), or they are amenable only to slow incremental changes. The model is not only probabilistic, but the probabilities decline as we move from (1) to (7). The fall will be especially sharp after effective presidential governance as a president's control diminishes. Moreover, the harm that weak EOP structure and incompetent staff causes far outweighs the good that strong structure and competent staff can effect. This asymmetry, it is critical to underscore, does not derive from logic but from experience. I emphasize factors (1) through (3) because the quality of EOP structure and staffing; of expert policy information, analysis and advice; and of presidentially formulated policies are the points of maximum presidential control. If the president mishandles these factors, the likelihood of good outcomes is materially reduced.

We should not fall into the trap of absolute determinism, stating baldly that failure early in the causal chain will bring deleterious policy outcomes. Exogenous factors can make presidents look good or bad without their having done much right *or* wrong — OPEC (Organization of Petroleum Exporting Countries) oil prices soaring in the 1970s and plunging in the early 1980s are a case in point. However, it is not only that the presidents have far more direct control that leads me to emphasize presidential governance and the first three factors in the model. A major hypothesis is that inept presidential governance has done great harm in recent presidencies and is a critical pivotal factor in the policy equation. Sound presidential governance is still only a means to the end of better societal outcomes, never an end in itself.

Postulating that inept presidential governance is a critical factor affecting outcomes raises a thorny problem: Can it be shown that what the government does through its inputs, such as organizational structure, or its outputs, such as policy decisions, affects outcomes? In short, does analytic structure, staffing, and process affect outcomes? There is no definitive answer. However, recent work by Irving Janis on how the quality of the U.S. policymaking process affected outcome variables for the effectiveness of U.S. crisis management in nineteen major international crises shows a strong correlation between the "quality of [the analytic] procedures used to arrive at a fundamental policy decision . . . [and] a successful outcome."[16] Janis observes: "The use of the vigilant problem-solving strategy must be considered as only one of the major determinants of successful versus unsuccessful consequences of policy decisions—but one worthy of special emphasis because, unlike all other determinants, it is largely *under the control of policy makers themselves.*"[17] Janis's list of steps in "vigilant" or "high-quality" problem solving is the standard policy analysis format that stresses determining objectives; undertaking an intensive information search; developing a wide range of alternatives; determining benefits, costs, and trade-offs; and providing for implementation and monitoring of the chosen alternative. The available evidence provides support for the claim that high-quality policy analysis facilitates effective decisionmaking, while at the same time recognizing the basic assumption of the causal model, that other variables may be much more important.

THE PROBLEM OF EXPERT POLICY INFORMATION TODAY

Three dramatic changes over the last three decades since the start of the first policy analysis unit at DOD have intensified the expert-information dilemma. First is the widening gap between policy complexity and the technical and organizational competence to treat it. Despite both dramatic improvements in our policy analysis tools and techniques over the last thirty years and a far greater number of competent policy analysts inside and outside government, policy analysts have fallen further behind in their ability to cope with increasingly complex policy problems. Rapidly increasing policy complexity complicates the federal decisionmaking process. Key policy actors and institutions are victims of mounting policy complexity. The uneven footrace between policy complexity and analytic competence has made the treatment of policy information more difficult and has decreased the credibility of experts. Today it is harder for journeymen policy analysts, chief policy analysts, and generalist policy advisers to cope effectively with policy problems. Richard Brandon has suggested that policy may be no more complex than in the 1960s but seems so today because policy analysts now know more. This knowledge comes partly from improved techniques and partly from competition among the growing number of policy analysts. The latter is the more critical development, as no analysis goes unchallenged in a world of competent analyst advocates on all sides of the issues. Findings in the 1960s may have been no more robust than they are today, but current policy analysts, in knowing more, see their proposals as less robust. Greater knowledge may bring less, rather than more, confidence in policy proposals because the more knowledge there is, the more difficulties the analyst can see.

The second big change is the increased politicization and centralization of the presidency. Presidents have became less trusting of career civil servants and far more willing to undercut White House agency linkages that support the development and flow of policy information and analysis. Since the end of the Eisenhower administration, power has shifted dramatically to political appointees in the White House, at the expense of the agencies and the EOP careerists. Terry Moe argues that a president does not want "neutral" competence, which is likely to be dispensed by civil servants, but rather "responsive" competence provided by political appointees.[18] Responsive competence, however, can degenerate into just plain responsiveness driven by personal loyalty to the "man," without much competence. Paul Light has made the counterargument in advising presidents to "hire expertise."[19]

Presidents from Kennedy to Reagan built up the analytic capacity in the EOP and the agencies, with Presidents Lyndon Johnson and Richard Nixon bringing policy analysis to a high point in the executive branch. Sound policy advice was at a premium as a critical element in White House policy formulation. At the same time, beginning with Kennedy, presidents were undercutting the usefulness of the expert policy information and analysis and the policies formulated from them by bad management practices that lessened materially the capacity of the departments and agencies to implement and operate programs. No matter how sound the policy analysis and advice to the president on specific programs and policies, no matter how well White House policies are formulated, the value is limited if the departments and agencies lack implementation and managerial capacity. By making White House political appointees dominant over politically appointed cabinet secretaries and agency heads, Kennedy and the presidents who followed reduced the agency autonomy and capacity needed for effective policy implementation and management. Although an increase in White House power at the expense of the agencies may make presidents feel more in control politically, the White House can formulate a policy, but the agencies must implement it.

White House policy formulation and agency implementation are often separated in practice. This can be fatal to good policy for several reasons. First, if the White House shuts the agencies out of presidential policymaking, EOP policy units are likely to be cut off from relevant agency policy information and analysis on implementation. Second, in this isolation, as presidential staff seeks to centralize policy formulation in the White House, significant implementation difficulties in presidential programs may not be detected. Or they may be ignored because of the staffs' lack of organizational knowledge or misguided view that implementation barriers will get worked out later as policy moves to the field. Third, if an agency is cut off from formulating key presidential policies when it bears the responsibility of implementation, it may react negatively to this top-down approach. Fourth, even if the agency tries to implement the policy as the president desires, barriers may block or slow down successful implementation. Fifth, White House anger caused by a lack of immediate success might fuel greater distrust of the agency and bring even more effort to monopolize policy formulation in the White House. Presidential policymaking is a seamless web. A president must understand the hard reality of interconnectedness and the formulation-implementation linkage if he is to succeed at the critical presidential task of balancing White House control and agency autonomy.

The third major change is the growing importance of the individual leader in shaping institutional policy analysis and the development of expert information. It is closely related to the previous change but so critical that it must be singled out. The prudent use of policy analysts and analysis depends less on White House or agency institutional structure and process than on the personality, style, experience, and competence of leaders and their top advisers. The point is not that issues of structure, staffing, and process are unimportant. These issues are the critical factors that can be addressed in prescriptive terms, independent of particular presidents. Moreover, we know a fair amount about how to shape and staff the presidential policy process to provide it with strong, competent staffs and with credible information and analysis derived from analytic competition. But, as I. M. Destler points out, "There is only one problem. The president . . . has to agree . . . [and] to behave in a way that reinforces rather than undercuts the system. . . . The president is both solution and problem."[20] Lately, presidents have been far more problem than solution, in part because they and their inner circles have lacked the competence and/or the integrity to act as needed.

REAGAN'S ANTI-GOVERNMENT, ANTI-ANALYTIC PRESIDENCY

Terrel Bell, Reagan's first secretary of education, described Counselor to the President Edwin Meese at the outset of the administration when he was Reagan's chief guide to policy: "Here was a man who literally detested the federal government. He viewed the upcoming Reagan presidency as a magnificent opportunity to smash the government programs that had created a 'welfare state.'"[21] This attitude of detesting government and of not really being a part of "it" — recognizing that "it" means "them," the bureaucrats — marked Reagan's two terms. In his account of trying to run the Department of Education (ED), Secretary Bell singled out for his strongest criticism the highly ideological political executives placed in his midst by the administration that did not fully trust him. Mismanagement resulted as these executives moved into key subcabinet positions. They understood little about how government worked, were overcommitted to rigid principles, and wanted no part of rigorous analysis that might not produce the answers they believed correct.

Reagan began his attack on analytic and institutional capacity immediately by cutting back precipitously on the size, competence, and influence of policy units in the EOP, except for OMB. The critical impact was to give OMB a monopoly on relative analytic competence, thereby mainly elminating meaningful competition at the top of the presidential policy process. Another far-reaching move was to appoint Meese as top policy adviser, despite Meese's limited policy experience and lack of analytic literacy. Meese became "policy czar," occupying the pivotal position linking the president and his other top policy and political advisers to the institutional policy process. When Meese failed to exert control over the policy process and provide policy guidance, OMB Director David Stockman, who had his own ideological agenda, played his, not the president's, game. Meese is a striking example of a top generalist policy adviser without the analytic competence to protect his president. In *The Triumph of Politics*, which he wrote after he left the government, Stockman said, "Designing a comprehensive plan to bring about a sweeping change in national economic governance in forty days is a preposterous, wantonly reckless notion. . . . [President Reagan] had been misled by a crew of overzealous — and ultimately incompetent — advisers."[22] Faulty policy analysis and a circumvented institutional policy process were central to Stockman's pushing through of budget and tax changes that led directly to the massive budget and trade deficits.

By reducing analytic capacity in the NSC staff and providing little management guidance or control in the policy process, Mr. Reagan laid the base for the NSC as a covert operator and its takeover by a "cabal of zealots," to use the words of Congress's Iran-Contra report.[23] There is a strong, clear, direct line between Reagan's anti-analytic actions that began at the outset of his first term and the Iran-Contra scandal. Could a sound policy process have saved the day? The Tower Commission, the President's Special Review Board investigating the Iran-Contra affair, concluded that the initiative lacked informed policy analysis and then wrote pointedly about the NSC process that was supposed to institutionalize in-depth analysis and deliberations: "Process will not always produce brilliant ideas, but history suggests it can at least help prevent bad ideas from becoming presidential policy."[24] However, the choice was made to avoid that process. Secrecy became an obsession. Hard analysis disappeared. Policy analysis and the policy process intended to vet the NSC staff efforts did not fail; they were simply not used.

In November 1988 the GAO characterized executive branch program evaluation and information collection capabilities as being "gravely eroded" and "drying up," and went on to label the drastic decline as a critical problem for democracy.[25] For eight years the Reagan administration cut back precipitously on using hard evaluative techniques, attacking the critical element of the ongoing analytic process that seeks to determine if programs are effective. If Congress itself had *not* mandated evaluation studies by the agencies in legislation, the Reagan cutbacks would have been even more dramatic.

Despite the mandated evaluations, Congress had to depend more and more on its own evaluation resources. The GAO foresaw critical constitutional problems from the drying up in the executive branch agencies: "Agencies may find themselves fenced off from evaluation-based debate about their own programs. . . . [The drawdown] could lead to a serious imbalance between the branches on who calls the shots on information that has become a vital influence in major debates on national policy and that is considered an important indicator of a credible government."[26] One result of eight years of Reagan's anti-analytic presidency has been an executive branch that turns out less and less credible information and analysis. It stopped producing much of the information needed to assess the effectiveness of federal programs and policies. The Reagan analytic gap meant that increasingly Congress and the public either did not know whether policies were working, or they were not sure that the executive branch information could be believed. The drastic cuts in analytic capacity and the misuse of policy information and analysis in the executive branch during the Reagan era came to shield that administration from hard scrutiny, thereby calling into question the accountability of the executive branch to Congress. This accountability is central to democratic governance.

In the same period the United States both showed significant economic gains and suffered the deleterious policy outcomes that appear to be but the tip of the iceberg.[27] The biggest objective gain was the reduction of the double-digit inflation that had become the major economic problem of the 1970s, to a level not seen consistently since the early 1960s. Starting in November 1982, after the worst postwar recession, the United States experiencd the longest peacetime economic expansion since monthly records began to be kept in 1854. Furthermore, wealth rose significantly, particularly in the stock and real estate markets. Juxtaposed against this prosperity were large budget and trade deficits, record indebtedness in both public and private sectors, a drug epidemic, a failing education system, a falling national savings rate, a deteriorating infrastructure, a financial system with grave problems, a growing disparity between rich and poor, the highest percentage of poor children in the advanced industrial nations, and a weakened federal government. Isabel Sawhill, codirector of the Urban Institute's Changing Domestic Priorities project that has tracked the Reagan administration since its inception, argued in her 1986 assessment of the Reagan economic performance: "The United States has experienced periods of *economic mismanagement* in the past, but few, if any of these instances, can rival the current government's tolerance of budget deficits that virtually guarantee poorer productivity performance in the future and a further erosion of America's relative standard of living."[28]

Reagan's performance was not better on the social side. The major indicators measuring the status of America's disadvantaged population worsened materially, as symbolized by the rising number of homeless people. Poverty returned to pre–Great Society levels with a devastating impact on children, especially those in female-headed families. During the Reagan period of extended growth, the poverty rate for children rose from 18.1 percent in 1980 to 20.4 percent in 1987, having reached a high of 22.2 percent in 1983.[29] In the period from 1979 to 1987, average family cash income in 1987 dollars for all families with children fell by over 20 percent for the lowest income quintile (from $8,502 to $6,733) and 8 percent for the next lowest quintile, while the highest quintile rose slightly over 12 percent ($66,219 to $74,264).[30] The Joint Economic Committee of the U.S. Congress noted that the official Census Bureau statistics show the largest income gap between rich and poor since the series started in the late 1940s and then stated that "the cutbacks of human resource programs in the early 1980s, especially Aid to Families with Dependent Children, Medicaid, and food stamps for working poor and near-poor families, clearly increased [income] inequality."[31]

To his credit, President Reagan restored U.S. confidence. But to do so he depicted an America that no longer existed — an America without limits. It was the politics of unreality that induced a false confidence and an ensuing consumption binge. The *Economist* described the massive consumer overspending and undersaving that characterized the Reagan era:

> Americans celebrated eight years of Reaganism with a spectacular spending spree. In the 1980s the annual rise in national output per head averaged just over 1%. But real personal consumer spending per head has risen by nearly 3% a year. People's savings have fallen . . . from 7% of disposable income in 1980 to a shade over 3% in 1987. . . .
>
> Rising consumption has been financed by higher borrowing. . . . Consumer installment-credit outstanding . . . more than doubled in the 1980s, from $300 billion to $660 billion. The plastic splurge has been even more striking. Credit-card debt was $50 billion when Mr. Reagan took office in 1981. Today it stands at $180 billion, over 5% of people's income.[32]

The massive borrowing from other nations was not used to build new private-sector capacity. Moreover, the federal government postponed badly needed public investment in physical and human capital. The postponed bills, as estimated by the GAO in late 1988, were staggering: $50 to $100 billion to shore up the bankrupt savings and loan institutions; $150 billion to clean up nuclear waste and modernize the environmentally hazardous nuclear weapons production system; $50 billion to repair or replace 240,000 deficient bridges; $315 billion to maintain (not improve) highways in their 1983 condition; and $20 billion to repair the deteriorating stock of public housing.[33] The GAO list ran to hundreds of billions of dollars, and the cost calculations are already turning out to be much too low. For example, the Bush administration in March 1989 projected roughly 500 more savings and loan (S&L) associations failing for a cost of $159 billion over ten years, but the Office of Thrift Supervision (part of the new S&L regulatory structure) in December 1989 estimated that nearly 1,000 S&Ls would fail in 1990.[34] The costs estimated by GAO at $50 to $100 billion seem to be moving toward $500 billion. Even more important could be the human investment needed in the areas of education and health. Recent surveys place the United States at or near the bottom among wealthy nations in comparisons among elementary and high school students in science, mathematics, geography, and history. There now seems little doubt that the United States has the least cost-effective health system among the advanced western nations, with by far the highest costs, not only in absolute terms but expressed as a percent of gross national product (GNP). Despite these outlays, the United States has relatively high mortality rates, and an estimated 37 million people are not covered by health insurance. Long-time civil rights activist Marian Wright Edelman, president of the Children's Defense Fund, after pointing out that the United States is eighteenth in the world in overall infant mortality and twenty-sixth for black babies, argues that "at a time when future demographic trends guarantee a shortage of young adults who will be workers, soldiers, leaders, and parents, America cannot afford to waste a single child, not even the poorest, blackest one."[35]

The Reagan administration's defense build-up and tax cuts not only took funds from the needy but drained scarce resources away from nondefense technology investment. The United States has a few more engineers in research than does Japan, but we have used them disproportionately in defense work, so Japan has a larger nondefense engineering effort than does the United States. The United States, which from the mid-1960s until 1981 had split federal research and development (R&D) evenly between defense and nondefense efforts, ended the Reagan years spending two-thirds for defense. In the Reagan era, U.S. nondefense R&D stayed roughly constant at 1.8 percent of GNP, while West Germany increased its civilian R&D to 2.6 percent of GNP, and Japan's nondefense R&D rose to 2.8 percent.[36]

Reagan's economic policies in the period 1981–1989 have materially increased the likelihood of (1) declining relative standards of living for today's citizens and for coming generations and (2) the end of the United States as the world's economic superpower. The danger is not that Reagan's harmful policies guarantee another Great Depression or a United States falling immediately from superpower status. As Benjamin Friedman, one of Reagan's harshest critics, observed: "Waiting for the sky to fall is waiting for the wrong thing."[37] The probability of a calamitous decline has been increased by the Reagan policies, perhaps more than critics are now claiming after the embarrassment of the sky's not falling because of the huge deficits.[38] The problem is not just a matter of economics. As the *Economist* pointed out, "[Mr. Reagan] leaves Mr. Bush a society not just economically spendthrift but spiritually flaccid, less prepared than a superpower should be to make the sacrifices needed to preserve its prosperity and freedom." [39] Moreover, Reagan's economic policy has severely constrained future policy options and made policy-making more difficult. Never has there been such a pressing need for a strong analytic capacity in the executive branch.

Beyond White House analytic capacity is the general capacity of the executive branch agencies to implement and manage current and new federal policies. It is becoming increasingly clear that the federal agencies, as a result of Reagan era cutbacks and mismanagement, are being overwhelmed by increasing workloads. In the Food and Drug Administration (FDA), personnel has declined from around 8,000 to fewer than 7,500. That seems a small drop, until it is realized that the AIDS (acquired immune deficiency syndrome) epidemic, unknown ten years ago, requires about 400 FDA workers, and another 675 staff persons are administering twenty-four laws passed since 1980.[40] More generally, the federal social agencies suffered the following personnel reductions between 1982 and 1988: Labor (15.8 percent), HUD (17.4 percent), Health and Human Services (22.9 percent), and ED (31.6 percent).[41] Such gross numbers probably disguise the number of the best staff members that left because of more lucrative job alternatives as federal pay dropped further behind nongovernmental salaries in that period.

The Reagan administration offers the strongest case during the postwar era of the negative impact of unsound structure, incompetent staff, unreliable information and analysis, and executive branch mismanagement on policy outcomes. The Reagan era declines raise basic questions about the capacity of the federal government to carry out its current legislative mandates, much less take on new ones. Reagan administration Internal Revenue Service Commissioner Lawrence J. Gibbs, after leaving the federal government, observed: "The wholesale [executive branch] disinvestment that has been occurring in the 1980s is like nothing I've ever seen. If things don't change, we will be left with a *hollow* government."[42] That hollowness is most pervasive in the domestic policy area, where unmet needs are particularly pressing. Hollow executive branch government means that a prior need to developing and mounting new programs is a restoration of the institutional capacity to deliver such programs effectively.

PERSPECTIVES

I have drawn on two sources. First are confidential, relatively unstructured interviews I conducted between 1980 and 1989 with former or then current elected officials, political executives, and career civil servants; media persons, mainly print journalists; and a number of people in independent research and consulting organizations and universities who follow the presidency. In a number of cases, several interviews were conducted with the same individual over the years of study. Most important among the interviewees were people who had occupied major policy analytic and advisory positions in the EOP or in agency analytic units (the people in the independent research and consulting organizations were often in this group) and a few journalists whose main focus was the White House. The choice was made to do interviews off-the-record so as to elicit the most candid comments. Readers cannot verify the specific source of a quote, although the individual's key position (e.g., former OMB political executive) is indicated. Second, the unusually large outpouring of books on the Reagan administration both by White House insiders and well-placed journalists provided a detailed look at the Reagan presidency before it ended. Journalists such as Hedrick Smith and Bob Woodward could not only obtain extended interviews with key persons but could also induce these people to speak for the record.

I concentrate on domestic policymaking, distinguishing it from both economic and national security policymaking, because domestic policy provides a richer base of experience for prescription than do the other two policy areas. First, domestic policy analysts, while coming late to the halls of government, came in a particularly intense period of governance starting in the mid-1960s when policy analysts diverged increasingly from tradition economists. Economists have been policy experts in government for a long time and were formally institutionalized at the presidential level in the 1946 Full Employment Act that established the CEA. Although economics probably remains the most frequent background for policy analysts, policy analysis is not just applied microeconomics, and policy analysts are drawn increasingly from other disciplinary and professional areas (e.g., public policy analysis and management schools). The importance of these distinctions will be spelled out in the next chapter. Second, domestic policy has brought the most vexing implementation problems under shared governance where the federal government funds and has management responsibilities for programs that are operated by state and local governments. Here is the best place to see the inseparability of policy formulation and implementation and the critical necessity to have a strong EOP institutional structure that both facilitates a two-way flow of information and analysis between the White House and the agencies and supports agency flexibility in implementation and management.

While much that follows is highly critical of policy analysis, policy analysts, and the institutional analytic process, the basic argument is for greater analytic capacity in the federal executive branch. Overall, the U.S. policy analysis experience is positive. It has contributed to federal policymaking in the executive branch and in Congress. Specifying the positive role of policy analysis is not to deny that its misuse is an ever present danger. Both the fallibility of the available analytic tools and the critical need for analytic competition among competent practitioners to scrutinize analytic products need to be emphasized. Be that as it may, expert policy information soundly analyzed is an essential element of both policy formulation and policy management. How else can the federal government cope with expert information to establish a credible base for the interplay among the president, the executive branch, Congress and the public that is essential to constitutional democracy?

My main concern is analytic institutions and the institutional presidency, not policy analysis practices per se.[43] Critical in this process is the linking of the top White House policymakers to the EOP institutional process that is aimed at developing expert information and analysis in support of policymaking and facilitating the execution of and monitoring of the president's policies. In the search for means to increase the institutional analytic capacity in the executive branch, the focus is on the aggrandizing of the EOP in recent presidencies and on links between the EOP and the agencies and the executive and legislative branches that must be strengthened if federal government legitimacy and competence are to be restored. Recent critics such as Terry Moe and John Hart argue that it does no good to admonish a president to put Humpty Dumpty back together again and constrain the EOP.[44] This may seem realistic advice, but it is unsound either for the nation or for a president. The United States is at a crisis point in the relationship between the EOP and the rest of the executive branch and between that branch and Congress. Something must be done. The 1988 election offered one ray of hope. In the campaign both candidates stopped the attack on the career civil service, despite the high electoral payoffs such attacks have had since the Nixon campaigns, and President George Bush underscored the importance of these professionals. The attacks had gone too far and threatened viable governance. That is a start but far from enough. Crises demand fundamental redirection.

An individual president's predilections and competence shape institutional analytic effort. At question are both what a president wants and what he can do. As Paul Light has argued, "The greater each president's information and expertise upon entering office, the greater the potential for converting the no win presidency into a winnable presidency. . . . Expertise is the most important resource that varies directly with the individual president."[45] Four skills loom large. First is political mastery, which is the *first* necessary condition for an effective presidency. A president without political mastery, no matter how well he measures up on other dimensions, is not going to have a successful presidency. Jimmy Carter is a classic example. Second, the president should have a probing mind, which analyzes information and ideas. No matter how much staff help the president has, his own critical thinking is essential in the White House policymaking process. Third, the president should be able to project long-range goals for the country. Fourth, the president should be able to think in organizational terms, understanding the complex bureaucratic processes that determine how federal programs work. Organizational mastery is the most important missing skill among recent presidents. As Fred I. Greenstein has observed: "Eisenhower's capacity to think organizationally — to conceive policy problems in terms of the formal and informal group processes through which they could best be clarified and implemented — is, of course far less transferable than the specific instruments and arrangements he employed."[46] If a president thinks organizationally, he is much more likely to see the value of sound information and analysis and of a strong institutional analytic process. Greenstein argued in his comparison with Roosevelt and Kennedy that "Eisenhower was far more concerned then either of them to build into his routines the requirements that policies be exposed to 'multiple advocacy,'" and then pointed out that "Eisenhower's keenness as an organizer of advice he received was rooted in his makeup and experience. . . . His formal procedure . . . [supported the] rigorous staff work and systematic institutional back-up for policymaking [that] is persistently lacking in modern presidencies, as is the teamwork that is an informal offshoot of this procedure."[47] More important yet, Eisenhower understood the inseparable linkage between analysis and management that demands federal agencies with sufficient managerial autonomy and capacity to put the president's policies into place.[48]

In speaking of the need for a president with analytic, strategic, and organizational competence, two points must be stressed. First, the call is not for the president himself to be a policy analyst but to think critically and to analyze, in the broad sense of that term. Second, it cannot be overemphasized that the first need is for political mastery because the three technical qualities can add up to a president who is far more technician than politician. That will not do; neither will being just a politician. That is the key point. Bert Rockman has noted: "[A] president whose only skill is policy analysis is not apt to be a president for very long. . . . On the other hand, statecraft without policy analysis is government by sheer instinct."[49] While an analytic staff cannot substitute for political leadership, it can to some extent fill in for a president's lack of technical skills. The main function of the institutional presidency is to provide this technical backup to a president and his top policy advisers, especially early in the administration. However, the president and his top advisers must both want to use this competence and have the skills to do so. A legacy of institutional competence should be awaiting the new president. It is this legacy that Ronald Reagan so depleted in his two terms of office. That is what makes the focus on the institutional presidency so critical.

In developing recommendations to improve the institutional presidency, the current constitutional structure is considered fixed. Since major constitutional changes moving toward a parliamentary system with political parties as an integral component are most unlikely, the critical institutional question is what structural and staffing measures not requiring constitutional change can improve presidential governance.[50] It is also worth noting that the structural and staffing changes recommended in later chapters would be needed with major constitutional reform. Parliamentary democracy needs competence at the top, too.[51] My approach, like Theodore J. Lowi's, sees "the personal president" as a deleterious development because the capacity to govern cannot reside in the White House alone; "building down" the presidency (Hart's "presidential branch") is needed.[52] The main argument is for strengthening the analytic and managerial capacity at both the White House and the federal agencies so as to restore a reasonable balance between the two. The presidency, now too powerful, is "built down." If balance could be restored, could the president, or more broadly, the federal government, govern, or has the Constitution, which may have been a splendid approach two hundred years ago, become hopelessly outdated with its independent Congress and powerful states? No one can say for sure. But it is clear that both the institutional presidency and the executive agencies are part of the problem and part of a solution, if one can be found. *The working assumption of the book is that structural and staff changes in the institutional presidency and the executive agencies without constitutional change can make the United States governable from the center.*

Recommendations to improve the institutional presidency in the post-Watergate years have fallen on deaf ears. In writing about the unresponsiveness of Carter and Reagan to structural and staffing reform proposals, Hart observed: "Presidents may have wondered why they are being criticized for not thinking institutionally when, from their perspective, it is the reformers who are at fault by neglecting to think politically. . . . Presidents and reformers are fundamentally at odds with each other over the very basis on which the reformers have argued their case. . . . [Presidents] see virtues in politicizing the EOP and centralizing power in the White House. . . . [C]abinet government and rational decisionmaking processes have little appeal to the one person who counts. . . . [Reformers] have not come to terms with the reality of the presidential perspective on the presidency."[53] The fact remains that a president faces both political and managerial problems and neither of the two separate but overlapping demands can be ignored in an effective presidency. Political management cannot substitute for organizational management when the goal is to lead the executive branch toward better government performance.

At issue is how an institutional reformer is to reach future *presidents and voters* and convince them that (1) presidents have two big problems: getting re-elected and establishing the base for leadership (political mastery), and running the machinery of government (organizational mastery); (2) both need to be considered, and this demands an artful balancing act between the two; and (3) the balance is out-of-kilter toward politics and reached crisis proportions under Reagan; and (4) the balance can be restored only through strong, well-managed agencies, and such strength is likely to come about only if there is forceful presidential leadership by a president with both political and organizational mastery. One answer is clear. The task will not be easy and may be impossible if the president lacks organizational mastery. The superrealistic approach, which holds that presidents are going to be more political and that the task is to help them become so without regard for the underlying management problem, is wrong. That view will foster the continuing decline of the American presidency because it fails to accept that policy and politics are intertwined and must be balanced.

2

The President's Policy Advisers
and Policy Analysis

Although policy analysis today across all levels and branches of government is both thriving and more widely and deeply embedded in the institutional policy process than ever before, it suffers from the complexity-competence conundrum and the rising distrust and ideology in American society. At the base of the crisis of policy analysis is the widening gap between what can be done with current policy analysis tools, despite material improvements in the available techniques, and what information is needed for sound policy-making, since policy complexity has increased rapidly in the last quarter century. Alice Rivlin, the Brookings policy analyst who headed both the (then) HEW analytic office in the Johnson administration and the CBO during its formative years, points out that "the tools of policy analysis have been vastly refined. . . . [C]omputers enable us to manipulate large data bases with great speed; elaborate estimating models can project just about everything; and sophisticated analytic models provide insight into policy options."[1] There is little question that analytic tools and techniques have been improved and that more and more technically competent journeyman policy analysts are being turned out. But in the race between policy complexity and analytic competence, competence is losing. Federal Reserve Board Chairman and former CEA Chairman Alan Greenspan put the matter quite succinctly: "Even though we've had an extraordinary increase in our tools, such as computers, we have not been able to keep pace with the growing complexity of economic relationships, both domestic and international."[2]

The increases in policymaking complexity in the postwar years, and particularly in the last quarter century, are staggering. Consider economics first. In the post–World War II period until the early 1960s, the American economy was dominant internationally, quite stable, and still relatively independent of the rest of the world. Economists were particularly bullish after the Kennedy-Johnson tax cuts that so successfully stimulated the American economy. Robert Nelson argues that CEA Chairman Walter Heller, the driving force behind the tax cuts, was a superb policy entrepreneur, able to operate successfully in the interface between policy and politics. Nelson also points out that "part of Heller's success was that he truly believed that economists had the macroeconomic answers and that it was his mission to do what it took to educate the president and the country."[3] The hubris of the economists even then was unjustified. But it is clear in retrospect that the United States experienced a golden period of stable relationships and independence from international economic events that ended dramatically with the first OPEC price rise in 1973. From then on, international interdependencies have been increasingly critical factors. Over the last fifteen years, macroeconomists at times have had to operate in the uncharted terrains of double-digit inflation, unemployment, and interest rates and of massive budget and trade deficits. The Reagan years took the United States from being the world's biggest creditor to its largest debtor, embedding the nation more deeply in the capricious global economy.

Changes are even more dramatic in federal social and environmental policies. Before the War on Poverty, a passive federal government had a most limited role. The little that was done in social and environmental policy was performed and mainly financed at the state and local levels. Roosevelt-era social security and public welfare programs were the exceptions. Then, beginning in 1964, the federal government launched a host of new social and environmental programs that over the next decade were funded by federal grants-in-aid. Such active federal governance created uneasy federal-state-local partnerships that raised fundamental problems in U.S. federalism. The ensuing policy complexity has proved exceedingly difficult to analyze effectively and has defied the improved analytic tools and techniques. The successful Reagan decentralization transferred more power and responsibility to states and localities (mainly the former) and appears to have reduced some of the fundamental federalism tensions. But the disregard of mounting social, environmental, and infrastructural problems, combined with the massive federal deficits of the 1980s, has brought a level of policy complexity even greater than at the start of the decade.

Most interesting is the foreign policy arena, in which momentous decisions in the immediate postwar years revived Western Europe and shaped the Cold War. With the Marshall Plan, the Truman Doctrine, and the Korean War, could foreign policymaking today be more complex than that faced by such giants as George Marshall, Dean Acheson, and Robert Lovett? What is unique about the early postwar years is America's towering world economic dominance, with a far higher standard of living and per-capita productivity than any other of the great powers. In that period the United States produced one-half the world's manufactured goods and one-third of all types of goods and had one-half the world's supply of ships. It was the only great power after

World War II not close to famine and bankruptcy. The U.S. GNP in 1950 was five to ten times those of Britain, France, West Germany, Japan or Italy, which today are the five largest Western industrialized powers after the United States. The U.S. GNP per capita was nearly two to five times those of these countries. Britain then was number two in both GNP and GNP per capita. Japan's GNP was less than one-tenth that of the United States. A well-armed, hostile Soviet Union was a real geopolitical threat, but it also was a war-devastated country that had lost 20 million people and had a total GNP one-third that of the U.S. The United States had attained a level of economic world dominance seldom seen before. It had ample resources to lead the West in the fight against communism. The Marshall Plan is the quintessential case of a handful of executive branch policymakers seeing clearly the overriding need for the United States to help Western Europe. In this short period of dominance the United States reached that ideal policy point at which policymakers could work through problems to find reasonable answers, and at which the country had sufficient resources to move toward these answers.

The Vietnam War crushed the two-decade postwar national security consensus and complicated the foreign policy process. "The confidence, the sense of destiny and the self-assurance that had so marked the men that had built the postwar world, was slowly stripped away by the corrosive acid of Vietnam. In the end, all that was left was a sense of duty."[4] Not only had American economic and geopolitical power slipped, but the decisionmaking milieu had changed radically, as Walter Isaacson and Evan Thomas point out, from one during the "few years right after the war when a small band of able and selfless men controlled foreign policy relatively immune from the politicians" to one where "TV cameras and congressional committees followed decisionmakers everywhere, and thus froze them."[5] Part of the complexity-competence conundrum has technical roots in that sophisticated analytic models still are limited in their underlying capacity to cope with the ever increasing expert policy information. But it would be a grave error to see the main problem as that of developing more sophisticated hardware and software to treat technical issues. Far more important are the limitations of policy analysis in integrating organizational and political factors and the findings of disciplines other than economics into the policy equation.[6] In individual terms, the journeyman policy analysts, who now have far more technical tools than did their counterparts of a quarter of a century ago, often appear less able to move beyond their more narrow economic-based analyses to broad generalization, where the demands are for breadth of knowledge and vision, not technical virtuosity.

Policy analysis is mainly a victim of complexity, not its perpetrator, and is caught up in the larger problems of governance. As one of the broadest thinkers on policy analysis and governance, Yehezkel Dror, has pointed out:

"Advances in technology, especially in communications and information processing, provide some limited help. But no breakthroughs have occurred in the capacities of governments, which continue to be constrained by inherent limits of rulers, politicians, organizations, and mass behavior. Comparison of slight improvements in the capacity to govern on one side, with radical changes in intensity of expectations and demands, in complexity of issues, and in consequences of mistakes on the other side, reveals a negative balance of growing relative incapacity to govern."[7]

DISTRUST AND IDEOLOGY

The difficulties in developing and analyzing expert policy information have produced a crisis of trust. When the conclusions drawn from expert information conflict with beliefs based on ordinary information and an individual's experience, especially if the experts' conclusions are counterintuitive, the nonexpert may opt for disbelief. Hugh Heclo poses sharply the issue of the basic threat to democratic institutions: "If the problem were merely an information gap between policy experts and the bulk of the population, then more communication might help. Yet instead of garnering support for policy choices, more communication . . . tends to produce an 'everything causes cancer' syndrome among ordinary citizens. . . . [M]ore experts [make] more sophisticated claims and counterclaims to the point that the nonspecialist becomes inclined to concede everything and believe nothing that he hears. . . . Policy activists have little desire to recognize an unpleasant fact: that their influential systems for knowledgeable policymaking tend to make democratic politics more difficult."[8]

   This rising public distrust of policy experts and their analyses provides fertile ground for a retreat into ideology, where the interpretation of the policy ambiguity bears little connection to reality. As more and more information and analysis become available, the overload demands careful synthesis and translation. Even more important than simple overload, however, is that information is amenable to quite different interpretations. If the problem were only in ordering information to make it intelligible, computers and journeyman analysts would be able to do the job. As Alex Cairncross observed: "The most serious problem for the practitioner is that theorists differ . . . on how the economy works — on what governs the level of output or employment or process. Where the disagreements go so deep as they do nowadays it is difficult to speak with authority on technical economic issues."[9] When Nobel laureates in economics can look at the same data and come up with diametrically opposite interpretations and policy recommendations, we can join Henry Aaron in asking: "What is an ordinary member of the tribe to do when the witch doctors disagree?"[10]

One outcome in the face of growing policy complexity is to use the experts more but trust them less. Despite the weaknesses of macroeconomic forecasts, with their erratic record, such forecasts are central to the budgetary process. Given the likelihood of wide variations in forecasts, does it help or hurt policymaking for decisionmakers to have such an abundance of choices that range so widely? The problem is not simply deficient tools and techniques. For a number of years the CBO made better economic forecasts than the EOP, not necessarily because the CBO had more prescient forecasters but because the White House demanded forecasts be "cooked" to produce the results needed to support a previously arrived at budget position. An economist interviewee who had been involved in major government forecasts and now is in the private sector said not only that there is no such thing as a nonpolitical government forecast but that much the same is happening in the private sector. In discussing forecasts by business economists made in 1989, he told me that a number of forecasters were much gloomier either about the U.S. economy, their own industrial sector, or both, than their forecasts showed. However, pressures for bullish forecasts came from their superiors who feared negative reactions such as a decline in the market value of their companies' stock. What does such behavior do to analytic credibility? A more dangerous response to growing policy complexity and the accompanying failure of experts to agree or to predict correctly is for policymakers to throw out conflicting evidence and opt for the simplistic solution that "fits" with political or ideological predilections. As Rivlin observes: "Never mind that the last cure-all is counter-intuitive, that it conflicts with common sense as well as with the accumulated evidence of how our system works."[11]

Two more changes in response to the rising complexity are mainly beneficial in knocking down some of the pretentiousness of the early policy analysis. One change is generally to reject the notion of policy analysis as being above politics and ideology. Partly, the continued claim of neutrality is a search by practicing policy analysts for academic acceptability — "we are pure scientists, too." But whatever role or stance academic policy analysts, particularly the economists, may take, successful practicing policy analysts seldom can completely avoid the role of advocate or the claim that rational analysis makes them more pure than their adversaries in the policy process. The second favorable aspect is to see that economics, which underpins the basic framework of policy analysis, rests upon an unproven "faith" in the competitive market as an ideal. As Robert Nelson has observed: "[E]conomists have had the greatest success in government as proponents for markets, for efficiency-related values, and generally for their framework for viewing the world, rather than as technical analysts of particular policy details."[12] Cast in this light, the basic analytic framework is not unambiguously more reasoned and objective than other forms of decisionmaking but is itself a value-based approach. For example, environmentalists may question the underlying value assumptions of economists' cost-benefit studies that argue against 100 percent cleanup because the last 5 percent brings far greater costs than benefits. Health specialists attack policy analysts who put a dollar value on human life in their calculations. Both critics view the efficiency rationale as a harmful ideological thesis that rejects basic humanistic values.

Policy analysis still suffers from the excessive promises in its early days of "optimization" and of the highly desirable options that policy analysts would create to solve policy problems. There is almost never a single dominant, satisfying, workable policy option to be extracted by the allegedly powerful, rational, objective tools of analysis. Policy complexity yields flawed options, all of which have reasonably high probabilities of failure or harm. Not all policy choices are equally good or bad. Some options can be catastrophic. Sound policy analysis can expose inherent weaknesses in an argument, illuminate the best option available, and provide warnings of potential problems. Indeed, as Peter J. May has suggested, damage control may be the most critical positive contribution of policy analysis. Despite its deficiencies, policy analysis provides a useful policy tool.

In sum, policy experts are advocates, do adhere to underlying unproven principles, and are as susceptible as other advocates to misusing information and analysis in the heat of the bureaucratic political process. Moreover, policy analysis, wrapped in scientific framework and rhetoric, has a greater likelihood of confusing people or of being accepted without sufficient skepticism than does ordinary discourse. But the other extreme, rejecting all analysis as hopelessly biased, is even more dangerous, especially when driven by rigid, unrealistic ideologies. There are useful expert answers. As May points out: "One of the most striking things about policy analysis is that it has proved to be robust as a paradigm for policy advice. Despite many criticisms of the 'rational model' of policy analysis over the years, nothing has supplanted it as an idealized paradigm for guiding policy choice."[13] A most pressing need is to find institutional means of reducing poor or misused policy analysis.

PRESIDENTIAL POLICY ADVISERS AND ANALYSTS

A president's most critical policy staffing choices are the top policy advisers. These key aides are the first critical linkage point in the policy chain that runs from the top to the field where presidential policies are delivered. These advisers are not necessarily policy analysts. What skills and experience should presidential policy generalists advisers have? Where are the generalists to come from? What kinds of technical people are needed? How should a policy unit be structured? What kinds of political and technical leadership are needed?

The White House needs policy generalist advisers who can see beyond the narrow microanalysis of the area specialist and integrate across policy areas. What a president needs most is policy-political synthesis. This capacity involves determining the relevance and quality of the underlying technical analysis of policy proposals coming to the president, the degree to which proposed policy meshes with the president's immediate and longer-run objectives, the impact on his political standing, and the potential for selling the proposal in Congress. Good analysis and advice at the top require a blending of technical, political, and program knowledge. Ben W. Heineman underscores the importance of integrating policy and politics: "Reconciling the tensions, even antagonisms, between the world of policy . . . and the world of politics . . . is, in my judgment, the supreme act of political leadership. EOP policy management is a crucial process for trying to make that marriage work."[14]

Heineman and Curtis A. Hessler, writing at the end of the Carter administration, make this key point about the difficulty of policy-political integration: *"The increasing professionalism of both the political advisers and the policy advisers has served to widen, not narrow, the gap in language and approach."*[15] Although some presidential units have a disproportionate number of inexperienced people whom policy specialists may view as amateurs, the critical problem is the distance between the *political* professional and the *policy* professional. Ideally, policy and political analysts would have what Heineman and Hessler label "double vision." With double vision the two professionals would be comfortable coming together to develop a policy-political synthesis. Without double vision the policy-political synthesizer must serve as the critical link and work with both sides, separately when necessary, to guide a process of synthesis that blends policy (technical, organizational, and programmatic) questions and political considerations.

Generalist policy advisers need sufficient knowledge of policy analysis to be good consumers of analytic products — to specify needed policy information and analysis, to monitor the development of the information and analysis, and to protect the president from improper use of analytic products. Such a skill level does not require that policy advisers come up through the ranks of analytic units or be practicing policy analysts inside or outside the government. Many staff positions require a relatively high level of analytic literacy, including the capacity to generalize across analyses. Members of the Senate and House Budget Committees are good examples, since a primary task is to interact with the congressional analytic staffs, particularly the CBO. Public policy and management school graduates are trained at least to be journeyman analytic consumers, but no law specifies this minimum competence level.

White House policy staffs are not necessarily analytic units. The Carter administration's DPS had a group of young, intelligent staff generalists under an exceptionally bright lawyer, Stuart Eizenstat, who had other lawyers in the top two positions under him. It can be argued that broad policy generalist advisers, more oriented to politics than to policy analysis, are preferable in a White House policy unit. In the case in which Eizenstat had to fill in a political vacuum, the argument may be even more persuasive. The fact remains, however, that sound, timely, relevant expert policy information and analysis need to be available in the White House policymaking process if there is to be effective presidential governance. Someone must bear the responsibility of seeing that such information and analysis are being generated for the president and translated into a usable form for the top policymakers. The head of the policy unit does not have to be a policy analyst, but he or she certainly needs analytic literacy and a competent generalist policy analyst among his or her top people. If policy units do not ensure that expert policy information and analysis are put into a form most useful to nonspecialists, of whom the president and the top policy and political advisers are the most critical, where is the institutional responsibility to lie? Such responsibility should go beyond mere translation of the final analytic product and involve efforts to see that analytic products, whether developed in an EOP policy unit or in an agency analytic office, has benefited from nontechnical inputs at early stages of their development. The issue is not how to choose between politics or policy, but how to balance them.

Key policy people must ensure that sound information and analysis are provided at lower levels, linked to the presidential policymaking process, and put in a form useful to the president and his inner circle policy and political advisers, who probably will not be policy analysts and may not be competent consumers of analytic products. The further down in the process that the policy analysts are pushed, the more difficult it will be to move sound policy information and analysis to the top. And, if sound policy information and analysis do not make it to the top of the process, inept presidential governance seems almost certain. It would be ideal if we could postulate the obverse — that sound policy information and analysis are highly likely to yield effective presidential governance — but there, alas, is the asymmetry. The fact remains that to have effective presidential governance, sound expert policy information and analysis are required, and the likelihood of obtaining them rests with the president and a few policy advisers at the top.

COMPETENCE, COMMITMENT, INTEGRITY, AND LOYALTY

Technical competence for a policy adviser implies in-depth knowledge in a policy area about (1) programs and basic technologies used; (2) the structure, organization, and procedures of the relevant agencies; (3) agency political-bureaucratic interaction patterns internally and externally, such as with the White House and Congress; and (4) the analytic and research techniques relevant to developing policy information and analysis. Technical competence carries a lot of baggage, and it will be useful at times to separate particular aspects, such as analytic competence. Generalist policy competence refers to the capacity to integrate across policies or between policies and politics. Technical competence is more micro- or detail-oriented; generalist competence is macro-oriented, toward the "big picture."

Commitment has to do with service to the presidency and requires a distinction between a president and the presidency. The latter connotes both a continuing process that stretches beyond the person in the office today and a duty of service, not just to the man, but to the institution. As Stephen Hess has put it: "[Commitment] must be to more than the person who is president. It also must be to the presidency and to a system of political democracy, civil liberties and government through the competition of balanced institutions."[16] Serving the presidency can imply serving the nation. It is difficult to translate into operational specifics. As John Hart has observed: "The idea of a president being free to shape the EOP to his own design, yet at the same time, being constrained by the longer-term interests of the presidency might appear to be internally contradictory. . . . Presidents . . . have been tempted to question the distinction reformers make between the president and the presidency, a distinction that is vital to the arguments used against politicization and deinstitutionalization."[17] It is a point well taken, but the concept is used for two main reasons. First, the notion of the presidency is a central one for post-Watergate reformers who seek to restructure the EOP. Second, it has been important within the EOP, especially in the budget office, and it focuses on institutional factors not tied to an individual president. Historically, OMB, particularly its predecessor, the Bureau of the Budget, had a high institutional commitment to provide presidents (and the plural here is critical) with hard analysis without partisan political spin. Individual OMB staff members have shown a strong commitment to the institution's well-established principles intended to guide its staff in how it serves a president and the institutional presidency. The staff members have ultimately internalized the standards that reflect this basic institutional commitment. This creates a tension for the permanent staff as the needs of a particular president and the presidency have come to diverge more. The increasing politicization of the White House and the concomitant decline of the career civil servants in the OMB hierarchy means that the top layer of OMB, made up of political appointees, is likely to serve only the president, not the presidency.

OMB no longer has career staff members at the top with institutional wisdom gained over many years and a commitment to serving the presidency. Of particular importance is the criticism of Paul O'Neill, who was an OMB career staff member, a program associate director (a political appointment under Nixon), and the OMB deputy director in the Ford administration and is considered one of the brightest and most thoughtful former OMB officials. In a September 8, 1988 talk, O'Neill told OMB staff persons that their "guiding light of motivation" should be "the objective of living up to a standard which says . . . in every decision the president has to make, he has from you . . . the best and clearest exposition of the facts and arguments on every side of the issue that it is possible for a human mind to muster."[18] In his most important statement O'Neill made the critical point about the loss of institutional commitment:

> Recent calls to create a non-partisan, institutional staff in the Executive Office are an indirect measure of the degree to which this key role is believed to have been eroded beyond redemption in the Office of Management and Budget.
>
> As you look for things to repair in the institutional fabric, I urge you to give this issue your priority attention. As our society and government become more complex, it is of the greatest importance that there be a point of institutional memory and neutral competence — better yet, neutral brilliance — available to the president and the presidency. We are doomed to repeat the mistakes of the past if we lack a trusted cadre of experts who can span the issues of partisan politics and survive the transition between parties in power. This is the role that is the raison d'etre of this office. If it slips further from your grasp it will, I suspect of necessity, be placed elsewhere. If that should happen, OMB will become another point of special interest — yet another office the president must protect himself from rather than one he can count on as his own.[19]

The concept of "neutral competence" should not be interpreted as purely rational, objective, and apolitical analysis — "we're just scientists." Instead, neutral competence is the analysis of relevant policy factors including political, organizational issues, and bureaucratic politics not slanted toward a particular president (decisionmaker). That is, under the same circumstances neutral competence would produce the same analysis whether the decisionmaker was a Republican or a Democrat, a liberal or a conservative. Along with current and former OMB staff I have interviewed, O'Neill and I believe that neutral competence is most needed at the top of the presidential process, where partisan politics so often becomes too dominant. Here the notion of balance is crucial. Both partisan politics *and* neutral competence are essential at the top. The career generalist's "neutral" analysis may not be comforting to a president and his top advisers; however, in the presidency analysis that is politically sophisticated but not slanted toward partisan concerns has become an increasingly critical missing element as the number of voices telling a president what he wants to hear continues to grow.

Integrity denotes an unswerving adherence to high moral principles — an individual (not an institutional) code of honor that guides behavior. Loyalty is used more restrictively to indicate an individual's faithfulness to a person.

If a broader definition were employed, loyalty could attach to an institution such as OMB or the presidency. As used here, integrity and loyalty are strictly individual traits, while commitment, which can apply to the individual, also carries an institutional dimension. Thus, OMB Director Stockman did not give his first loyalty to President Reagan in that, by his own admission, he had his own ideological agenda. He exhibited little or no personal integrity in that, again by his own admission, he cooked the books, and he certainly showed no commitment to the presidency. At the same time OMB still had strong institutional commitment to the presidency among its professional staff, who as individuals were put in a highly conflicting position.

There can be tensions either within or between these key concepts. High technical competence, as we will see in the case of policy analysts, can mitigate against generalist skills. Loyalty and competence can conflict in that the demand for faithfulness to a specific president can work against picking a less loyal person of high competence. Integrity and loyalty can conflict or at least make for hard choices or shaky compromises. OMB in the Reagan era provides a pristine case study of these strong tensions because of the particular combinations of competence, commitment, loyalty, and integrity both in the same individual and in critical personal relationships. These combinations led to the budget and trade deficits and OMB's decline in institutional commitment. Stockman's technical and generalist competence dominated from the outset. In contrast, Counselor to the President Edwin Meese, Reagan's top policy generalist during this period and the key staff person above Stockman, had great loyalty but neither technical nor general analytic competence. Donald Regan, who combined the top policy generalist and chief-of-staff jobs in the second term, was not a competent policy generalist. National Security Adviser John Poindexter had great technical competence, no generalist competence, and apparently neither integrity nor loyalty. Stockman's dominating competence greatly increased OMB's clout from the low period under James McIntyre in the Carter years, but his lack of commitment and integrity raised serious questions of institutional commitment and credibility. Stockman's successor, James Miller III, in combining limited competence (he came to be nicknamed "Miller Lite"), lack of commitment to serving the presidency or his organization, and unswerving personal loyalty to President Reagan, decreased OMB's power in Congress and further compromised its credibility.

LAWYERS AND POLICY ANALYSTS

Where are competent top policy generalists to be found? Two areas that make strong claims for such roles are law and policy analysis. The legal profession historically had been a training ground for future politicians and had a near-monopoly as the supplier of legal technicians. Practitioners were ready to take the issue at hand without necessarily having in-depth substantive knowledge and apply their skills of legal logic and advocacy. In the New Deal, lawyers became generalist policy advisers who drew on their broad framework in carrying policy issues far beyond their narrow legal boundaries. The 1960s brought new generalists — the policy analysts — from a different background and with a distinctly different analytic rationale from that of the law. Critical was the powerful normative framework that users believed was applicable to almost any policy problem. As Richard Nelson observed: "[T]hose who consider themselves policy analysts seem to profess an almost universal validity for their intellectual tradition."[20] Lawyers and policy analysts clashed and still clash in Washington policymaking. But it would be a serious error to miss the key similarity in their approaches: Both operate with the basic belief that their respective conceptual frameworks permit the treatment of a broad range of policies and support synthesis and integration within and across policies and politics.

Policy advisers are needed at various levels to synthesize complex government policies and integrate political factors. But at the lower levels, technical issues are most salient, and hard analysis predominates. As we move toward the top of an agency or of the White House, policy advisers must have a more generalist outlook, treating policy areas beyond their special knowledge and not infrequently beyond much knowledge at all. The top presidential policy generalist adviser needs some knowledge of the tools, techniques, and methodologies used to develop information and analysis in the policy area being considered. Increasing policy complexity demands of the top policy generalist both greater policy and political knowledge and greater methodological sophistication.

Like policy specialists, presidential policy generalists are burdened by the growing gap between complexity and competence. Complexity has made obsolete the broad generalist whose main qualifications are long service to the leader and unswerving loyalty and ideological consistency. Today the need in the White House (and at the top of the federal agencies) is for generalist policy advisers capable of working with a broad range of specialized expert information and analyses. At the same time, today's generalist must still have the capacity to treat the big policy-political picture. The problem is one of balance — a balance that shifts as the policy adviser moves toward the top, where the emphasis is upon breadth at the expense of depth. At high levels the capacity for informed judgment looms larger. As an astute interviewee, who is one of the top-level people in a congressional agency, noted: "The central skill comes down to the ability to exercise informed judgment in dealing with technical analysis in a political environment. The generalist must be able to distinguish gold from garbage, but does not need the training required to do the original analysis."

The problem of developing sound policy-political syntheses that blend technical, program, and political information and analysis is well illustrated by the cases of law and policy analysis. The basic argument is that the law is too "soft" and policy analysis too "hard" for preparing competent top generalist policy advisers. The former fails to provide enough analytic-quantitative skills and experience to cope with policy evidence; policy analysis is biased against evidence not easily treated by these tools. Academic training for both law and policy analysis (particularly in economics departments) has one strong similarity: The predominant skills and orientation acquired by graduates do not equip them to be broad generalist policy advisers. We need to consider the legal and policy analytic concepts and frameworks that shape the training of lawyers and policy analysts and the probable job experiences that might prepare them to be top presidential policy generalists.

Lawyers

The United States is the most litigious society in the world, with far more lawyers per capita than any other nation.[21] More important than size is the way lawyers are educated in the United States. As Marshall Dimock points out: "The unwritten law of the legal profession is that the lawyer has the potential to deal with any technology, from physics to medicine and from psychiatry to insurance, because he is resourceful and adapts quickly. He may not know, but he is expected to act as though he did. He knows he is not omniscient, but protocol requires that he act as if he thought he were. He likes a cockfight."[22] Law schools have built their curriculum around the adversary process that is central to the U.S. judicial system. Validation of evidence results from the clash of opposing views. Lawyers learn how to argue and to challenge legal evidence. The encounter of two competent partisans — especially if there are sound rules of evidence and a fair and knowledgeable judge — can produce a level of informed scrutiny that reduces or eliminates inaccurate facts or poor analysis. But much depends on competence. Law schools have been weak in giving their students the tools and techniques of policy and quantitative analysis. The deficiencies are clearly manifested in the courts. Of the three branches, the judiciary is the only one that has not acquired a cadre of substantive specialists. The law itself — that is, the framework — apparently is presumed to be sufficient. Ascertaining the "truth" through confrontation by partisan adversaries remains the preferred means.

The adversary process that dominates the legal profession in the United States has critical implications for the way expert information is treated — how it is gathered, analyzed and presented. Nearly two decades ago a top lawyer–policy analyst, Peter Szanton, wrote:

Though lawyers regard their profession as analytic, it normally involves analysis of a limited kind. Lawyers assess the probative heft of qualitative information, and they analogize and distinguish. These are the logical processes of common sense. Common sense, as the systems scientists keep reminding us, is a very poor predictor of the complex interactions of large social systems. . . .

[T]o meet the emerging responsibilities in both public and private sections, lawyers will need a far greater familiarity with the uses of quantitative analysis, the perspectives of rational resource allocation, and the techniques of planning and management than typically they now possess. Those are the requirements, I believe, which should most powerfully influence the next wave of curricular changes in the law schools.[23]

The law schools' failure to heed Szanton's warning has had serious implications for lawyers' capacity as policy generalists.

Another top lawyer–policy analyst, Ben W. Heineman, Jr., has castigated law schools for the flight by law school professors from policy concerns, as evidenced both in the writing of "highly theoretical and arcane articles, divorced from any decisionmaking reality . . . articles that approach an almost theological abstruseness" and in a withdrawal from policy and politics because *"law professors often find the political process distasteful."*[24] Embedded in this retreat is the law schools' continuing predilection for the adversary process. Heineman's criticism is particularly relevant in terms of policy analysis: "[D]espite decades of criticism, the basic analytic technique used by law professors is destructive, not constructive. The case method is, of course, habitually derided as elevating logical consistency to an overarching ideal. The real problem, however, is that the method induces a corrosive, critical cast of mind and, given the closed world of an appellate opinion, does not aid its practitioners in thinking constructively and creatively about complex problems."[25] If Heineman is right about this increasingly narrow scholasticism and the aversion to politics and broad policy in law schools, new generations of lawyers may be less trained for or oriented toward becoming generalist policy advisers. The point to be underscored is that the weaknesses derive from the underlying analytic framework and orientation rather than from the lack of intellectual capability. Indeed, as Heineman points out, the decline in demand for academics in areas such as philosophy and history brought some of the nation's brightest students to law school. At issue is whether these students will receive an education that will prepare them to be leading policy generalists at the presidential level.

Lawyers become substantive experts and masters of the legal aspects of a subject area. At the same time in policy areas much is written that draws heavily on economic and statistical reasoning and methods. To the extent that lawyer analysts are cut off from certain analyses and research because of their lack of quantitative and policy analysis skills, they may be at a real disadvantage with policy analysts. Furthermore, lawyers often overrate or misunderstand what policy analysts do. Lawyers often "buy" the image of the policy analyst as a premier numbers person. A lawyer on President Carter's DPS told me that the unit could not engage in policy analysis because it did not have a major computer system, although other EOP analytic units had them. Even this sophisticated, policy-oriented lawyer missed the fundamental point that the framework of policy analysts is what is important, not computerized number crunching. With the coming of the minicomputers tied into major computer systems, this view of what is required to do policy analysis makes even less sense. But it is certainly true that policy analysts over the years have contributed to an image of themselves as number specialists. Lawyers also befuddle people with jargon and "in" concepts, but in the policy areas their comparative advantage from such tactics may not be effective.

What can be said about lawyers' experiences? Lawyers often get into policy through electoral politics frequently as staff members of an elected official, and such political experience generally is useful. The lawyers emerge as sound political professionals capable of a high level of political synthesis. In contrast, they are seldom students of large-scale organizations. They become administrators of big public organizations, but usually it is a different career path than that for lawyers who become policy advisers. Given both lawyers' political backgrounds and lack of intense policy specialization, they may well be oriented toward being generalist policy advisers. The last point may seem a left-handed compliment — lawyers are generalists because they do not know enough to be specialists — but it is not. Intense specialization may be inhibiting, or it may indicate a propensity not to engage in broad generalization.

Policy Analysts

Policy analysts are likely to be strong in policy substance and modern analytic-quantitative techniques — "hard-edged" — with a well-delineated framework for approaching policy problems. The shaping disciplines of policy analysis — operations research, statistics, and economics — traditionally have downplayed politics and internal organizational processes. Policy analysts may pick up knowledge about politics and organizations from on-the-job experiences, but their career routes do not necessarily lead in this direction — certainly not as much as the lawyers' path in the public sector. The mark of policy analysis has been a powerful normative framework that permits a broad approach in treating a policy problem. The big question is whether the underlying tenets of that framework make it likely that different kinds of evidence will be treated reasonably — I am tempted to say "fairly." What expert information is sought and how available information is interpreted and used are the crux of the policy information problem. The policy analytic framework permits the incorporation of different kinds of information and approaches. It also provides a general basis for policy integration. But the fact that the broad framework allows the treatment of wide varieties of expert information does not ensure in specific cases that policy analysts will pursue certain kinds of information (e.g., on political or organizational issues) or that they have the competence to handle such information when it comes in. *The great danger is that the broad framework, which in conceptual terms permits integration of wide varieties of information, is going to be put in the hands of a "narrow" policy analyst who has neither the necessary knowledge to cope with these certain kinds of information nor the orientation to see that such information is important.*

Although universities are turning out more people highly qualified to do sound narrow (partial) analyses, this technique-driven education may inhibit development of policy generalist skills and orientation. Techniques and tools often are oversold in their power to cope with complex policy issues. Moreover, because of the tremendous investment in acquiring quantitative methodologies, the tendency is to devalue the importance of the political and organizational issues less amenable to the hard techniques. Or, perhaps even worse, fledgling analysts may come to believe that their analytic techniques and esoteric models are sufficient to integrate substantive, political, and organizational issues into an analytic equation. As in the case with law students, the problem is not lack of intellectual capability but deficiencies in the analysts' framework and orientation. The best and the brightest are provided sophisticated tools that at the same time make them both far more capable as technicians and less likely to become sound policy generalists.

In interviews conducted after the Reagan years, interviewees were extremely negative about the supply of competent policy generalists. One interviewee, who had served in government and now is in one of the top Washington think tanks, said she was having a hard time finding bright, younger policy analysts with the breadth to manage major projects. She thinks the federal government analytic offices in the Reagan period were not turning out such people. Another interviewee, also with government experience and now at one of the most respected think tanks, made the point that economics had become so mathematical that a bright young economist is not willing to come to his organization because it is difficult to go from that think tank back into a good university department. The two policy research and analysis organizations in question are at the top of the prestige list in economic and domestic policy work. A veteran OMB civil servant went further in saying that even the economists at public policy schools are teaching economics that is not useful for policy generalists.

Experience is the key factor. Policy analysts can hardly avoid political and organizational experiences in an agency, congressional, or EOP analytic office. At the same time, strong analytic offices have tended to bring together people of similar training and orientation — a critical mass — so that the policy analysts do not necessarily work closely with those who treat political and organizational issues. Moreover, strong analytic offices will foster professional norms that stress objectivity and mitigate against politically-oriented approaches. At the same time, certain kinds of broad policy experiences do contribute significantly to the development of generalist policy analysts. Breadth of experience is the best indicator of the capacity to be a policy generalist, save, of course, a proven track record itself. Unfortunately, no institutional setting alone necessarily leads to the development of competent policy analyst generalists. The need remains for the policy generalist virtuosos.

3

Domestic Policy Analysis
in the Executive Branch, 1964–1980

Domestic policy analysis in the executive branch developed in its present form in the period 1964–80. The first twelve years were the most creative in both the agencies and the White House, reaching a high point in the Nixon years. The Carter administration continued without notable change, and the Reagan administration decreased policy analysis. The policy analysis momentum shifted after 1976 to Congress as the 1974 Congressional Budget Act began to be prominent in congressional decisionmaking. This critique of executive branch domestic policy analysis begins in 1964 with the start of OEO, which developed the first domestic policy analytic office. To keep this treatment in bounds, three restrictions are imposed. First, only a few successful agency domestic policy analytic offices are considered. This is not intended to suggest that no analytic efforts failed; many did. Second, White House policy units start with the relatively big DPS staff established in 1970, even though domestic policy advisers such as Clark Clifford (Truman), Theodore Sorensen (Kennedy), and Joseph Califano (Johnson) had real power in domestic policy decisionmaking.[1] Third, neither national security nor economic policy staffs are discussed with the exception of Ford's Economic Policy Board (EPB), which illustrates analytic competition or "multiple advocacy." In excluding national security and economic policy staffs from discussion, we are not considering analytic offices that have generally been far more influential in the agencies—and in the White House—than have domestic policy units.

DOMESTIC-AGENCY POLICY ANALYSIS

In October 1965, while policy analysis stood almost uncriticized in the glow of the success of the DOD analytic office (started in 1961), PPBS was launched government-wide. In 1969 the Bureau of the Budget (BOB) (now the Office of Management and Budget, OMB) and the GAO conducted separate surveys of sixteen domestic agencies to determine whether the agencies had "made substantive progress toward the development of PPB systems for policy decisionmaking."[2] The scorecard was dismal; only three agencies were rated as having made substantial progress. Certainly the effort to install PPBS as a government-wide system in which policy analysis within the domestic agencies would yield a flow of useful decision documents to BOB should be rated an outright failure. The case of the individual agencies is more complex because BOB's topdown directive that decreed that PPBS be established in the various agencies does not imply that the agency heads wanted the new approach. The BOB-GAO studies found that only five agency heads supported PPBS analysis. If the others did not want PPBS, it is hardly surprising that it was not implemented. Of the five who did, three succeeded.

Where PPBS was well implemented in the domestic agencies, agency analytic success at the White House level was more limited than that of the 1961 analytic office at DOD. This was so because of the restricted influence of the agency head with the president, not because of the lack of analytic influence within the agency. For example, at OEO in the Johnson administration a Rand alumnus, Joseph Kershaw, the first director of the Office of Research, Plans, Programs, and Evaluation (RPP&E), was influential with Director Sargent Shriver. Kershaw's successor, Robert Levine, another ex-Rand researcher, was agency head Bertrand Harding's closest policy adviser. During that period, the OEO analytic office sold Shriver on the negative income tax and on the delegation of the OEO manpower programs to the Department of Labor. In the former case, Shriver could not get the Johnson administration to adopt a negative tax. The manpower program delegation, however, was a precipitating factor in the federal government's reorganization and redirection of its manpower program efforts, which led to the development of the 1967 Concentrated Employment Program, the precursor of many of the manpower programs of the next several years.[3] Even more impressive than single events was the continuing day-to-day influence, especially in the Harding-Levine period. That such real influence did not always lead to proposals accepted at the presidential level is simply part of the power game.

The point is not to deny differential agency power. There can be little doubt that Robert McNamara was the most powerful cabinet member in the Johnson administration. But to think that domestic agency heads do not still have power with Congress and within their agencies is to misunderstand the whole power process. Nor should we assume that the analyst has no power. Yet it is harder to influence the entire system when the agency head is not a key insider with the president. As William Gorham, assistant secretary for planning and evaluation at HEW (now Health and Human Services) during the Johnson administration, points out:

The analytic function [at HEW and OEO] was added in both organizations at a high level, reporting to the top administrative officer. Access was good. But in neither of these agencies did the top officials have the degree of final authority over budget, legislation, or even internal administrative matters that was enjoyed by Defense officials. On most issues worthy of note, the White House, Bureau of the Budget, Congress, and frequently the state and local governments had either greater, equal, or important subsidiary roles. The effect of this diffused authority (which has very positive values for some purposes) was to narrow the range of subjects being handled and to limit the potential impact of the analytical staffs working for the secretary of HEW and the director of OEO. Under such circumstances, the analysts need not pack up and go home. What they must do, to become effective, is to have much wider interaction with analysts serving the other parties to the decisions concerning them.[4]

The Analyst and Agency Power

The policy analyst's main rival as a staff adviser in an agency historically has been the budget officer (comptroller). This is hardly surprising since the final budget — both the dollar amounts and the written documentation — represents the ultimate outcome of the annual agency resource bargaining process. The two most successful analytic offices in the Johnson administration — Systems Analysis at DOD and RPP&E at OEO — both "solved" the budget relationship problem in separate ways. At DOD the chief budget officer, Charles Hitch, was a recognized authority on policy analysis and had been part of the Rand group that had developed the basic concepts that underlay PPBS; the budget function was captured by a PPBS theorist. By 1965, when Systems Analysis became a separate office, its power had been established under a Hitch disciple. At OEO a small budget office that had been part of the Office of Administration was moved to RPP&E early on, so the director of RPP&E headed the budget activities for the agency. This change enhanced RPP&E's position as the primary agency *staff* office responsible for determining major budgetary issues. The placing of the macro-level budget function in RPP&E removed the potential threat of a combination of the budget activity with related functions in the Office of Administration that might have permitted the emergence of a strong comptroller in that office.

Where such a clear superiority over the budgeter did *not* exist, there was the likelihood of a battle for influence, despite what the formal organization chart said. This is well illustrated by the changing situation at HEW over a decade. That experience, presented in the following case study, shows clearly the more subtle elements of the agency power struggle among top policy advisers. An able, influential comptroller at HEW during the Johnson administration was the classic example of the strong budget person who knew how to use budget information for power. His many years at the agency prior to PPBS had brought him wide influence within and outside the agency in HEW's various congressional committees. HEW, with its great diversity and multiple appropriations, faced a huge logistical problem each year in moving its budget through the Congress—a job requiring a great amount of mundane work to answer what were often routine questions about the details of a complex agency. But this service function also included working with Congress members to see that their special problems within the scope of HEW were addressed. The servicing of Congress put HEW's comptroller in that rare situation for a policy adviser—having an outside constituency. And the power base in the Congress enhanced his position to speak on important *ex ante* budgetary decisions in the agency.

In response to the BOB October 1965 directive establishing PPBS government-wide, Secretary John Gardner appointed William Gorham, who had served in DOD under McNamara, as head of the Office of the Assistant Secretary for Planning and Evaluation (OASPE), granting him responsibility for carrying out policy analysis within the agency and supplying what at the time appeared to be a reasonable number of staff persons. Although never as influential with the secretary as some of his Republican successors or his counterparts at OEO, Gorham was able to establish a base of reasonable influence with Gardner. However, OASPE was never able to dominate the budget office. In fact, probably the reverse was closer to being true.

When Wilbur Cohen replaced Gardner, and Alice Rivlin succeeded Gorham in 1968, the influence of the senior analyst with the secretary declined precipitously. The situation is a most interesting one for our purposes. On paper not much changed. Moreover, both Cohen and Rivlin were able individuals. Rivlin, who became the first director of the highly successful CBO, ranks as one of the top analytic office heads. Cohen, just out of graduate school, had been involved in the development of the original Social Security legislation in the mid-1930s. Between that time and his appointment as secretary, he had two distinguished carreers, as an academic and as a civil servant and political appointee at HEW. It may have been his deep knowledge of the agency that led him to doubt his need for help from the relatively new analytic staff headed by a young female analyst. It may have been his extremely strong ties to the agency's senior budget officer built up over a number of years. Whatever the reason, analytic influence dwindled to the lowest point in either the HEW or OEO settings during the period discussed in this chapter.

Nixon's first HEW secretary, Robert Finch, appointed his close California associate, Lewis Butler, as assistant secretary for planning and evaluation. Butler and John Veneman, the undersecretary who was also from California, were Secretary Finch's two principal generalist policy advisers. OASPE under Butler gained both additional staff and clear supremacy over the comptroller in the pecking order. However, Butler's influence seemed to be based more on the past relationship than on the use of analysis. As Joon Chien Doh observed: "Doubt exists . . . regarding whether the secretary has really understood PPBS: uncertainty pervades concerning whether he has been supporting the system."[5] Whether because of Finch's personal deficiencies, Butler's relative inexperience as an analyst, the earlier, primarily political, relationship between the two men, or some combination of these factors, policy analysis as policy analysis was in a somewhat suspended state at HEW during Finch's tenure. But let us not miss the point that the influence of the top policy analyst was high.

When Finch became a counselor to the president, Elliot Richardson, who replaced Finch as secretary, appointed Laurence Lynn, an economist whose background was similar to those of the earlier senior analysts at HEW and OEO, as assistant secretary for planning and evaluation. Not only was Lynn able to strengthen the staff and reestablish the analytic orientation, OASPE retained at least in part its superior status established under Finch vis-à-vis the comptroller. Moreover, Lynn was able to develop a more normal working relationship with the comptroller's staff to reduce conflicts. Although Lynn never achieved direct influence with the secretary comparable to that of Finch or of Lynn's successor (perhaps because Richardson's tenure was relatively short), his was an important transition period in restoring analytic excellence while retaining the *real* position gain over the comptroller. It is worth noting that Lynn moved to the Department of the Interior to head its analytic staff, and this was a period of particularly strong influence for that office, which reinforces the claim that policy analysis flourished in the Nixon-Ford years.[6]

Lynn's replacement, William Morrill, an experienced program examiner policy analyst, built on this base to become one of the most influential advisers to both Secretaries Casper Weinberger and David Mathews. During Morrill's tenure, OASPE grew into the largest and most diversified policy analysis and research office in the domestic policy agencies. A look at changes in size over time is interesting. OASPE and OEO's RPP&E began in 1965 with professional staffs numbering twenty to thirty and at most doubled by the end of the Johnson administration. By the beginning of 1975, OASPE had about 150 professional staff positions filled by people with a wide range of social science (still predominantly economics) and program examination skills including a number of specialists in experimentation and large-scale data management.

Large staff alone does not bring influence. However, in an agency such as HEW, with its vast size and great complexity, a big staff may be a necessary prerequisite for the analyst to gain adequate control over information.

Recall that the HEW comptroller's early advantage over the analyst in 1965 stemmed in part from his office's command of detailed information. The 1965 OASPE staff did not have much direct experience with HEW; 80 percent of the members came from outside the department. In his analysis of three federal agencies based on the Johnson administration and very early Nixon administration experience, Doh rated the Department of Agriculture analytic unit (another agency success story) superior to that of HEW, in part because of the experienced analytic staff in Agriculture, all of whom came from within the department.[7] My assessment of OASPE during the Johnson years was that the staff was too small and lacked the kinds of policy analysts labelled as program examiners. Program examiner policy analysts, as compared with the prototypical economist policy analysts, generally lack high-powered research skills and experience but have more in-depth knowledge of programs and an appreciation of organizational process and practices. Thus, program examiner policy analysts and research-oriented analysts have complementary skills and experience. Moreover, the program examiners should be indispensable to the policy analysis unit head in battles with other offices. Here program facts and bureaucratic nuances are often critical. At RPP&E in the Johnson years a program examiner policy analyst always served either as the deputy or the number three person in the hierarchy, and program examiners were well represented on the analytic staff. During that period the research-oriented policy analysts were in one division, the program examiner policy analysts in another. In policy areas such as manpower and community action, however, RPP&E teams contained policy analysts from both divisions. Based on my experience both as a staff person from the Research and Plans Division (the research-oriented policy analysts) working on a manpower policy team and as the division head working with several teams, I have seen the value of such interaction.

Particularly under Morrill, who had a program examiner background, OASPE brought in such people and gave OASPE more control over detailed agency information. Morrill and OASPE's great influence in HEW during the tenure of two secretaries can be attributed in part to Morrill's considerable bureaucratic and political skills matched by few other policy analysts. However, the large and able staff that provided the senior analyst with control over information and a response capacity to informational and advisory requests were also important in making Morrill such a formidable figure in the HEW influence game. Finally, the developmental aspects of OASPE should not be overlooked. In a vast, complex agency such as HEW, gaining real control over information may demand both personnel with extended knowledge of the workings of the agency bureaucracy and an established system of information control—both of which may require time to put in place.

During its first decade OASPE, except for the period of Cohen's tenure as secretary, had a significant impact on the agency decisionmaking process.

Twice in the Republican years, the top analysts, Butler and Morrill, had the secretary's ear and exercised considerable power. The variability is interesting, too. Rivlin, an able analyst, had a most limited influence although her boss was not only bright but research oriented. Despite his limited policy analysis training and experience, Butler had far more power than did Rivlin. Although Butler was teamed with a secretary who had little facility for analysis, Lynn, who was a capable analyst, had considerable influence with the highly analytic Elliot Richardson. Morrill, also able, was influential with both Weinberger and Mathews.

I cannot overemphasize how crucial to the impact of the analytic office is the personal chemistry between the top analyst and the secretary. Also of importance are the needs of the secretary. The "ideal" setting is that of an able analyst such as Rivlin, Lynn, or Morrill, and a reflective secretary who is interested in being presented information and alternatives and willing to read and to listen. Illustrative of this type is Elliot Richardson, who headed several agencies in the Nixon-Ford administrations. Richardson was described by one of the unnamed policy analysts interviewed by Arnold Meltsner in his study of federal policy analysts:

> He is by nature analytical. He is by nature a man who wants to approach problems objectively. He is by nature a man who is perfectly willing to put aside for a time the obvious and sometimes overwhelming political forces that may be pushing him in certain directions in order to think carefully through what the problem is and determine whether or not or how he personally wants to operate, what proposals he wants to make, how he wants to rationalize the positions he wants to take. He's very much willing to do this, and therefore he very much has provided a very strong stimulus to the development of good analytic capabilities, not only in my office but insofar as possible throughout the department.[8]

In contrast, Morrill gained great influence with Mathews because Mathews needed help to cope with an agency he did not understand.

PRESIDENTIAL POLICY ANALYSIS IN THE NIXON-FORD YEARS

Presidential policy analysis in the domestic policy areas flourished during the Nixon-Ford years, as illustrated in two case examples. OEO'S Office of Planning, Research and Evaluation (PR&E) presents a transition situation in which an *agency* analytic staff served the White House through the OEO director, who was also a presidential assistant. The Domestic Council is not an outright success but a failure or a near miss, depending on the accounts one is willing to accept. Yet it, too, is important in showing the potential for power and abuse by policy advisers at the presidential level.

A Presidential Think Tank

In the Nixon administration, OEO underwent major functional changes that had a visible effect on the analytic office. Much to everyone's surprise, President Nixon, who had attacked OEO in his campaign, lured Donald Rumsfeld from his Illinois congressional seat by promising to continue OEO and to give Rumsfeld a voice in overall government policy toward the poor. Rumsfeld was appointed both OEO director and assistant to the president. Also, in PR&E the research effort in support of policy planning increased materially under the able direction of John Wilson and Thomas Glennan. At full strength RPP&E's two research-oriented divisions numbered about twenty professionals. PR&E had three research-oriented divisions with a combined staff numbering over fifty professionals. The total research budget increased from slightly over $7 million in the last year of the Johnson administration (fiscal year 1968) to $23 million in fiscal year 1971, with roughly two-thirds of the funds allocated for major field experiments, such as the New Jersey negative income tax.

Almost immediately, PR&E's policy analysis efforts shifted from direct OEO concerns to those of the White House and the newly created Domestic Council. Through Rumsfeld the office provided a flow of analysis to the White House. In support of analysis, PR&E engaged in major research activities such as a continuation of the New Jersey experiment, the funding of a companion rural negative-income tax experiment, and planning efforts for a major health insurance experiment. None of these studies concerned OEO's direct operating programs. OEO apparently carried too many political liabilities from its past to spring rejuvenated as an experimenting agency. But for a brief period, PR&E operated like a social policy research office relatively independent of a specific social agency.

The Domestic NSC

In his Reorganization Message to Congress dated March 12, 1970, President Nixon stated, "The Domestic Council will be primarily concerned with *what* we do; the Office of Management and Budget will be primarily concerned with *how* we do it and how *well* we do it." The division of labor between the Domestic Council staff and OMB was crucial. The former was to be the administration's analytic arm for domestic policy just as National Security Council (NSC) staff was for foreign policy and its head, John Ehrlichman, was to occupy a position similar to that of Henry Kissinger. OMB was to be downgraded or removed from major analytic activities, instead concentrating on management, administration, and assessment. Important in assessing presidential policy analysis are how well the Domestic Council worked, how viable the division of labor between the council and OMB was, and how the reorganization and later changes altered OMB.

Raymond Waldmann, who served on the Domestic Council staff, has argued that the staff was a success as an analytic office. During the last two years of President Nixon's first term, which Waldmann called the heyday of the Domestic Council, he claimed that the Domestic Council staff "succeeded to a degree never before attempted in gaining centralized political control over the Executive Branch for the president. . . . It kept information, analysis, and proposals flowing from the Oval Office and reactions, decision, and presidential priorities flowing to the agencies."[9] There is another side to the Domestic Council staff's "success." The staff, at least on the drawing board, appeared to have the main function of serving the cabinet members who made up the council. However, as Thomas E. Cronin observed: "[T]he Domestic Council staff at the White House became, at least under Nixon, a kind of operating center. . . . Some of the Domestic Council staff soon became more prominent in policy decisions than the members of the Council — the cabinet officials — whom they were supposed to assist."[10]

Where the Domestic Council staff ran into problems was with OMB. First was a pure power question. Although Ehrlichman enjoyed insider status in the Nixon administration, the status was not comparable to that of Kissinger in national security affairs. The proposed split between the Domestic Council and OMB was not implemented fully, in part because of the power of OMB Director George Shultz, who was at least a coequal to Ehrlichman in the presidential policy process. Furthermore, the Domestic Council staff suffered vis-à-vis OMB because of the council's lack of established institutional channels to information such as those that existed in budgeting. Finally, there is the matter of competence to do analysis. Cronin's question that applies not only to the Nixon administration but to earlier ones is especially apt: "But is it now enough to have a small band of staff lawyers or former public relations specialists manage the nation's domestic policy?"[11] Apparently not, if the objective is to have a separate, strong analytic office for domestic policy and a strong, professionally competent, relatively nonpolitical central budget office. As Hugh Heclo has observed, "It was an ill-starred division of tasks [between the Domestic Council staff and OMB]. Thinking about what to do turned out to be difficult without having the people around who could tell you how to do it. Since they had much of the necessary experience and expertise, OMB staff members were increasingly drafted into Domestic Council operations — and even directed by council leaders not to inform OMB colleagues of their work (a secrecy which, predictably enough, was rarely pledged and even more rarely maintained)."[12] At least in an analytically oriented presidency, sound policy information and analysis had a critical place in the institutional process.

The politicization of OMB is crucial to an understanding of presidential policy analysis in domestic policy. OMB (then BOB) prior to the Nixon reorganization had few political appointees, so it relied heavily on its career, professional staff in decisionmaking. Here unquestionably was *the* elite career staff in the federal government, where career staff held most of the top spots, were at the center of power, and yet were viewed as the ultimate nonpartisan analysts. Up until the Eisenhower administration, there were only two political appointees, and at times the director or the deputy director was career staff. Eisenhower raised the political appointees to five, but only two were in the key "line" positions.[13] The heads of the major budget divisions were careerists, who as a class rivaled any British treasury mandarins in prestige and power. A call from a program division chief to the secretary of an agency for lunch would send the cabinet member scurrying to arrange a date as soon as possible. The division chiefs were the most powerful GS-18s (then the highest civil-service grade) in the government. The decision-making chain went from careerist division chiefs straight to the deputy director and the director.

Despite its flaws, BOB was a place "to look for [budget] analysis with a minimum of political body English."[14] At "old" BOB, a president could find a hardheaded, independent judgment based on information and analysis. The politicization of the central budget agency came about mainly because of Nixon's unceasing effort to gain control over the permanent bureaucrats in the agencies or on his own staff. The reorganization and subsequent changes created a new layer of political appointees between the career staff and the OMB Director and hence the president. A panel of the National Academy of Public Administration (NAPA) has observed, "The emergence of a powerful White House staff which has progressively assumed the role of speaking for the president has seriously diminished the responsibilities of the career, professional staff of OMB and its capacity to provide the kind of objective and expert counsel to the president which characterized earlier operations."[15] The issue of the politicization of OMB, which suffered declining power in the Carter years, becomes an even larger question with Reagan and David Stockman.

Analytic Competition: The Case of the Economic Policy Board

The argument for openness and analytic competition rests on the fallibility of the available analytic tools in coping with policy complexity. Recognizing such weaknesses as the impossibility of producing certain kinds of badly needed policy information, the pitfalls of faulty analysis, and the need for analytic scrutiny and challenge is a vital stage in the building of a more effective institutional process. This fallibility of the analytic tools and techniques makes open competition among strong analytic units so critical. In this setting, advocacy and an adversary relationship have an important place in the development of sound information and analysis in support of policymaking. Proponents of "multiple advocacy" recognize that those who argue about

policy are partisans and maintain that competition among such policy adviser advocates in an open, managed policy process can improve the level of
information and analysis available for policymaking. Management of the process is central to healthy competition. At the presidential level, the need is
for a managed policymaking process that fosters competition among competent top-level generalist policy adviser advocates and keeps analytic firepower
in rough balance among the competitors. Fair competition is expected both
to raise the level of the policy debate and to protect the president from analytic errors and abuses. The critical elements of a viable process of presidential multiple advocacy include a president who wants multiple advocacy and
is willing to pay the price for it, competent generalist policy adviser advocates and specialist analysts distributed fairly among the key competitors, a
policymaking process that moves sound analysis to the top, and an honest
broker to micromanage the process for the president. The honest broker is
the key staff person, whose central function is to foster fair competition
among policy adviser advocates so that the president has as full a range as
possible of well-analyzed alternatives. The honest broker's effectiveness requires that he or she be judged as neutral, fair, and objective by the top
generalist policy adviser advocates in the presidential policy process. The
honest broker contrasts sharply with both Kissinger, who controlled the process tightly to keep out other policy adviser advocates, at least in face-to-face
encounters, and presidential policy process managers who seek outside arguments but are themselves strong policy adviser advocates likely to have privileged access to the president.

The best example of successful multiple advocacy is the EPB.[16] The EPB
was established as the focal point for all presidential economic policy when
there was a serious economic crisis that the Ford administration thought
demanded policy responsibility consolidated in a single body. Roger Porter,
a key EPB staff member, has asserted that Ford also saw the EPB as a means
of restoring the cabinet role in White House economic policymaking with
Secretary of the Treasury William E. Simon as chair and most of the cabinet
as members.[17] However, the board was dominated by a five-member executive
committee, all of whom except Simon were EOP staff—the heads of CEA,
OMB, the Council on International Economic Policy, and L. William Seidman,
who was executive director of both the EPB and the executive committee—
surely strong evidence of how much economic policy responsibility centered
on EOP rather than on agency staff, including political executives.

Porter, who not only served on the EPB staff but has written the definitive
work on it, has argued that the EPB was effective in meeting President Ford's
needs for wide-ranging, well-staffed economic analysis. Porter cited a senior
official who maintained that "[the EPB's] most important strength was that
it provided a mechanism for reaching into various departments and finding
staff expertise on issues," and another official who claimed that "it was a

model for interdepartmental communications, cooperation [and] resolution of issues."[18] Two men were critical in this successful case of multiple advocacy. President Ford was impressed by solid evidence and comfortable with oral debate. He was willing to hear people out, to listen to different points of view *and* to do homework, which could include reading a number of economic tracts. In addition, Ford was comfortable with acting as a neutral judge during much of the give and take, seldom indicating which way he leaned. Such neutrality is a critical stimulant to open debate. Seidman, who had been a key assistant to Vice-President Ford and had a good relationship with him, was that rare creature, a relatively modest assistant to the president. He was willing to allow Secretary Simon to be the administration's point man on economic policy, since Simon enjoyed the role of public spokesperson. Seidman was also comfortable with the honest-broker role. He perceived managing the presidential policy process rather than individual policy advocacy as his main task. Seidman was willing to act "as a surrogate for the executive in attempting to assure the quality of the search and analysis phases of policymaking that precede final action . . . [and] to insure that the executive will have a number of well-considered, well-presented options to choose from."[19]

Multiple advocacy is not necessarily a technique for all seasons.[20] First, it demands a particular presidential personality. Neither brilliance, in-depth knowledge, nor an analytic orientation itself insure that multiple advocacy will be a president's preferred mode of operation. Second, an honest broker is hard to find. Third, multiple advocacy stresses conflict and is time-consuming and the best debater does not necessarily offer the wisest policy advice. To some extent these problems can be countered with strong management and a stress on written documents, but high skill in process management and much time are demanded. A viable multiple-advocacy process is hardest to implement at the start of an administration, just when it is most needed, as the Reagan experience illustrates dramatically. A president may see the need to avoid openness if he wants to exert immediate control as was the case in 1981. Unlike Reagan, Ford had no agenda; he also inherited an ongoing administration with seasoned policy adviser generalists in place.

Porter underscores three weaknesses of the EPB process that are significant for understanding deficiencies not only in that multiple-advocacy process itself but in policy analysis generally: political insensitivity, domination of a prevailing ideology, and lack of strategic thinking. Porter quoted a White House staff member who argued that the EPB "tended to talk too much to itself. . . . [I]t needed in it, more of a political component."[21] As Porter recognized, President Ford to some extent may have provided the political spin. But top-level policy staff members need political sensitivity so that policy and politics can be integrated. Though the EPB shied away from partisan politics, it was dominated by a single political ideology characterized as "the 'old time religion' in economic policy."[22] A dominant ideology can restrict unduly the alternatives developed for the president and so dominate process. As Porter wrote after his service at the EPB, "A shared economic philosophy is more a reflection of the individuals selected to fill major administration positions than of the way advising the president is organized. In the end, people count as much as process."[23] Finally, Porter faults the EPB for not having an overall strategic plan. The deficiency flowed not from the structure or staffing of the EPB, but from President Ford's style of taking problems one at a time without any strategic concern for interrelationships or impact on administration goals.

CARTER'S DOMESTIC POLICY STAFF

The Domestic Policy Staff under Stuart Eizenstat vividly illustrates the strengths and weaknesses of a White House domestic policy unit in its service to a president deeply concerned with policy and information.[24] Carter was extremely intelligent and thought much like a narrow analyst. At the same time he did not think strategically. In her Carter biography Betty Glad laments, "[Carter] lacks, it seems, a well-thought-out conceptual framework to guide his concrete political choices. He immerses himself in the technical details of programs that interest him, testing various strategies and rhetorical appeals. Yet he fails to bring the components together in an integrated approach that would give him a sense of direction and set up priorities for his various programs."[25] The strategic problems of the Carter administration were captured by the following statement, repeated by an interviewee who could not recall the source: "Secretary of Defense Harold Brown looks at the trees; the president himself looks at the leaves; National Security Adviser Zbigniew Brzezinski looks at the biosphere; and the forest goes unnoticed." In their study of welfare reform, Laurence E. Lynn and David de F. Whitman state: "Carter seemed to encourage his advisers to focus on discrete, technical issues, rather than inspiring them to a noble calling. . . . In the hundreds of pages of memoranda and in the records and recollections of discussions generated during the seven months of welfare-reform debate within the administration, there is scarcely a word about how welfare reform was related to the problems of the cities, federal-state relations, the economy, or equality of opportunity by race and sex. . . . This was a classic case of missing the forest for the trees. Only Carter could have been the chief forester; instead, he was just another lumberjack."[26]

A member of that administration, considered one of the brightest persons around Carter, told me that Carter was exceptionally intelligent and quick. He was able to grasp new, complex ideas rapidly and discuss them with surprising understanding. The interviewee thought Carter had a first-rate analytic mind and would put him up against any of the recent presidents for quickness and capacity to master complex issues.[27] Moreover, Carter liked engaging in analysis. Indeed, Carter often looked much like the classic policy analyst *qua* engineer–operations researcher who seeks a pristine optimum solution without concern for political, institutional, or bureaucratic reality. In discussing Carter's political personality and style of leadership, Hargrove wrote:

1. He liked programs to be comprehensive attacks on problems rather than incremental steps.
2. He was hostile to interest groups or any form of particularism that might block comprehensive solutions.
3. He believed that there were "correct" answers to problems that rational people could find.[28]

These grand comprehensive attacks on problems should not be confused with vision. Comprehensiveness is on the "means," not the "ends," side. In reality, the grand solution is not broad but rather a kind of tunnel vision representing a stress on rationality, solvability, and the power of science, combined with a disinterest in and lack of understanding of organizational processes and a distaste for politics. There is a second, equally perplexing aspect of Carter's behavior. Carter did not demand a high level of domestic policy analysis or see the value in building a strong analytic staff in support of the domestic presidency.

Carter remains an enigma in the areas of analysis and organization. Even his intelligence and analytic mind seemed to hinder him. He focused too much on detail, and his insight into the complexities of problems made it difficult for him to stick with a decision. An interviewee observed, "I once spent two hours in the office of the head of an economic agency, while he sounded off to me about the fact that there simply was no economic policy, because everyone knew that if you lost the argument one week, you could come back and reargue it the next, and Carter would change his mind. No one could implement the decision since it was not perceived as permanent." Another bewildering aspect of Carter's presidency was his approach to organizational issues. One of his strongest claims in the 1976 election campaign was that he had reorganized the state of Georgia, reducing the number of state agencies from 300 to 22 and that he would do the same for the federal government. He was the first presidential candidate to offer government reorganization as a major theme. Early on he established a reorganization project and created a new associate director position at the top of OMB. But Peri Arnold, who has studied presidential reorganization attempts in this century, argues that "Carter sought to use reorganization as a way of attracting voter attention and loyalty, but he gave little evidence of realizing that it might be a means for dealing with governance."[29] Carter was not an "organizational man" president. He seemed to see organization as lots of little connected boxes on an organization chart with a main goal of eliminating them — "box count" was equivalent to "body count" in Vietnam. Carter had no concept of organizational dynamics as central to governance.

Stuart Eizenstat and DPS Operations

A *National Journal* article written early in the Carter administration quoted one cabinet member's aide as saying that Eizenstat seemed to him to function as a "high-powered research assistant."[30] Over time, however, Eizenstat became Carter's most important generalist domestic policy adviser — the only head of a domestic policy unit in the inner circle and the only member of that inner circle consistently looked to for advice on domestic policy substance. Eizenstat and his rise are both intriguing and important for an appreciation of the dynamics of a policy office and the development of a generalist policy adviser. Eizenstat himself is an appealing figure — bright, hard-working, fair-minded, and seemingly without the burning drive for power that often almost oozes from young White House insiders. No evidence in my interviews suggests that Eizenstat sought power or tried to increase the responsibilities and size of DPS as a means of gaining preeminence in domestic policy. One interviewee told me that Eizenstat never really understood how much power he had and "at times seemed not to understand that he had much power at all." Yet, Eizenstat finally emerged to dominate domestic policy.

Eizenstat grew tremendously in his job, and after four years he had most of the traits needed by a competent generalist policy adviser. But a long period of on-the-job training at the top for a generalist policy adviser can be a costly endeavor. A member of the Carter administration subcabinet told me after reading an earlier version of this chapter, "You are far too nice to Stu. He is a super person — of the highest quality. But you should not judge Eizenstat by how he acted at the *end* of the Carter administration. By that time, Stu was much more sophisticated. But he messed things up for two years getting to that point."

DPS was not a policy analysis operation. The issue was not the intelligence of the staff, of Eizenstat, or of the other lawyers at the top. Though there were a few competent policy analysts on the staff, the framework of policy analysis did not guide DPS efforts. The staff reminded me of a British Cabinet Office unit — the Central Policy Review Staff (CPRS) — that was referred to as the "think tank." CPRS differed from the usual British staff by bringing in outsiders. These people were unusually young (in their twenties and thirties), bright and brash, but like most high-level British civil servants they were generalists with nontechnical educations from Oxford or Cambridge.

They were Britain's version of the DOD "whiz kids," but unlike them, CPRS members were not hard-edged policy analysts.[31]

DPS roughly doubled in size over time, finally numbering 55–60 members, of whom about half were professionals. The three top people, all lawyers, were Eizenstat, assistant to the president for Domestic Affairs and Policy; David Rubinstein, deputy assistant for Domestic Affairs and Policy; and Bert Carp, deputy director of the DPS. There were ten associate directors in the following areas: Agriculture and Rural Development, Economics, Transportation and Labor, HUD, Government Reorganization, Human Resources (Health), Human Resources (Employment), Arts and Humanities, Civil Rights, and Justice. There were also at least seventeen assistant directors with subspecialties in the areas under the associate directors.

Over time DPS took on more and more policy development responsibilities. The staff continued to work with the agencies that did the major analyses and with their counterparts in OMB. One high DPS official stressed the good working relationships at lower levels with OMB and said that "OMB was involved at all stages." From its earliest days in the Carter administration, DPS produced a covering memorandum for the president that summarized the agency positions and offered DPS's own recommendations on domestic policy decisions. Over time DPS recommendations became more important. In the pecking order, DPS moved to the top.

Articles in 1979 issues of the *Congressional Quarterly* and the *National Journal* offered glowing descriptions of DPS at the height of its influence.[32] Several staff members had congressional or executive branch experience. A high percentage of the professional staff were lawyers. The DPS staff has been criticized for a lack of depth and *substantive knowledge*. Ben W. Heineman and Curtis A. Hessler assert, "DPS has consisted of forty to sixty people who specialized (*though they were infrequently expert*) in a variety of substantive areas. They attempted to manage great numbers of interagency issues and to maintain close liaison with all manner of constituencies. Too often, DPS has been a complicating factor throughout the government, an institutional rival of OMB in the routine business of government . . . and a powerful magnet for interest group pressures on the White House and thus on the president.[33] If the *National Journal* and *Congressional Quarterly* pieces are too positive, Heineman and Hessler may be too harsh. There were competent people on the DPS staff, including a few sound policy analysts. At the same time, tremendous pressures on Eizenstat and his staff led to a harried pace that often cut into quality. Weaknesses were magnified as the staff became increasingly overburdened and grew more powerful. The brashness of some of the younger staff and the inadequacies of weaker staff members became more obvious.

Eizenstat: An Assessment

Eizenstat clearly was talented, intelligent, and industrious. Moreover, he had a fundamental integrity and also was able to be highly objective. But he was not without liabilities, even after he had gained the necessary on-the-job experience. A sympathetic EOP policy analyst asserts: "Eizenstat himself is very objective. He may come into a meeting with a position worked out by his staff that they think he agrees to, take that position, get evidence to the contrary, and turn around on his opinion. However, he did look at things primarily in political terms. *Also, it is unclear whether or not he appreciated how little policy analysis he got from his staff*" (my emphasis).

Eizenstat was a man in the middle. On the one hand, the highly political types in the inner circle, such as Hamilton Jordan, often saw the bookish Eizenstat as politically naive. In the narrow sense of their perspective, cast in terms of short-run electoral politics, he probably was naive at times. On the other hand, as the only member of the inner circle with policy credentials, it is hardly surprising that some of the policy analysis types questioned his policy purity and capability. Eizenstat had a different, and much wider, view of politics than did the other key members of the inner circle. He believed strongly that the president needed the broad Democratic party coalition, not simply in electoral politics but in terms of the capacity of a Democratic president to govern. Close ties with the congressional Democrats and the key interest groups in the Democratic coalition were critical, not just in reelecting the president, but also in policy development over time. Especially in the early period, the Carter inner circle members who could have been expected to handle these relationships did poorly. As one interviewee put it, "Hell, Ham never even returned phone calls." Jordan especially, but some of the other inner circle too, appeared at times to think that politics consisted of campaigning every four years for office and taking polls. In a White House that was weak at the top in relationships with Congress and key interest groups, Eizenstat had problems. An interviewee who served in the Carter subcabinet observed, "Stu was basically unable or unwilling to deal with Jordan. If he couldn't deal with Ham, there could be no fusion of policy and politics. To be sure, the ultimate responsibility was Carter's. But Stu could have done more than he did."

Eizenstat was often labeled as analytically naive and far too political by people from OMB. Criticism flowed in part from the budget professional's mentality that likes to cast policy analysis as nonpolitical, and in part from "sour grapes" because of the relative configuration that made Eizenstat more powerful than OMB Director James McIntyre. However, Eizenstat does appear to have placed too much emphasis on the political aspects of policy issues in his role as generalist policy adviser. One explanation is that the failure of the political types in the inner circle to have any concern for policy except in the narrowest electoral terms forced Eizenstat and DPS to overcompensate. Or possibly Eizenstat's political biases, combined with his own lack of knowledge of policy analysis *and* that of his top aides, better explain the overemphasis on politics. The EOP policy analyst, quoted earlier as indicating Eizenstat's bias toward politics and lack of appreciation of how little policy analysis he got from his staff, went on to observe about the other two top people in DPS: "[Bert] Carp was really good at political analysis, but was almost exclusively [doing] political analysis without any policy analysis. Rubinstein was super bright but very young and inexperienced. Further, he was a lawyer with no analytic framework. So the three people at the top simply did not push for policy analysis."

The DPS problem was one of balance at the top. A strong policy analyst in the leadership group could have provided an analytic counterweight and technical quality control in DPS. A few more competent policy analysts in DPS could have demanded both better analysis and analysis more relevant to the president's specific policy needs from the agency analytic units, which were dominated by policy analysts, and have provided the analytic competence to monitor the agency efforts — a fighting-fire-with-fire argument. One reason Eizenstat did not bring on such people may have been that he did not have much of an understanding of policy analysis and at times seemed to see it as mainly technical number-crunching. It is these kinds of personal elements that bedevil those of us who would offer prescriptions on the structure and staffing of the EOP.

Eizenstat had management problems within DPS and in DPS's relationships with both other EOP units and agencies. Once he became the main domestic policy adviser, too much work became a continuing state of affairs that kept Eizenstat and his staff under constant pressure and mitigated against extensive staff interaction or critical analyses. In the main, DPS staff simply did not have much time to think, and this problem flowed at least in part from Eizenstat's mismanagement. An EOP policy analyst said, "Eizenstat felt the president wanted to be involved in a tremendous number of issues and did not block or cut off issues to protect him. This meant that Stu's plate kept getting more and more full. Eizenstat was programmed with a vengeance. It was extremely difficult to get him to spend much time on an issue. A member of Congress tried to get Eizenstat to bring in good people and talk out a problem. But Stu never would reflect deeply on an issue in this manner — he claimed he never had the time."

Some of the young DPS activists were abrasive and caused external relationship problems that Eizenstat handled poorly. A Carter administration EOP staff member cited the case of an intelligent young staff member who had considerable experience and expertise in the assigned specialty area gained as an outside activist but who had no credentials from within government or the academic community. This was the kind of situation likely to bring problems with older, more credentialed agency or EOP career staff. The former EOP staff member questioned whether the young staff person could have worked out these relationships alone, and he drew a broader conclusion: "Stu never really did understand this kind of bureaucratic dynamics, and this was a real weakness that diminished the effectiveness of his staff. Stu did not appreciate either power or bureaucratic politics and that meant he did not appreciate how to use his staff, did not appreciate how threatening and abrasive some of these people from the outside seemed to be."

Some of Eizenstat's management problems were clearly at the subpresidential level. Others were at the point of relationship between Eizenstat and the president where Eizenstat can be faulted for not getting the president to see that he was handling too many issues and needed priorities so that he could concentrate his attention. Many of Eizenstat's organizational problems, however, flowed from the basic weakness in the Carter White House itself. Carter seemed to have almost no understanding of the dynamics of policymaking when bureaucratic politics and personalities loomed so large. Operating under these adverse circumstances and when compared with people who occupied similar positions in past administrations. Eizenstat fares well. He stands out in the Carter administration as an unusually modest and likable individual.

Eizenstat and DPS filled some of the vacuum Carter created. It was Eizenstat, not only the ablest member of the inner circle concerned with domestic issues, but also the only one who could live comfortably in the world of politics and policy, who had increasingly more power thrust on him. Eizenstat labored hard and with some success in serving his president, but he erred badly at times and was often a poor manager. In short: (1) he was the only member of the Carter inner circle who tried to live in both worlds of politics and policy; (2) he overemphasized politics in the policy-politics equation; (3) he did not appreciate how little rigorous policy analysis his staff did, nor did he recognize its importance in complementing his lawyer generalist orientation; (4) he was not a good manager of staff resources; (5) much criticism of Eizenstat is criticism of the Carter presidency, in that the overloyal Eizenstat tried to carry out faithfully the president's bidding, even though he did not necessarily agree with it.

DPS ended up being much less than the sum of its parts. My assessment rests on the assumption that policy analysis should be a central function of the domestic policy unit. For a policy analyst looking at a policy staff, such an assumption is so basic that it is more implicit than explicit. But is it a fair assumption? A case might be made that the White House domestic policy unit should be made up primarily, or perhaps even exclusively, of broad generalists whose orientation is more political than policy-dominated. History supports such a claim. Unlike the NSC staff, domestic policy units do not have a tradition of strong policy analysis. The two most prominent heads before Eizenstat were also generalist lawyers: Joseph Califano and John Ehrlich-man. Beyond history, the vacuum at the top in the Carter administration that Eizenstat tried to fill forced an imbalance that overemphasized politics over policy. Eizenstat and his staff were drawn more and more into political activities, including some lobbying on the Hill. Nevertheless, Eizenstat failed to appreciate the necessity of both policy analysts and generalists, and that resulted in a policy staff not capable of ensuring a flow of sound, timely, relevant expert policy information, analysis, and advice to the president in the domestic area.

SOME CAUTIONARY THEMES

Policy analysis units have had a significant impact on federal policymaking. Even in the Reagan years, when policy units declined in competence and influence, and policy analysis itself all but disappeared, the administration occasionally used policy-analysis rhetoric (particularly in cost-benefit analysis) and analytic units (mainly OMB) to underpin its policies. The big question, then, is not whether policy analysis and the information experts are powerful, but how the power can be better used. Policy analysis is most dangerous under two circumstances. First is its misuse as a cover for justifying policy recommendations or decisions based on other criteria, such as ideological predilections. I would prefer not to label such a justification effort as policy analysis, since in my definition of policy analysis, it occurs *before* the choice among alternatives is made; such an effort would be better depicted as "ersatz" policy analysis. However, in a verbal or a written policy presentation, listeners or readers may not be able to determine that the ersatz policy analysis came after the fact. Sound policy analysis is likely to contain some element of justification. We must be careful not to ignore normal analytic practice that tries to make the case for the policy adviser advocate's position. As Giandomenico Majone observes, "There is nothing intrinsically reprehensible in selecting the particular combination of data, facts, values, and analytic methods that seem to be the most appropriate to convince the people who have to accept or carry out a decision."[34] But the competent analyst should do the rigorous analysis first to provide a sound basis for a policy recommendation.

The second danger is when policy analysis is too technical and narrow, both hindering nontechnical inputs and excluding important factors that do not mesh well with the underlying analytic framework. The first danger of ersatz policy analysis carries well beyond methodology and structure and is most difficult to combat within the structure of policy analysis itself, because what passes for technical analysis is "working," in the sense of doing what the leader wants by justifying his or her policies. This second major danger, however, involves both method and structure. The overuse of esoteric techniques has led to abuse by and mistrust of policy analysts. Simpler approaches, combining relatively straightforward analytic and research techniques with bureaucratic-political knowledge and judgment, will often yield valuable information and recommendations for policymaking. In part this view reflects the notion that analytic and research information should be scrutinized by nontechnicians. The more straightforward the techniques, the less likely that wrongheaded analysis and research will slip through under the cover of "high-powered" methodology. The prescription, however, is not simply a negative one. Straightforward technical approaches that can be understood at least at the conceptual level by nontechnicians appear to be the ones most likely to benefit significantly from inputs of organizational and political wisdom. They are most likely to lead the analyst to asking the right question, which can be the most difficult — but not the most esoteric — of the analytic tasks. Such techniques seem the ones least likely to cause errors and abuses. They are also likely in the short term to increase capability in the analysis-decision system, so that more complex approaches can be employed, if needed, and to restore confidence in the use of scientific techniques. One strong argument for having a program examiner policy analyst at or near the top of an analytic unit, as well as on the staff, is that these analysts are likely to work well with the nontechnicians and to assure that policy analysis is "on target" for top decisionmakers.

Policy analysis as presently practiced is weak in treating political and implementation feasibility. The analysis of political feasibility is shunned by "objective" policy analysts trying to avoid partisan politics; "political analysis is somebody else's job." But as Peter J. May has argued:

> There is a continuing difficulty in integrating political considerations — in a small "p" rather than partisan politics sense — with hard analysis. This is both an organizational phenomenon and a difficulty for the craft of analysis in blending hard and soft analysis. The lifespan and credibility of policy analysis units may be jeopardized if they become tainted by particular ideologies. . . . The dilemma is that in order for an analysis or analytic unit to contribute a realistic set of policy options, ideological and political factors need to be considered. The typical assumption is that someone else will provide the political analysis — the assistant secretary of an executive agency, or the member of Congress or committee staff. Yet, one of the salient lessons of the implementation literature and emerging policy design literature is that political considerations are not simply an overlay to be applied to hard analyses of options. They are fundamental to the design and eventual implementation of the options.[35]

Unfortunately, the bulk of work in political science has little or no relevance to the necessary political analyses.[36]

The second technical weakness—the analysis of implementation feasibility—arises from different causes than does political feasibility. First is the well-known proclivity of economists to ignore organizational dynamics, arguing that market forces will solve the organization problems. This is a questionable enough approach in treating the private sector, let alone the public sector, where institutional rather than market forces dominate. Second, and closely related to the problems of analyzing political feasibility, is that the work on implementation produces soft information that is difficult methodologically to integrate with hard data. Although the broad analytic framework allows the use of soft data, narrow policy analysts are ill-equipped both technically and psychologically to use it. However, as Henry Aaron, both an outstanding economist and a former analytic office head, warned his fellow economists in his Ely lecture at the 1988 American Economics Association meetings: "[A]nalysis that prescribes rules before devoting serious attention to whether they can be implemented and sustained is at best incomplete and at worst irresponsible."[37] The problem is that a policy decision is a seamless web of technical, organizational, and political factors, ultimately demanding reasoned judgment. Robert W. Komer caught one aspect of the policy problem: "It is . . . tempting to suggest, as one key lesson of Vietnam, that 'policy is easy to decide, execution is much more difficult.' But this would be a grievous oversimplification. For sound policy formulation must itself take fully into account the capabilities of the institutions involved to execute it effectively."[38] It makes no sense to recommend a policy alternative until the necessary implementation analysis has been carried out to determine the likelihood of successful implementation. The world does not neatly divide a policy decision into the policy proper, implementation, and politics so that different specialists can tackle each one separately.

In discussing deficiencies in policy analysis we must consider value analysis. In the Reagan years not only did ideology come clearly to the fore, it got entangled with a "hard" approach when cost-benefit analysis became the Reagan weapon of choice in attacking government regulation. Cost-benefit analysis, which historically underlay the early policy analysis when it was cast in its most value-free and rigorous form, in recent years has become even more pretentious than policy analysis in its claims to purity and rigor. But for all the claims, cost-benefit analysis is equally flawed and usually more narrow in its approach than other policy analysis techniques. The areas of politics, implementation and cost-benefit analysis can *all* benefit from greater simplicity and wider scrutiny and challenge inside and outside policy analysis.

One final point: Beyond analysis is judgment. As Alain C. Enthoven and D. Wayne Smith point out: "Analysis is no substitute for judgment and the analyst cannot do final judging. But judgment can be a poor substitute for fact and analysis. Policy should result from a combination of judgment and analysis."[39] The problem is that few can move competently across the various segments of a policy decision. That is why the generalist policy adviser is so critical in the presidential or agency policy equation and why the top policy analysts in the policymaking process must think in terms of integrating the various areas and of translating policy proposals into usable form for policymakers.

4

The Reagan Era: First Term

In the Reagan years there was a radical shift from policy analysis to political ideology. The terms "ideology" and "ideologue" can carry with them pejorative images of irrationality and distortion. In these terms ideology is based on unshakable assumptions and is not amenable to factual challenge. The argument is not that Reagan was an ideologue in the conventional sense of having a rigorous, at least internally consistent set of interrelated principles or of leading a movement based on such principles, but that his guides to action were principles he did not challenge with "hard" evidence.[1] In this form, Reagan's ideology of the right became prevalent and a threat to institutional policy analysis in the executive branch. The ideology of the left can be equally threatening; it can lead to unthinking support for expanding social and environment policies while ignoring strong analytic evidence of weaknesses in parts or all of particular policies. The true believers of the left and the right are alike in their treatment of both evidence and opposition to their views. The political spectrum is better characterized not as a straight-line continuum from right to left, but as a circle, with the extremes coming together. In the Reagan era the country moved to the right politically, as did the Reagan administration, led by the true believers, who occupied so many key positions in the White House and the agencies. As the increasing policy complexity defied the best available analytic techniques, the conflict between policy analysis and political ideology opened the door for Reagan's politics of unreality. His leadership and style of governance rested on unshakable principles, extreme optimism, hands-off management, and indifference to details, and it had no place for rigorous analysis that might challenge ideology.

CHARISMA AND THE POLITICS OF UNREALITY

Reagan's two terms, the first eight-year presidency since that of Dwight Eisenhower, were remarkable. Most remarkable was Reagan's ability to recover from a scandal that was a jolt to presidential popularity unmatched in the postwar years, except by Watergate. The Iran-Contra scandal propelled Reagan downward from ratings of close to 70 percent public approval to 42 percent. Yet, in the January 1989 polls he was back at 68 percent, with the highest final rating for a president in the postwar years. President Eisenhower's ending score of 59 percent approval is the closest rival; Nixon had a 24 percent approval rating when he resigned. After the last four presidents had either been driven from office or defeated for a second term, President Reagan left in triumph, with roughly half of the people in a *Washington Post* survey believing he would be rated as an above-average president and only 10 percent seeing him as below average.[2] How did President Reagan from his inauguration until the Iran-Contra scandal come to dominate American politics and, to a degree, world politics?[3] How did a president with an arguably limited attachment to reality and little organizational understanding come to be seen as a masterful leader with broad vision who brilliantly delegated responsibility? How did Reagan recover from Iran-Contra?

The key to understanding Ronald Reagan is his political charisma, Max Weber's critical leadership concept. Charisma induces followers to grant an extremely high degree of power, value agreement, esteem, and loyalty to a political leader who is confident of his mission. The term "charisma" is used restrictively, following Ann Ruth Willner, who in her major work on political charisma found only seven charismatic national political leaders in recent decades — Hitler, Mussolini, Castro, Khomeini, Sukarno, Gandhi, and Franklin Roosevelt.[4] Willner, who categorized John Kennedy as a "postmortem" charismatic, does not treat President Reagan.[5] However, I consider him the only truly charismatic president since FDR.

Political charisma cannot be defined precisely, but it can be identified by four key elements. First is people dominance. The charismatic leader can reach and move both elites and the public without coercion. Most critical is the followers' willingness to believe. As Willner has argued, "Followers believe statements made and ideas advanced by their leader simply because it is he who made the statement or advanced the idea. It is not necessary for them to weigh or test the truth of the statement or the plausibility of the idea."[6] Second is agenda and mood dominance. David Broder wrote in 1988 that "it is not an idle boast when the president told officials of his administration the other day that they had brought about 'a fundamental change of direction' in government. . . . Reagan has redefined the fundamental principles that guided two or more generations of government policy."[7] His mood dominance is even more impressive. President Reagan took a country that had lost confidence to a state of healthy confidence and beyond to an over-confident lack of reality. He created a politics of unreality that produced unparalleled consumer consumption and the lowest savings levels on record for a booming economy.

Third, charisma acts as a shield. A charismatic leader can survive political and economic setbacks that would crush an ordinary president. This is not to argue that the charismatic political leader is immune from harm: He can lose credibility if his magic does not work. Reagan's magic was clearly in question after the deep 1982 recession, when unemployment rose above 10 percent (the first and only time since the Great Depression) and after the Iran-Contra scandal. As the Iran-Contra scandal shows, for the charismatic leader a remarkable recovery is possible—perhaps, likely—from the most debilitating of political defeats.

Last is the most amorphous characteristic, "myth creation." The charismatic leader can have almost magical qualities. The assassination attempts on the lives of President-Elect Roosevelt and President Reagan and their concomitant heroic behavior gave both leaders a special quality. Suddenly in real life, Ronald Reagan acquired the heroic role John Wayne made famous in movies, the archetypical American hero. Reagan was able to do what the average man would do in his dreams. "Make my day," he said. It is our Walter Mitty dream in purest form.

Reagan's charismatic power flowed from his deep beliefs—he was an ideologue, not a liar. As Werner Stark wrote thirty years ago, "The liar tries to falsify the thought of others while his own private thought is correct, while he himself knows well what the truth is[;] a person who falls for an ideology is himself deluded in his private thought, and if he misleads others, does so unwillingly and unwittingly."[8] But charisma was the foundation, the indispensable ingredient that made the message believable. An ordinary president—all other presidents of this century, except FDR, are ordinary—could never have sold Reagan's message. It would have been too sugar-coated, too simplistic for anyone else. The message was an image of a just, powerful, unbounded country, a land of milk and honey and equal opportunity. Here in all its splendor was the American myth, made acceptable to so many Americans who wanted to believe, by a charismatic president who was himself the truest believer.

The Reagan message depicted either a mythical United States that never existed, or one that had once existed but had ceased to do so. The latter was the United States' hegemony in economic and geopolitical terms in the first years of the postwar period. David Calleo observed: "SDI [Strategic Defense Initiative], in part at least, is merely the latest phase in the vain effort to return to America's global invulnerability of 1950. . . . [T]he American political system finds it very difficult to face the reality of a plural world in which the United States is no longer supreme. . . . [T]he American consensus has grown into a conspiracy to avoid reality. American policy, requiring a supremacy that cannot be sustained, lacks the guiding principles to determine priorities."[9] But principled, sound priorities demanded relinquishing the dream of U.S. supremacy to face a world complexity that conflicts with Reagan's image of the United States. Nowhere is this conflict more apparent than in President Reagan's overall tax and budget policy, which cast aside rigorous analysis to produce immediate gratification and great future economic risk. David Stockman, admitting that he was "the original architect of the fiscal policy error," rightly cast Reagan's 1984 America in Orwellian terms:

> The brash phrasemakers of the White House had given George Orwell a new resonance. . . . In 1984 we were plainly drifting into unprecedented economic peril. But they had the audacity to proclaim a golden age prosperity. . . .
>
> Reagan had been induced by his advisers and his own illusions to embrace one of the most irresponsible platforms of modern times. He had promised . . . to alter the laws of arithmetic. No program that had a name or line in the budget would be cut; no taxes would be raised. Yet the deficit was pronounced intolerable and it was pledged to be eliminated.
>
> This was the essence of the unreality. . . . The White House's claim to be serious about cutting the budget had . . . become an institutionalized fantasy.[10]

"Illusions", "Orwellian," "institutionalized fantasy"—the imagery of the politics of unreality is clear. Reagan's budget and tax policy enveloped the White House, the administration, Congress, and almost the entire country. Only Walter Mondale's home state of Minnesota did not opt for Ronald Reagan after Mondale uttered the forbidden words of the politics of unreality, tax increase—what satirist Mark Russell called the "T" word.

The charismatic political leader does not have to turn his back on reality or spurn hard information and policy analysis. Roosevelt did not. Charisma only makes the task much easier. Under Reagan hard information and analysis were dangerous to the interaction between the president and the public. Gary Wills explains: "If one settles, instead, for a substitute past, an illusion of it, then that fragile construct must be protected from the challenge of complex or contradictory evidence, *from any test of evidence at all.*"[11] It is not surprising that the Reagan administration shunned policy analysis and demolished the institutional analytic process in the executive branch. Rigorous policy analysis was at best irrelevant and at worst dangerous because it challenged Reagan's basic verities.[12]

An article in *Fortune* written at the height of Reagan's second-term popularity claimed, "Reagan has introduced government to the how-to's of efficient management more successfully than any modern president."[13] Here, *Fortune* asserted, was a big picture leader who picked the best people, gave them room to manage, and waited to make the key decisions. The Iran-Contra scandal and a host of insider books stripped away this carefully crafted facade to expose a far different picture of a disengaged president who "acts for his own administration as he did for GE [General Electric], as symbol and spokesman."[14] The portrait of Reagan's leadership style that emerges from the unending flow of insider books reveals several factors that support his anti-analytic bent: an unshakable conviction in his principles combined with equally unshakable optimism, his disinterest in and haziness about details, and his striking lack of knowledge about his government and its programs.

Another side of the Reagan leadership style is that the administration was "an active presidency without a highly active and involved president."[15] Reagan had priorities that were clearly articulated. Martin Anderson, a favorable critic who served as Reagan's first head of the OPD (an EOP policy unit discussed shortly), argued that Reagan "stubbornly held to his major, long-range goals . . . [while being] as agile and deceptive as a pro football halfback in making his way to those goals"; he was willing to try one approach, abandon it if it did not work and move on to a new tactic; he was tough and relentless in pursuing his highest-priority goals. Anderson observed that "Reagan may be unique in that he is a warmly ruthless man."[16] Reagan was also a master of negotiation. His style was to ask for far more than he expected to get, hold out strongly for this unexpected result, and then accept quickly an offer below his stated demand but much above what he would have settled for. An interviewee who was a Reagan critic argued that "Reagan's rigidity — or perception thereof — made him a terrific bargainer."

The dark side of this relentless pursuit of his goals was Reagan's limited capacity to understand policy difficulties, particularly implementation. The interviewee critic saw Reagan as the master of the "big lie," repeating the same "untruths" over and over "until the press began to give this untruth equal coverage." Even Anderson admits that Reagan's management style "made no demands and gave almost no instructions." Anderson summed up his views: "[E]veryone overlooked and compensated for the fact that he made decisions like an ancient king or a Turkish pasha, passively letting his subjects serve him, selecting only those morsels of public policy that were especially tasty. . . . He just sat back in a supremely calm, relaxed manner and waited until important things were brought to him. And then he would act, quickly, decisively, and usually, very wisely."[17] That Reagan sat back and waited and then made rapid decisions is not in dispute, but how wise the decisions were is open to debate. Even Anderson recognized that Reagan's management style, with its extreme delegation (also not in dispute), depended most heavily on the quality of his policy advisers and delegatees.

REAGAN AND INFORMATION

The Reagan administration engaged in a successful war on federally developed and analyzed policy information. The outcome was only somewhat lessened by congressional action both to mandate information gathering by the executive branch and to undertake the development of more policy information, particularly by GAO. We see a clear retreat from a historical responsibility of the federal government that dates back to the first census in 1790. In 1985 a *Society* article by Eleanor Chelimsky, assistant comptroller general for program evaluation and methodology in GAO, argued that Reagan's first-term cutbacks in federal data systems had "severe effects both on data availability and data quality"; that the administration's claims that it had done so because it no longer needed the data were unconvincing in that "they distort long-established national policy"; and that the notion that states, localities, and businesses can collect their own data was "only dubiously feasible."[18] Chelimsky's *Society* piece carried the caveat that the views expressed were her own, not those of GAO, but three years later, GAO in its *Transition Series* argued the Reagan cutbacks had "gravely eroded" data collection capabilities of the executive branch and that the administration, in not developing good information, had failed to carry out the "responsibility of [the U.S.] government to the people of this country."[19]

A fundamental policy information question is whether current statistics such as those for the GNP, productivity, and savings are really measuring what is happening in the economy. In the *New York Times* Jonathan Fuerbringer wrote that "statisticians and economists, both in and out of government, say that a combination of budget cuts and deregulation — much of it a legacy of the Reagan Era — is eroding important [statistical] yardsticks and undermining policymakers striving to guide the economy."[20] Current measures are deteriorating because government staffs and data collection have been cut, because deregulation of industries such as airlines and reductions in paperwork from businesses has reduced the variety and the amount of collected data, and because data sampling techniques have not been improved. The Bureau of Economic Affairs, for example, has had an 18 percent staff decline since 1979. Further research funds needed to improve data collection have had to be shifted to current operations so as to have sufficient staff and sample size to support the collection of basic data. Here is another example of government underinvestment, in this case in R&D to upgrade data gathering techniques.

The threat to policymaking is particularly large because some of the numbers, such as GNP, most watched by policymakers, are highly suspect when they are first released. Better estimates of these early figures are made at later dates as more information becomes available. But relatively good estimates may be long in coming. For example, in July 1988 the Department of Commerce concluded that GNP change for the spring quarter of 1986 was down (negative growth) instead of up as previously estimated. Revised figures showed that the summer quarter of 1986 was weaker than earlier estimated but still positive. Since the National Bureau of Economic Research defines a recession as two consecutive quarters of negative GNP growth, the "booming" economy of 1986 had barely escaped a recession as seen from the mid-1988 figures. In another case, new estimates in August 1989 indicated that May 1989 retail sales were materially higher rather than down a bit as first reported. Are policymakers to wait months or years for "good" figures before acting? No obvious answer appears, but the problem of acting on early numbers is clear.

What is the quality of the basic economic data that support the decisions made by government at all levels, decisions that can affect billions of dollars and millions of lives? Such data are the primary fuel that runs the decision process. If these numbers are inaccurate, not timely, or not relevant for key policy decisions by governments and businesses, the policymaking process can collapse. Loss of confidence in them can paralyze the process. On the other hand, misplaced confidence in faulty statistics — not knowing how bad the numbers are — portends bad policies. Although policymakers and the public need to understand that available methods technically cannot yield faultless numbers, it is reasonable to expect that every effort within reason is being made to obtain sound data.

A look at the quantitative reductions in the capacity to generate sound policy information and analysis during the Reagan years starts with Research and Development funding. Defense R&D funding increased 81 percent between 1980 and 1987 in constant 1980 dollars, while all other federal agencies overall had their R&D budgets reduced by 20 percent in the same period. Defense rose from 44 percent to 64 percent of federal R&D budget obligations between 1980 and 1987. Between 1980 and 1986 funding (budget authority) for major statistical units, such as the Census Bureau, Center for Education Statistics, National Center for Health Statistics, and Bureau of Labor Statistics, fell by 21 percent in real dollars.[21] Cutbacks in program evaluation funding have been particularly severe in the Reagan years and would have been far deeper without congressionally mandated set-asides. Evaluation funds decreased by 37 percent in constant dollars between 1980 and 1984, and professional staff dropped 22 percent in the same period. A later study showed that fifteen evaluation units had experienced a decline in professional staffs of 52 percent. The GAO *Transition Series* on program evaluation reported that evaluation studies in the executive branch were produced increasingly for internal consumption and that executive branch evaluation studies to support "congressional oversight and public scrutiny were limited in number and were primarily studies mandated for Congress, which set aside funds for this purpose."[22]

GAO also charged that "the capacity to perform program evaluation [and research are] drying up [in the executive branch], not the least in such areas as defense, health care, education, and the environment, where it is precisely needed most."[23] The National Institute of Education's research awards fell in number from 476 in 1980 to 168 in 1985; roughly 65 percent; 79 percent of the research awards were congressionally mandated in 1984, as compared with 55 percent in 1980.[24] In the Office of Planning, Budget, and Evaluation — ED's analytic office — contract awards for evaluation fell from 119 to 25, or nearly 80 percent.[25] In the Department of Health and Human Services' Health Care Financing Administration (HCFA), which funds Medicare and Medicaid, funding for studies within its major research office, the Office of Research and Demonstrations, fell 43 percent in constant dollars between 1980 and 1987. The GAO reports that at the same time program costs rose 50 percent in real terms. Also, mandated studies in ORD rose from 2 percent in 1980 to 43 percent in 1987.[26]

The quantitative cutbacks are dramatic, and the qualitative ones may be even more so. A theme cutting through the various details GAO studies is the deterioration of evaluation quality. The study of HCFA research is subtitled "Agency Practices and Other Factors Threaten Quality of Mandated Studies"; the report on education is subtitled "Changes in Funds and Priorities Have Affected Production and Quality." Nowhere is this more the case than in defense. In 1983 Congress established the Office of the Director of Operational Test and Evaluation (DOT&E) to check on DOD weapon systems because of "fundamental [congressional] concern . . . that weapons were not being tested thoroughly or realistically and that complete and accurate information was not being disseminated."[27] In its 1988 report on the DOT&E effort GAO claimed that DOD in weapons testing used "golden crews" (persons atypically high in skill or experience levels), engaged in tests that lacked realism (e.g., employed easy targets or tested under ideal weather conditions), reported results improperly, and made incomplete or inaccurate statements.[28] The overall assessment was that the effort "has fallen short of the objectives sought by Congress when it established DOT&E."[29] Congress was not being supplied the information needed to assess whether the multibillion dollar weapons systems of the Reagan era worked.

Peter May has made estimates of full-time equivalent (fte) staff changes in the top agency policy analysis offices as compared with congressional analytic units — all personnel numbers shown are fte staff. Agency-level analytic office professional and support staff in Commerce (27 to 23), Energy (197 to 60), HHS (165 to 75), HUD (198 to 140), Interior (35 to 31), Labor (61 to 40), State (41 to 36), and Transportation (32 to 21) fell overall almost 43 percent between 1980 and 1988; while CBO, Policy Analysis and Research in the CRS, and the Office of Technology Assessment had over 900 full-time equivalent professional and support staff in both 1980 and 1988.[30] GAO, which declined from 5200 to 5020, because its size overwhelms everything else, and its staff had many auditors, has been excluded. However, an interviewee with in-depth knowledge of GAO said the growth in GAO analytic staff was large during the 1980s, particularly in the period 1985–1989 (part of the shift in GAO from auditors to policy analysts). Analytic capacity shifted visibly to Congress.

YEAR ONE

President Reagan's first year marks the most dramatic changes in the EOP and the cabinet since the coming of the institutional presidency in Roosevelt's second term. As is often the case, part of the impetus for change came from perceived failures or excesses in previous administrations. From the Carter failures, the Reagan people saw the need for a guiding agenda and a fast start, strong control at the top, as well as a competent legislative staff ready to work with Congress immediately. Beyond that, the incoming Reaganites had strong views about cabinet government as practiced during Mr. Reagan's California governorship and a less-than-fully-worked-out view of policy integration at the top. Finally, a critical element of the agenda — cutting back on domestic programs — for all intents and purposes reduced domestic policy to budget policy.

The first year of the Reagan administration is particularly noteworthy because of the dramatic changes in the EOP and the fast start that brought landmark legislative triumphs comparable to those of Roosevelt in 1933 and Johnson in 1964–65. This dramatic year crystallizes one of the most crucial problems of presidential analysis and advice: A president is likely to be strongest politically at the time when his institutional analytic competence is lowest because his new staff has not had time to work through internal organizational issues or to gain the kind of wisdom that comes from experience on the job. This crucial start-up problem flows from the fact that the political dynamics of the presidency push toward a fast start, particularly in the domestic and economic policy areas. But can the president wait for a careful build-up of analytic staff competent to engage in hard analysis to support early decisionmaking? As James Sundquist laments: "If an administration spends any time trying to make up its collective mind as to what it wants to do, as in the case of the Carter administration in 1977, it is destined to be lost for the whole four years."[31]

An Iron Hand at the Top

Control at the top laid the foundation for the Reagan administration's fast start. First were the agenda and the budget to guide action. Second was staff power that centralized control in the Triumvirate. Third was the Legislative Strategy Group under Baker that operated with skill on the Hill not seen since Lyndon Johnson's Great Society effort. In sharp contrast to Carter, President Reagan had a strategic vision. Chester A. Newland observed: "More than any recent presidency, strategic planning and activities characterized Reagan administration policy management with respect to the economy and general domestic affairs. Much of the planning for the initial months was done before the election and during the transition."[32] A prominent role in agenda development was played by right-of-center "think tanks," particularly the American Enterprise Institute (AEI), the Heritage Foundation, and the Institute for Contemporary Studies (ICS). As Peschek observed: "Nearly all the hard-line positions developed at the AEI and ICS during the Carter administration were translated into concise policy proposals for the incoming Reagan team in the Heritage Foundation's *Mandate for Leadership*. In the late 1970s, Heritage had ceaselessly attacked Carter's foreign policy in papers, newsletters, and the journal *Policy Review*, reaching a widening circle of would-be policymakers. Expanding from its New Right origins, the Heritage Foundation brought together neoconservatives and old-line hawks into the growing conservative policy network."[33] The central focus of the agenda was the budget. What shaped much of the first year of the Reagan administration was the lightning move to capture the budget before the cabinet had settled in its offices and many of the subcabinet had even been appointed.[34] The speed was amazing; the critical budget decisions were made at the top by the president and a handful of inner circle members with little input from the agencies. The early Stockman initiative that put in place so quickly what the Reagan administration wanted was central both to Reagan's policies and to the emerging EOP structure.

Reagan used three men to give him the most powerful, disciplined staff control that has been seen in many a year. Edwin Meese, his trusted lieutenant from California days, was made policy chief of the White House staff and had cabinet rank (most unusual for a White House aide). James Baker was then given the more traditional position of chief-of-staff, with responsibility for overall White House administration. They were joined by Deputy Chief-of-Staff Michael Deaver, the staff person closest to the president and Mrs. Reagan, whose main responsibility was protecting the interests of the president. Much of the early momentum of the Reagan administration was in selling the Reagan package on the Hill. Baker put together a political juggernaut of staff members who could "work the Hill" and, if needed, generate strong outside pressure on members of Congress from their districts and their states. This effort often made politics far more important than policy (Meese's bailiwick), leading one White House watcher interviewee to observe that "merchandising is everything in this administration." The "Triumvirate," and the members of Baker's staff, and a few others became the "Legislative Strategy Group." That group, dominated by Baker, was the foundation for his moving to the top of the White House staff pecking order.

A Policy Czar

The early Reagan administration's institutional decisions to downgrade policy analysis and to make Meese policy czar—the top policy adviser generalist— helped establish the base for Stockman's rapid rise to power. Because of the distaste for powerful aides such as Henry Kissinger, who had stood between the president and the cabinet, the Reagan administration moved immediately to make the heads of both the OPD and the NSC staffs report to Meese rather than to the president. That Meese and the rest of the Triumvirate were as firmly ensconced as Kissinger had been above the cabinet apparently did not bother President Reagan. Most critically for our purposes, the quality and the size of the OPD and NSC staffs dropped dramatically, and in filling the staff philosophical consistency and loyalty became far more important criteria than policy experience and capability. As Dick Kirschten wrote in 1981: "The 99-member NSC staff recruited by [National Security Adviser Richard] Allen is seen as generally unskilled in dealing with the bureaucracy and possessing a hard-line, ideological tilt unsuited to a staff that is supposed to coordinate policy, not to shape it. Their academic and professional reputations are regarded as rather mediocre. 'They're not the kind of people I'd like to have around if I were responsible for advising the president,' observed a veteran NSC consultant."[35] Ronald Brownstein and Kirschten succinctly captured what happened with the domestic policy unit: "From the time Reagan moved into the Oval Office, no one has ever bothered to turn on the lights at the White House's Office of Policy Development."[36] Hence OMB's policy analysis capacity was unrivaled in the White House in the critical first year of the Reagan administration. It was not that OMB was so good, but that its potential rivals had such limited analytic capability.

When the Reagan administration first came to Washington, Meese, the Reagan insider, was "Mr. Everything," a "deputy president" with unchallenged staff authority for overall administration of policy and strategy. Baker had yet to emerge on top.[37] Lou Cannon caught the basic Meese-Baker relationship and Meese's superior policy role during the critical 1981 period of the tax and budget efforts: "[Baker] took a back seat to Meese on policy recommendations. . . . [Meese] was the conceptualizer, the synthesizer, the translator of Reagan's ideas to others and the policy funnel into the president. . . . Meese was Reagan's geographer."[38] No matter how inept a guide, Meese was the unquestioned top policy generalist adviser, standing between the president and all other key policy advisers including Stockman.

Meese treated expert policy information and analysis in a manner that was generally characteristic of the Reagan administration. Janet Mayer and Doyle

McManus describe this style: "Like Reagan, Meese could cheerfully bend the facts to fit whatever case he was trying to make. When he was White House counselor in Reagan's first term, some reporters found his 'background' briefings so unreliable that they flipped a coin: the losers get the exclusive session with Meese."[39] Meese, with his fierce loyalty to the president, his limited perception of integrity, his lack of analytic competence, and his lawyer's training, came easily to treat numbers as something to be used as needed. At the same time his lack of analytic competence meant he was not able to tell when the numbers were turned on him and the president he wanted to protect when Stockman played his own game.

The Administrative Presidency and the Cabinet Councils

Another key element in exerting control from the top was appointing likeminded subcabinet members at the outset of the administration and establishing a number of cabinet councils. Unlike earlier administrations that sought to balance the cabinet and subcabinet by appointing persons with different views, the Reagan strategy made philosophical consistency and loyalty to Reagan himself the two most important criteria for selecting the cabinet and roughly 600 key subcabinet appointments at the top of the federal departments and agencies.[40] As Paul Light observed: "They [the White House] appointed people [to cabinet departments] who would cut their boss's throat to please the president. . . . They [the appointees] are ideologically committed. There is no allegiance to the department, but to the Oval Office or the conservative cause. No administration has penetrated so deeply."[41] The indirect control through like-mindedness and loyalty of subcabinet members is more likely to ensure that the president's needs are met than is a White House staff trying to force recalcitrant political executives into line.

Another key element in the evolving relationship in the Reagan administration between the White House and the cabinet were the several cabinet councils established in the first term. The seven councils covered such broad areas as commerce and trade, economics, and human resources. Each was chaired by the president and had a cabinet-level chair pro tempore who directed the council and took the chair when the president did not, which was most of the time. Staff members from OPD served as executive secretaries to each council. OPD provided a limited level of staff support and coordination. Staff support also came from the agencies. The cabinet councils were potentially the most innovative of the Reagan EOP changes, promising both to restore agency executives as key White House generalist policy advisers and to reduce White House interference with agency operations. However, the extended council system that operated in the first four years did not fulfill its promise. After extensive study, Newland offered this evaluation: "As they developed the councils did become important to facilitate coordination of secondary-level domestic policy development, interpretation, and implementation. [But the councils did not become] the principal center of highest policy processes. The councils . . . never achieved the capacity to provide general policy direction; they became principally occupied with details required to carry out Reagan's agenda. More than other forces, the budget initially drove other policy not the reverse."[42] Policy was controlled tightly from the top, and the councils reinforced this control. In the first 200 days of the administration, when the most far-reaching policy decisions were made, David Stockman and his budget dominated domestic policy. Stockman's partial fall, however, did not elevate the cabinet councils to the top. The inner circle still ruled with an iron hand. Small and medium-sized decisions were all that the councils found on their plates. That the councils could be a device for highest-level decisions is not out of the question, but this did not happen in the first four years of the Reagan administration. The councils did help tie the cabinet and subcabinet to the White House, thereby reinforcing loyalty and commitment to the agenda. In this sense, the cabinet councils became a crucial part of the Reagan administrative presidency strategy. In his second term President Reagan materially changed the extended domestic policy council system by reducing it to two bodies with an economic group chaired by Treasury Secretary Baker and a domestic council chaired by Attorney General Meese. The move thus put two more key persons between the president and the rest of the cabinet and became more an additional layer than a channel for rank-and-file cabinet members.

David Stockman and the Triumph of Analysis

David Stockman's *The Triumph of Politics* was the first major insider book on the Reagan years, comparable on the domestic policy side to Henry Kissinger's foreign policy memoirs. Unlike Kissinger—and this is one of the most remarkable aspects of Reagan's first two hundred days—Stockman, the key analyst of this period, operated almost completely independently of the president. Stockman's day in the woodshed symbolically being punished by President Reagan after the *Atlantic Monthly* article was, according to Stockman, the only time in those critical months he had ever been alone with the president.[43] The adviser who could legitimately be labeled the vicar of domestic policy was not a member of the Triumvirate that was in daily contact with the president. Nor did Stockman appear to be close to other top advisers. Thus he could assert that "the president, the secretary of the Treasury, and the White House senior staff . . . were almost entirely innocent and uninformed [about the details of the Reagan Revolution]."[44] Stockman's claim to be the master of the tax and budget revolution in the policy formulation period has validity. Though it must be recognized that future research drawing on now unavailable papers or testimony may invalidate it, the available evidence strongly supports the claims that in the post-World War II era no presidential aide has operated so independently of the president and that no policy analyst in the domestic policy arena has exercised so much White House power.

The president and the Triumvirate trusted Stockman, who combined a radical ideology claiming his first loyalty, with arrogance, indefatigability, and an amazing grasp of budget numbers for one so new in the director's job. As Hugh Heclo observed: "Bright and hard-working (eighteen-hour days at least six days a week were the norm), David Stockman as a freshman congressman in 1976 had devoted himself to learning the intricacies of the federal budget in the way other young people work at mastering video games."[45] With his reputation for infallibility, which was only partly deserved, Stockman flourished in a policymaking environment with limited competitive mechanisms. In later years he was to attain a high level of budget mastery. One interviewee argued that over his entire stay at OMB, Stockman was both the most capable director, with the greatest combined mastery of budget details and macroeconomic issues, and the most successful in accomplishing his *own* goals. However, a less admiring interviewee maintained that Stockman looked so good because of the string of less than outstanding OMB heads immediately preceding him, but that Stockman was not more able than say Charles Schultze (a Johnson-era director) and some others before that time. Another critical interviewee, who watched Stockman perform on the Hill, said, "Stockman's brilliance is overrated. His excellence was articulation. He could pull a few numbers and technical details to make a weak ideological argument sound analytic. A large part of his success was arrogance and bluff." Although he was clearly competent, Stockman looked so good because Reagan EOP analytic capacity was so weak. He was probably not as competent an analyst as strong earlier directors such as Schultze. Stockman used his great capacity less for sound analysis in search of feasible alternatives and more for justification of his and Reagan's agenda. He had less institutional commitment and integrity than any of his predecessors. As another interviewee told me, it was too bad Stockman had so little formal training in policy analysis because he lacked any standards of analysis against which to test the outcomes from the application of his great talents.

The period Stockman treats in *The Triumph of Politics* — the transition and first year of Reagan's first term — is illuminating because politics brought a wide opening in the honeymoon period that allows us to see politics and policy analysis in full action. No policy honeymoon is guaranteed in a new administration's first days. Jimmy Carter's rocky start is a striking example. Even Reagan's policy timing was critical. As Stockman observed: "I reckoned that the 'window' for successfully launching sweeping change in national economic policy would be exceedingly brief."[46] At the outset of his first term Reagan had a vision of a future America with high growth, low taxes, no inflation, a strong defense, and a balanced budget; only Stockman had any notion of how to get there. Stockman made the most of this open policy window by producing a budget for approval before cabinet secretaries had begun to settle in and before much of the subcabinet had even been appointed. Opposition forces did not have the time to marshal cases or rally their supporters. The lack of competition made for low-level analysis and some glaring errors that might have been reduced if the system had contained more safeguards. But with moving quickly seen as essential by the president and the Triumvirate, Stockman was perfectly placed as the only person in the early administration to have both the relative competence to take charge of the Reagan Revolution formulation phase and the reputation as a super policy analyst and strategist. Nowhere can we see more clearly the power both of ideas and of an advocate analyst in the right spot, where politics and policy converge. It was the perfect stage for the policy entrepreneur.

In the honeymoon period the mixture of political power at its greatest, staff confidence at its highest, and staff competence at its lowest can be lethal when the policy window is open. In a chapter about the first few weeks of the Reagan administration, appropriately entitled "Blitzkrieg," Stockman wrote: "I instilled so much confidence by appearing to know all the answers, but I was just beginning to understand the true complexities and mysteries of the federal budget. . . . If the Reagan plan had been incrementalist in nature . . . the low level of fiscal literacy among the upper echelons of the new administration might not have mattered. . . . The changes would have been made by the budget bureaucracies at OMB and the agencies. But a plan for radical and abrupt change required deep comprehension—and we had none of it. . . . Designing a comprehensive plan to bring about a sweeping change in national economic governance in forty days is a preposterous, wantonly reckless notion."[47] The case at hand involved the particularly dangerous situation in which the driving idea was of a partisan policy adviser analyst at the top, with neither integrity nor loyalty, and with the institutional setting insulating him from scrutiny by policy analysis peers.

Stockman was not deliberately subverting the Reagan agenda; both men shared a similar radical ideological view of the world and similar goals. But Stockman was overconfident of his knowledge and skills, overambitious, and overcommitted to an ideology that demanded maximum change. He ran too far, too fast, unchecked by policy analysis from above and below. Had there been a generalist policy adviser above him with both the analytic competence and the authority to rein Stockman in, the game might have been played differently, with more favorable results.

In the early days of the Reagan administration Stockman had an undeserved reputation for infallibility. He admits that his gross error contributed to the doubling of the defense budget, that he spent April 1981 "rigging the [budget] numbers to the point that even we couldn't understand them," and that he blatantly cooked the books, inventing $15 billion per year of phony cuts in order to bring Reagan's first full budget deficit under $100 billion.[48] Four factors can be singled out in this dramatic abuse of power: secrecy, arrogance, brilliance, and ideological zeal. Secrecy was central. Nothing comes across more vividly in Stockman's account than the fact that he alone in the executive branch had a full picture of what was being done in tax and budget policymaking. This monopoly position came in part from his mastery of budget numbers and concepts. More important, however, were his efforts either to block information from getting to potential user groups or to allow them only partial knowledge. Stockman used his quickly completed budget drawn up in secrecy to end-run the cabinet. When forced to deal with the cabinet and with Congress later on, he did his own negotiating, often accompanied only by his massive briefing books that so symbolized his command of budget intricacies. Interviewees from the CBO said that they knew what Stockman knew, and no doubt as budget numbers emerged on paper, they did. But there is no way to reconstruct as of 1981 the numbers in Stockman's head that he used so adroitly in going from committee (or subcommittee) to committee. Here he hid numbers to his advantage, especially when he also cut off the career budget staff members.

Secrecy and arrogance were intertwined. Particularly important for our purposes, Stockman practiced top-down budgeting within OMB with a vengeance in looking to the senior OMB career staff not for ideas, general critiques, or plans but for backup data or detailed technical assistance. This tactic was not only to cut off criticism. Stockman was confident that he needed no one else to do his thinking or even to test his thinking—just someone to do his calculating and to fill in details.[49] Stockman was much more likely to seek out a lower-level specialist (with whom he could discuss the arcane budget issues that he was willing and able to grasp) than he was to call together the senior career staff for strategic thinking. Only Stockman's most trusted inner circle, brought over from his congressional staff, was privy to his grand schemes. Even here, I have been told, Stockman kept the full master plan to himself.

Stockman's analytic brilliance must be qualified in two ways. First, at the beginning of the Reagan administration, Stockman knew far less than he did later, and we should not confuse the later Stockman with the earlier one. Though Stockman came to OMB with an amazing amount of knowledge about details for an outsider, he lacked the mastery of a number of budget intricacies and interrelationships. An interviewee, who had been a high level EOP staff member and then an outside adviser to Stockman, indicated that in this early period the gaps in Stockman's knowledge made for faulty analysis. Stockman argued that the original budget plan was "fatally flawed" and observed that "[Reagan] had been misled by a crew of overzealous—and ultimately *incompetent*—advisers."[50] Second, pure analytic brilliance does not necessarily carry with it wisdom, probity, prudence, integrity, or political

sensitivity. Because brilliance so often combines with arrogance, it can mitigate against these other desirable traits. This flaw may be the Achilles heel
of the brilliant analyst. It is hardly surprising that Stockman lacked the deep
institutional memory gained from experience, or that he denied needing it
because such memory often is cautionary and indicates the need either to
rethink an approach or to go slowly, but he also claimed political naivete
with an unrealistic attitude toward politics.[51] Information and analysis in
Stockman's hands were weapons to be used fairly or unfairly in the larger
battle. Stockman was held in check neither by presidential loyalty, an adherence to analytic standards, challenges from other advocate analysts, nor an
underlying commitment to serve the presidency. Information is a dangerous
commodity in the hands of the ideologue, and particularly so in the case of
an ideological policy analyst who uses complex concepts and numbers masterfully as weapons to score points.

An overriding message of *The Triumph of Politics* is the president's need
for a competent top generalist policy adviser who has the integrity and capacity to cope with key substantive areas, to determine how recommended policies fit with the president's interests, to link the president to the institutional
analytic process, and to protect him from analytic abuses. Meese lacked this
combination of skills and knowledge. Loyalty was not enough. The building
of safeguards central to the prudent use of policy analysts and their work
depends less on White House structure and process than on the personality,
style, experience, integrity, and competence or incompetence of the president
and, to some extent, of his top advisers. After discussing the fact that he
knew large domestic program budget cuts would have to be made later, Stockman writes that "history cannot blame the president for not considering this
crucial question; I never provided him with a single briefing on this."[52] Apparently it does not occur to Stockman that the president is fundamentally responsible for the actions and competence of his top appointees. That Reagan
had Meese, rather than a competent policy adviser both loyal to him and
knowledgeable about economic and budget issues, that Reagan himself was
anti-analytic, that this trait had misshaped his EOP staff, and that neither
the president nor Meese knew how to manage the presidential decisionmaking process so that analytic competition would have checked Stockman
were dramatic indications of inept presidential governance. A critical demand
in competent presidential governance is to choose the right person for the
particular job.

POLITICAL DOMINANCE AND INEPT GOVERNANCE

From the perspective of the White House, it is useful to distinguish among
control exerted to enhance or protect the president's political standing, con-

trol over the formulation of the president's policies, and control over the implementation of the president's policies. From a policy focus, political standing is not only a key factor in electoral politics but also a central element in selling the president's programs in Congress. Formulation concerns the determination of the president's policies and raises issues about the White House-agency relationships. For example, where will the underlying analysis be performed? Implementation is used broadly at this point to include both selling the president's policies and getting them in place. In the former case Congress is the main target, although a president may go over Congress members' heads to the people as a selling tactic. Generally, putting a program in place requires a downward focus toward the agencies and ultimately subnational governments. But selling some policies in Congress goes most of the way toward implementing them. For example, a presidential goal of cutting back grants to states and localities is fulfilled once Congress adopts the cutback.[53] Selling other policies in Congress may be far easier than field implementation.

Both Martin Anderson, the insider, and Stephen Hess, the outside observer, have stressed the importance of policy implementation relative to policy formulation in the early days of the Reagan administration because the policies were ones that Reagan had spent two decades *promoting*.[54] I emphasize the term "promoting" used by Hess because a policy well promoted is not necessarily one well formulated, as is strikingly illustrated in the Stockman case. However, the big issue at the top during Reagan's first year was selling the president's tax and budget package in Congress. The selling did most of the implementation—that is, marginal tax rates were lower, federal funds to states and localities were lower, and major new funds were available for defense spending. That translating increased funds into greater national security demanded far more implementation, did not worry the Reagan administration. Selling itself became the symbol of Reagan prowess.

After year one Jim Baker and Dick Darman replaced the Triumvirate but with a far closer personal relationship to each other, and with Baker as the clearly acknowledged senior partner. Their three years was a period of virtuoso political manipulation in which almost all the effort at the top consisted of protecting and projecting the product—the highly salable, charismatic, optimistic president. Media management (the projecting) was a less difficult task than protecting the image. That is, Reagan was easy to sell if his image as the powerful leader of a smooth-running presidency could be maintained. But protecting the image turned out to demand Baker and Darman's absolute control of the product.

The two men's tight control in the period between the passage of the 1981 tax and budget package and the start of the second term, however, did not focus on effective presidential governance or policies but on the president's image as leader as perceived by Congress and the public. This yielded a wide gap between the created vision of firm leadership and the reality of inept policy and governance, indicating how politically powerful was the combination of Reagan charisma (the source of the image) and Baker-Darman mastery.

Properly packaged and protected, Ronald Reagan was the perfect product — he sold himself. To insulate and isolate the president, however, demanded extremely tight control of the "performer" to minimize his verbal errors and to mitigate those that got out, since no amount of control could keep Reagan from deviating from his carefully crafted script. But in the main he was an able performer willing to be directed, just as he had been in his Hollywood days.[55] Baker and Darman's big problem was not the usually passive president but those around him who might corrupt him. Such control took great effort, as Bob Woodward pointed out: "Baker and Darman got the daily phone log of every call in to Reagan and every one that he placed. Separate logs were kept for the regular phone lines and the secure line. . . . There was a weekend log, even of Nancy's social calls, lunches and dinners. . . . A talk with the president after a simple greeting or a quick hello could become, in the mind of the visitor, a firm expression or even a decision. So Baker and Darman followed up everything, making sure nothing escaped their net. The president was obviously comfortable with the system, and no one broke through."[56] At the same time Baker and Darman isolated the president less than Don Regan did in the second term, but they had a much better system of damage control and greater skills in handling emerging problems. The two realized that the president leaned ideologically toward hard-line positions and was unwilling or unable to analyze the case on his own. Since President Reagan was comfortable with face-to-face debate and counterarguments by advocates (as long as they were not acrimonious), Baker and Darman sought to let in different ideas.

The downside of the Baker and Darman control system was its impact on sound policy analysis. The dominant style was the quick fix, the frantic search for data to quell the problem of the moment. One astute interviewee captured Baker and Darman's effort (my emphasis): "They do care about policy, but not to the extent of taking any political risks. They're interested in selling the president's policy. But both take what they can get and do not overplay their hands. *They are the best fire fighters in the history of the White House.* But they do not have a lot of time to ponder about policies. Their style is to jump on the hot issue of the day or put out the threatening blaze of the day. Baker and Darman simply do not have time for policy thinking. *What they do mainly is policy reacting.*" Extended policy analysis simply was not a prized commodity at the top of the Reagan White House. Moreover, the two were fast enough on their feet to do the quick-and-dirty analysis themselves, and Darman had both a quick analytic mind and sound analytic experience. Baker and Darman also used a small number of people to help, such as Roger Porter of the OPD staff. Stockman was more valuable to them with his diminished power after the *Atlantic* article. But Baker and Darman kept their circle small, to exact maximum power and control. Ultimately, there was a question of competence to manage the flow of information and analysis into the inner circle.

The result was the tightest control from the top over information and analysis since the Nixon-Kissinger era. But there was a marked difference. Nixon was a pro-analysis president and a consummate user of the analytic product. Both Nixon and Kissinger were highly analytic and took a strategic world view of American foreign policy. Both wanted lots of information and extended policy analysis. What President Nixon did *not* want was the game of bureaucratic politics being played; he did not want open competition among strong agency analysts. To meet these demands, Kissinger institutionalized a strong flow of information and analysis coming up but kept tight control to insulate the president from the actors themselves while allowing in their information. It was access and a forum for influence, not information and analysis, that was blocked.[57] In contrast, policymaking at the top of the Reagan White House operated with a few people using a most limited amount of information and analysis. The value of policy information and analysis was seen mainly as fuel feeding quick efforts to put out fires. The two "conservative, anti-government, anti-bureaucracy" presidents arrived at diametrically opposite answers on the usefulness of policy analysis, making it clear that policy analysis is an available means to serve any political persuasion. Where it cannot compete is where ideology completely rules out facts that threaten its basic tenets.

The Baker-Darman years were not ones of major new policy initiatives but were dominated by efforts to protect the gains from the 1981 budget and tax package—lower marginal income tax rates, higher defense spending, and lower federal outlays for grants-in-aid to states and localities. In this the administration was mostly successful. Although some new taxes were enacted, and the deep recession brought increased grants-in-aid, marginal tax rates stayed low and the rate of growth of the grants to subnational governments was kept well below earlier levels. Moreover, once the recession ended and economic growth became strong in 1983 and outstanding in 1984, policy pressures on the administration subsided. There was a smooth surface of still water masking a great turbulence below as deficits mounted and the administration engaged so often in inept governance. The politics of unreality was in full bloom, and Baker and Darman were the chief architects.

Bell's Story

In its September 15, 1986, edition *Fortune* observed that President Reagan "is painstaking in choosing subordinates but otherwise avoids details. . . . His leadership style strikes a constantly recalculated balance between idealism and realism."[58] Crucial to this image was the choosing of managers from the business sector who brought competence, realism, and hard analysis to the problems of government that mere bureaucrats could not handle. It is remarkable how well the image sold when the reality was so different. Many of the key people in the subcabinet positions were not businessmen but hard right ideologues who operated in secret, distrusted everyone who was not one of them, and spurned numbers and analysis except to justify their ideologically driven actions.

The destructiveness of ideology and inept governance is told in Terrel Bell's *The Thirteenth Man: A Reagan Cabinet Memoir*, which treats his four years as the administration's first secretary of education.[59] President Reagan and his inner circle came to Washington, having promised to do away with ED. They ran into criticism when Bell, a moderate Republican, not an ultra-conservative, was appointed secretary. Because of criticism that Bell would not try to eliminate ED, he was forced to appoint to key subcabinet positions several extreme right or "movement conservatives," who were his enemies, and he, their special target. These conservatives were scornful of those who compromised rather than fighting to the end on ideological principle and labeled the compromisers "pragmatists," a group containing not only Bell but Vice-President George Bush and Chief-of-Staff Baker. The conservative ED political executives were like a secret society and a power unto themselves seeking to force both the secretary and his political executive allies and the career civil servants to conform to what they saw as the pure Reagan doctrine.[60]

What stands out in the case of the movement conservatives, as it did so often in the Reagan administration, is an obsession with secrecy; a commitment to ideological principles so strong that unlawful acts were seen as acceptable means; heavy-handed, often inept implementation efforts that showed little understanding of how organizations operate in the field; and a distrust of the federal government and those in it who offered information, analysis, and advice that did not support the guiding principles. In all incoming administrations where a political party change occurs there is some distrust of the previous government. This distrust translates into suspicion of the remaining high-level civil servants. The ED movement conservatives went far beyond this to a distrust of everyone who was not one of them, including Bell and other less ideological Republican political executives, and finally to a desire to destroy the institution itself. All tactics were fair. The movement conservatives, like Reagan, saw themselves as outside the government, not the leaders of that vast array of agencies and programs. They especially detested the career "bureaucrats" whose advice and analysis might counsel caution or a different direction. Ironically, they were often ineffective because they either understood little about how government worked or were so overcommitted to rigid principles that they allowed no organizational deviation and accepted no contradictory information and analysis.

The rigid ideological political executives in the key subcabinet positions saw little or no value in sound policy analysis or rigorous evaluative data. An interviewee who served on a congressional staff told me: "The ED analytic shops were stacked with movement conservatives. Those of us in Congress who were inclined to try to salvage funding quickly learned through our contacts in the department that the movement conservatives' idea of analysis was to give studies to their friends to 'prove' their ideological positions." Congress prevented this ersatz analysis sometimes by a detailed mandating of studies. In this atmosphere agency analytic units withered, shrinking in size and influence. When the Reagan administration simply sought to stop government activity, the lack of solid policy information and analysis was not a major hindrance. But when the Reagan administration wanted to make changes that required sophisticated implementation in the field, the analytic gap and managerial gap were critical obstacles.

Bell's experiences with President Reagan also illustrate both the immense power of political charisma and its limits when there is no underlying base of competence. Reagan and Bell were brought together by the National Commission on Excellence in Education's April 1983 report entitled *A Nation at Risk: The Imperative for Educational Reform*, which chronicled "a rising tide of mediocrity" in education that threatened America's commercial preeminence. *A Nation at Risk* observed that "if an unfriendly power had attempted to impose on America the mediocre educational performance that exists today, we might well have viewed it as an act of war."[61] Much to Bell's surprise, President Reagan joined him in the crusade for educational reform. It was Reagan's political charisma at its best. Moreover, it was an opportunity to turn his charisma to the critical leadership task of transforming a badly working elementary and secondary education system. Reagan could do what an ordinary president such as Jimmy Carter could not do—mobilize the nation. But it was not to be. Bell, who initially believed Reagan's support was a sincere effort to bring fundamental reforms in education, finally had to confront the true Reagan that his friends had warned him about. Bell lamented:

I had heard the president speak persuasively and with too much conviction to think that I would see the last of his efforts once he had won his second term. . . . [However, the] commitment lasted only as long as the election season. . . .

We would have changed the course of history in American education had the president stayed with us through the implementation phase of the school reform movement. And this would have won a place in history for Ronald Reagan as the man who renewed and reformed education at a time when the nation was, indeed, at risk because we were not adequately educating our people to live effectively and competitively in the twenty-first century.[62]

Bell points out that the education reform effort got as far as it did because Reagan provided outstanding leadership. Organizational follow-through was missing, however, so the potential of strong leadership was not realized. In the end Reagan cast off his chance to lead toward better policy. His unswerving ideological tenets that a federal role in education is bad and that no money is necessary were key barriers. Pouring money into education is not a panacea, but new funds can be a critical stimulant. Reagan also would not or could not connect better education with his top priority, greater military power. Nor could he see the critical link between education and international competitiveness. Finally, he could not recognize that from 1981 to 1989 he embodied the federal government and could have used that organizational vehicle to lead states and localities toward the badly needed educational reform. The result was good electoral politics but incompetent, ineffective goverance and a costly policy failure.

In his disillusionment with Reagan Bell appears to be saying that Reagan's support for educational reform was all electoral politics. I think not. Reagan did want a more productive America and a stronger military capacity. But he and his team had limited understanding of how to govern, how to move toward their desired policy, as opposed to political, goals. The Reagan people generally did not understand the need for rigorous analysis to provide substance to ideas and for sound management in execution. Reagan and the movement conservatives remained outside the government, attacking it or abusing it.

5

The Reagan Legacy

The long shadow of the Iran-Contra scandal dominated Reagan's last four years.[1] It was a classic example of how not to govern that almost brought down a president who in 1984 had scored a landslide victory and in the middle of his fifth year had the highest approval rating at a comparable period since polling began.[2] Iran-Contra reinforces the first-term message of the dangers of incompetent policy adviser generalists, excessive secrecy, and hiding or distorting information. In Chief-of-Staff Donald Regan and National Security Adviser Vice Admiral John Poindexter, President Reagan brought together the "too general" and the "too narrow" generalist policy advisers in an explosive combination. Regan was able to move far beyond the Baker years in centralizing control of the White House staff. He also built a staff loyal to him, not to the president. Conservative columnist George Will said that "the aides in close contact with President Reagan today are the least distinguished such group to serve any president in the postwar period."[3] Poindexter was the opposite of Regan. As Keith Schneider of the *New York Times* wrote: "Poindexter was regarded as the consummate military aide. . . . 'He was a nuclear scientist and a military man,' said . . . [a] former staff member, who said he believed that Admiral Poindexter did not understand the politics of the situation . . . [Poindexter had risen rapidly in the NSC] without sitting on the interagency committees, without having to cement relations with Congress and without having to talk to reporters — in short, without gaining the broad political and public relations experience most accomplished officials need before becoming senior members of an administration."[4] Adding to the problem was the Regan-Poindexter relationship. Regan had handpicked Poindexter, but the two were not close, and Poindexter chose to operate in secret from everyone, including from Regan (sometimes especially from Regan).[5] More broadly, "secrecy became an obsession."[6] A knowledge gap widened. As Hedrick Smith observed, "Regan knew little about foreign policy and left the substance to Poindexter, and Regan lacked the political horse sense to give the president independent judgment on the political risks in his foreign policy ventures."[7] With these two incompetent generalist policy advisers at the top in a closed system that tried to keep out other voices, the president and the nation were ill served. In Iran-Contra the question of how the Congress can operate if it cannot believe the White House or expect to be informed of far-reaching operations became fundamental, confronting the constitutional issues of accountability and separation of powers. Is Congress supposed to create an information system independent of the information structure of the executive branch, spy on the White House, or work a mole into the EOP? Credible information and analysis are critical to governmental legitimacy, but top-level staff members, taking a cue from the president, saw information as a weapon to be hidden or used to serve ideological demands. Also like President Reagan, they often had no understanding that the validity of information and analysis needs to be assessed in the president's interest.

THE 1986 TAX REFORM ACT

If Iran-Contra was the low point, the tax package, passed October 22, 1986, and called by Senator Russell Long the most important change in the U.S. tax system in fifty years, was the second term's high point.[8] It was a striking piece of legislation, the passage of which reinforces the case for the power of Reagan's political charisma. As noted earlier, only three presidents of the modern era have brought notable domestic policy changes — Roosevelt, Johnson, and Reagan. Johnson was not a charismatic leader, but he benefited from Kennedy's postmortem charisma. It was all downhill for Johnson after the Great Society victories. FDR, in contrast, came back after the first hundred days of 1933 to lead another round of dramatic legislative changes in 1935, including his great triumph, the Social Security Act. Only history will tell if the 1986 tax legislation is of such importance. But even today, it is clear that the 1986 Tax Reform Act was a change of major proportions; its most prominent features were only two tax rates (15 and 28 percent) and a major reduction of loopholes.[9]

The passage of the 1986 tax bill had many heroes. Hedrick Smith argued that "Reagan's bill was literally saved by the ingenuity and astonishing legislative skill of Bob Packwood," the Oregon Senator who chaired the Finance Committee. Smith claimed that Reagan was not a "central player — certainly not the coalition leader" in the final legislative round in 1986.[10] Nevertheless, the tax package got to the stage where Senator Packwood could exert his legislative mastery because of Reagan and because of Baker and Darman in their roles as secretary and deputy secretary of treasury respectively. Baker and Darman had inherited a plan developed at the treasury while they were at the White House and Donald Regan was secretary of treasury. Baker and Darman, who were considered pragmatists par excellence and were noted for their tactical skills in working out viable compromises, were the key operators in the executive branch. And Reagan himself was at his best holding the effort together in its darkest political days.

To compare the tax reform success of the second term with the educational failure in Secretary Bell's account of his first-term experience is instructive. In both cases President Reagan's political charisma was a central factor in making the effort highly visible and in providing an opening for action. Beyond that, the differences are striking. In the tax reform effort, two of Reagan's most trusted people, Baker and Darman, were out front, and Regan, the father of the tax package, was at the president's side. No movement conservatives lined the pathway. Moreover, while the president may not have understood a great deal about the tax reform package, he could support its basic thrust of tax reduction and simplification. Finally, the battleground was Congress, where Baker and Darman were masters, joined by other experts at the congressional game such as Packwood and Rostenkowski. Once passed, a new tax bill impels action; the new rates are a fait accompli. Moreover, while various aspects of tax reform can be implementation problems in the field, the difficulties are minor compared with the shared governance of complex domestic policies to improve education through federal grants-in-aid to fifty states and thousands of localities. In education, Reagan's ignorance of programmatic and organizational issues dominated and was reinforced by his simplistic view that the federal government is destructive and education is purely a state and local issue. Making major improvements in elementary and secondary education demanded both political and organizational mastery from the president. With tax reform, Reagan's political mastery was enough.

A TRANSFORMED OMB

OMB has experienced greater institutional change in the Reagan era than at any other time in its history. The most important changes include moving from "bottom-up" to "top-down" budgeting, shifting from a primary focus on budget preparation in conjunction with the executive branch agencies to a main concern with selling the president's budget in Congress, and taking the lead role in President Reagan's regulatory reform effort. David Stockman was the driving force in these institutional changes, pushing them through as he dominated the agency to a degree heretofore not seen. His successor, James Miller, continued the Stockman changes, shifting OMB even more toward White House centralization and politicization. By the end of the Reagan era, OMB was more critical to White House policymaking, more political than ever before, and less credible.

Top-down budgeting has two connotations. One is that OMB, not the agencies, dominates the budget. Rather than budget estimates starting in and working up through the agencies to form the base of the president's final budget, a preliminary budget comes out of the White House with many numbers locked in, so agency discretion is small. The second connotation of top-down budgeting is that OMB political executives in conjunction with some inner circle members make the budget. Here not only the agency political executives but also OMB professional staff are kept out of the major budget decisions. In September 1988 a NAPA panel observed, "Now all OMB staff report to the director or deputy director through one or two of *eleven* appointees (who are supported by 10 to 20 noncareer staff)."[11] There is considerable controversy about the extent to which budget policy was torn from the hands of the career staff in the Reagan presidency. Chester A. Newland charged for the entire EOP: "[T]he Reagan policy apparatus is structured and staffed around strictly partisan and personal presidential loyalty, largely excluding professional expertise. The gradual politicization and de-institutionalization of the EOP since the late 1960s had culminated under Reagan in an unprecedented partisan political system. . . . Institutionalized expertise and professionalism are rarely present at high levels within the EOP."[12] OMB professional staff interviewees claim that the degree of professional staff exclusion has been overstated. To begin with, OMB had gained relative to other EOP analytic staffs because of the decline in capacity of these other staffs. The weakening of the other White House analytic staffs in the Reagan years meant that OMB staff was used more widely than ever before.

Here a key distinction is needed between budgeting that sets major priorities, such as defense spending, and budgeting that operates on the details after the big budget decisions have been made. An interviewee who watched OMB from the perspective of a congressional staff noted that during the Reagan years

the macro-budgeting decisions were decided ideologically at the top without any regard for analytic input about program effectiveness. However, once the broad framework was set, the agencies, and the [career staff budget] examiners had a lot to say about programmatic details. This is obviously a more restricted role for analysis than in its heyday. Whether to cut/add is decided ideologically; how to cut/add is decided by analysis. You might also differentiate between two phases of budgeting—the president's and the actual legislated budget. OMB professionals got used for technical tasks that actually determined the way in which much of the budget bargaining was played out—"scorekeeping," or assessing the budgetary impact of legislation.

Top OMB political executives cannot possibly handle the microbudget effort so career staff members get involved in the details, which often are quite important. It is similar to situations in which the big, glamorous decisions are made at the top by presidents, Congress, and agency political executives, but the details that finally give policy its dimension and shape are left to be worked out below. That these lower-level — but still important — decisions are influenced by analysis is a positive feature. The position of OMB analyst is still viewed as desirable. Obviously, poor decisions at the top, unguided by analysis, can greatly reduce the importance of those at the next level.

Whether the OMB staff is used properly and whether it has a significant role in the policy process are two different questions. Having the OMB career staff person working actively on the Hill to help sell the president's budget may not fit the image of the old bureau or be in OMB's long-run interest. At the same time OMB may dominate the policy process. This use of OMB career staff in which it has a "new role as a 'packager' and 'seller' of the budget in Congress [has caused] some OMB staff members . . . [to] fear they could jeopardize their traditional reputation as a source of 'neutral competence'."[13] OMB moved to the Hill with a vengeance after Stockman spurned the previous practice of delivering the budget to Congress and moving on to other work. Stockman's basic argument was that the president's budget had no meaning unless Congress passed it. The budget became a full year effort as OMB career staff worked with other professional staffs, such as those on the CBO and the two budget committees. OMB career staff have told me that these congressional relationships that so disturb "OMB purists" are similar to those in the past but with congressional professionals rather than with agency career staff. However, one of my most perceptive interviewees, who has served at OMB and on a congressional staff, pointed out that while the OMB professionals were viewed as competent, the Reagan political appointees, who generally dealt with a completely different set of people, gained little trust or respect. The interviewee argued that on the Hill, the Reagan OMB was seen as two institutions, not one.

One institution was made up of the technicians who were assessed as highly professional. This supported the career staff argument that there had been a shift in focus from the agencies to Congress, with the permanent staff still performing at a high professional level in the interaction with their technical counterparts. A totally different picture, however, emerged with the second, or political, institution. Director Miller typified the problem; he was viewed as arrogant but not particularly competent. He was so loyal to President Reagan that he was ineffective. The *National Journal*'s Lawrence J. Haas contrasts Miller with Stockman: "If loyalty has kept Miller in the White House, it has hurt him with Congress. Legislating is a process of compromise. Because Miller has refused to bargain with Congress as Stockman had, and can't match his line-item expertise anyway, lawmakers have wanted less to do with him. What could he offer, they concluded, except the same cuts they had rejected year after year? In some offices, he isn't welcome at all, aides said."[14]

This activity by the political executives dominated the Reagan era OMB's image of having no long-term institutional view and of being suspect in the numers it produced. The Reagan OMB came to be seen as a political vehicle of the White House, however much its professional staff denied it.

OMB competence in the Reagan era appears to have declined; however, the case for the decline is not nearly as clear-cut as it is for greater centralization and politicization and less credibility. The point has already been made that the level of incoming recruits to OMB continued to rise over time in line with the overall upward trend in substantive and technical analytic competence. Greater OMB efficiency has come from a computerized Central Budget Management System developed for Stockman in 1982, which allowed comparison of administration and congressional proposals, since the two had different cost-accounting systems. On the negative side, while demands on the OMB staff grew, as the office again became central to the White House in the Reagan era, the agency's own budget between 1981 and 1989 declined by over 12 percent in real dollars, and staff fell from 610 to 570.[15] These changes led Miller to say, "People have been expected to do a lot more with less. . . . People are strung out. They're under real duress."[16] Although former budget staff members have told me that OMB personnel revel in a hair-shirt mentality, these cutbacks almost certainly materially reduced competence.

Two other factors have probably diminished the careerists' generalist policy adviser skills. First, the staff in earlier days worked just as hard during budget season as the present staff does. However, in the few months that they were not under the pressure of the budget, they had the time to reflect, to visit programs, and, I would argue, to hone their institutional knowledge and generalist policy adviser skills. This loss of "down time" is a critical factor that has made current OMB staff more number crunchers than policy analysts. Being "number-fixated" is an occupational hazard of budget offices generally, and the loss of time for reflection has exacerbated the problem in OMB. Their institutional role makes the budgeters think differently in focusing much more on dollars and narrow efficiency than on effective governance. "Down time" in OMB was a corrective factor against this narrow mind-set. Second, to be better technically often is to be more narrow, to be more uncomfortable with analytic synthesis. Reinforcing this tendency is the fact that careerists today are lower in the organizational structure than they were in earlier periods. The careerists of the golden days can probably be adjudged superior to their current counterparts as generalist policy advisers. Nonetheless, it does not necessarily follow that OMB is less capable of serving the function of generalist policy adviser than BOB was. To argue that would require us to say that the *combination* of political appointees and careerists at the top in the BOB days had a greater capacity to generalize than do today's OMB political executives assisted to some extent by the careerists.

One important exception to the Reagan administration's anti-analytic bent in many ways proves the rule—OMB's use of cost-benefit analysis (CBA) in the regulatory reform area. As Frank Fischer has noted, "[C]onservative politicians . . . found cost-benefit analysis to be conveniently compatible with their own biases . . . [and it] emerged as a major *political* methodology of the Reagan administration."[17] CBA was the perfect analytic weapon to turn against the government regulation that the administration wanted to stamp out because it gave off the aura of rigor and could be used narrowly to exclude the "soft" variables the administration preferred to ignore. The Reagan administration that generally spurned hard analysis was happy to put the burden of rigorous proof on those who pushed for greater government control over the environment. CBA also meshed well with the budget mentality of the OMB professionals who wanted cutbacks as deficits mounted. The limited nature of this discussion of Reagan regulatory reform in focusing only on OMB's cost-benefit analysis efforts must be underscored. The larger issue of the overall Reagan deregulation strategy, which included changes in managerial philosophy and personnel cutbacks in regulatory agencies, is not addressed.

Cost-benefit analysis has been around for a long time and had been used extensively in assessing the expected benefits and costs of physical projects such as dams. While CBA has generally been packaged in terms of its hardness and neutrality, the technique is but one of the many flawed policy analysis tools available and can be attacked on the same grounds as other policy analysis techniques. CBA did not provide the administration a super weapon to attach and destroy regulation. It was more the opposite case, with OMB power fostering the use of cost-benefit analysis, guided more by ideology than by scientific principles. This OMB analytic effort, with its narrow focus and its scientific base, caused turmoil among those who supported government regulation of the environment and the work place.[18] But as this section spells out, the Reagan administration attack on government regulation with analytic techniques was not successful, and the CBA experience offers stronger evidence of the limits of policy analysis than of its brute power.

OMB's move toward regulatory rulemaking has had major implications for the institutional use of policy analysis. Executive Order 12291 issued in February 1981, just after Reagan became president, and Executive Order 12498 issued in 1985 brought regulatory reform under OMB's Office of Information and Regulatory Affairs (OIRA) that had been established under the Paperwork Reduction Act of 1980. Executive Order 12291 was cast in information and analytic terms. It required that "administrative decisions . . . be based on adequate information," that "regulatory action shall not be undertaken unless the potential benefits to society for the regulation outweigh the potential costs to society," and that agencies must submit formal Regulatory Impact Analyses for major rules, which were defined as those likely to have either a $100 million or more impact on industry each year or major impacts on consumers, industries, and subnational governments. The order was a concerted top-down effort to make OIRA the lead organization in Reagan regulatory reform—the supreme enforcer with strong support from the White House to get the job done.

Implementation became the major stumbling block in an inept performance that was reminiscent of BOB's failure in the mid-1960s in putting PPBS in place as a government-wide policymaking vehicle. Regulatory reform was the latest unsuccessful top-down attempt by the budget office to impose the president's will on the agencies through a complex new process. Just as with PPBS, the agencies fought back with superior resources. Former OIRA head James Tozzi said, "OMB does not have extreme power. . . . OMB can't send regs to the Federal Register, only the agency can. . . . [An] agency outnumbers OMB by an order of magnitude in resources; they outgun us on data and research money."[19] NAPA's Panel on Presidential Management of Rulemaking in Regulatory Agencies noted: "OMB's generalist staff is derogated as lacking the technical expertise necessary for competent judgment in many proposed rulemakings; for the most part, OIRA desk officers are economists, lawyers, and policy analysts with little or no previous experience with government or the programs under its review."[20] Many of the OIRA desk officers were typical public-policy school graduates with strong quantitative and economic skills. For some it was their first job after graduation. The result was that OMB was not selective in regulation reviews; it spent too much time on minor efforts without concentrating on priority issues, a similar failing under PPBS. Most condemning is this NAPA panel charge: "Virtually every agency official who has commented on the review process has complained that OMB attention is often focused on 'nit-picking,' on relatively minor provisions of proposed regulations, on choice of wording, and on other differences that do not seem to have much importance. Agency officials widely share the perception that desk officers are expected to be adversaries of agencies, that they are recruited with the promise of being able to push agencies around."[21] This nit-picking, confrontational style by government staffs, in which they enforce rules and regulations but have limited understanding of them, is found in much of the work on program implementation.[22] In this regulatory mentality, control is equated with compliance.

A long-standing complaint against analytic offices is that many of the bright, quantitatively oriented staff persons are young and brash, are not masters of their substantive areas, and have little or no understanding of or appreciation for organizational structure and procedure that are often critical factors in arriving at policy decisions. When the original DOD analytic office was labeled the "whiz kids," it was a characterization with pejorative as well as positive connotations. That the new whiz kids at OIRA often fared badly against deeper, more experienced agency staffs is hardly surprising. The new OMB budget examiners are likely to be no more experienced than the OIRA desk officers, and they also face more experienced staffs. But there are big differences. First, the inexperienced budget examiners had far more clout, stemming from budgeting's historic, prestigious place as OMB's main function. Second, the young budget examiners reported to immediate superiors who were veterans of earlier budget battles. Third, *the* critical element of the yearly budget exercise often is the funding level so the budget examiner can go after dollars by telling an agency to cut a certain percentage without having in-depth mastery of the program area. Fourth, the top-down regime initiated in the Reagan years meant that cuts came from on high, so the frontline budget examiner was overseeing a direct White House command. Fifth, the budget examiners faced a task requiring less technological, substantive area and organizational mastery than was demanded to carry out the regulatory reform mission. Sixth, as an interviewee pointed out, the big budget and taxes successes of the final term—the tax cut, the military buildup, and the domestic cuts—had strong public support. Regulatory reform in the environmental and safety areas did not. The strong public support translated into unified support by congressional Republicans and much pressure on Democrats to go along. The mixed public support of regulatory reform let a number of pro-environmentalists, including key Republicans, thwart Reagan.

The OIRA setting illuminates two important aspects of effective institutional policy analysis—the bureaucratic status of the analytic unit and the technical and organizational mastery demands of the analytic environment. In early 1981 OIRA was a new office, having been established late in the Carter administration to oversee the Paperwork Reduction Act. However, OIRA did not acquire the regulatory charge until the February 1981 executive order. Such new offices outside of the main budget function historically have performed poorly at BOB/OMB. For example, the ill-fated, inept implementation of PPBS government-wide had fallen to a new office that was not in the mainstream of BOB decisionmaking. Furthermore, the attempts to make the "M" in OMB an important element of the agency effort had also failed. Relatively speaking, the regulatory reform effort does not look so bad, compared with other OMB efforts outside the budget function. The fact remains, however, that the Reagan administration, in one of its highest-priority areas, was able to make only limited headway with cost-benefit analysis.

Lack of technical and organizational mastery was probably more important than the newness of the office in OMB's failed implementation effort in regulatory reform. The main problem was that the knowledge demands were great and did *not* necessarily carry big dollar implications. Major regulatory efforts may have huge cost implications for the firms in a regulated industry, but not for the federal budget, where the costs involve regulators and procedures, rather than program grants, so OIRA was not involved in budget cutting per se. Budget cutting is OMB's strongest suit. Instead, OIRA was thrown into an extremely complex environment dominated by technological, substantive, organizational, and procedural issues. In short, the competence demands were relatively high and did not play to the strong suit—quantitative policy analysis—of the OIRA desk officers, for example, the 1976 Resource Conservation and Recovery Act (RCRA), which charges the Environmental Protection Agency (EPA) with the management of hazardous wastes. A Kennedy School of Government case study of EPA underscored the technical complexity of the hazardous waste area, pointed out that the RCRA regulations ran to 214 pages of the *Federal Register*, and observed: "In the case of standards for disposal, the rules at the time of the Reagan inauguration were still in the interim status stage. Comments from industry and other parties ran into the thousands; the RCRA docket at EPA occupied an entire storage room."[23] The case study, which told how career EPA employee Gary Dietrich survived and indeed thrived under EPA Director Anne Gorsuch, quoted another career EPA staff person on Dietrich's mastery of the regulations: "[H]e had an encyclopedic knowledge of the regulations and regulatory process. He knew every thread and exactly how they all came together."[24] These rules and regulations, which could be a quagmire for a policy analyst not steeped in them, were central to regulatory reform.

Another factor further complicating the hazardous waste regulatory environment was the large numbers of interested outsiders, including corporations being regulated, interest group organizations, and environmental interest groups. All were able and willing to go to Congress and the media with complaints. Why OMB expected that inexperienced policy analysts could quickly master this complex setting, which called for both highly technical knowledge about the nature of hazardous waste risks and the available treatment and a deep understanding of bureaucratic and interest group politics, is far from clear. If there is a plausible answer, it is analytic hubris—the belief that persons with strong policy analysis skills can quickly get on top of substantive policy areas, no matter how complex. This notion comes from the early days of policy analysis where there was a strongly held view that if a choice had to be made between having a person on an analytic staff with good analytic skill but with limited substantive knowledge, and an individual with substantive mastery but no policy analysis tools, the former should be chosen because the analyst could pick up the program and policy knowledge faster than the substantive person could acquire the analytic skills. That choice in the early days was often a real one in the domestic policy areas, as few substantive people had analytic skills, and almost no analysts had programmatic mastery. However, even then it was a choice with great risks that were exacerbated if the analyst was young, arrogant, and too dependent on the "hard" tools of analysis. Today there are people who can go both ways with technical and organizational mastery. Moreover, it is recognized that if the array of necessary skills is not found in one person, a team can be created. That OMB chose in the highly complex regulatory areas to go with OIRA desk officers with mainly analytic skills was a failure to use extensive past experience, including that at OMB. It lay at the heart of the poor implementation results in a highest-priority area. Possibly, OMB decisionmakers were misled by the experience of young, inexperienced budget officers, but they should have seen the clear differences in the two settings.

OMB in the Reagan era placed too much emphasis on high-powered, quantitatively based analytic skills. That incoming staff today are better equipped with quantitative techniques than were their predecessors may mean less than meets the eye if the current people themselves overvalue the analytic tools and undervalue substantive area and organizational mastery. Career staff has also been pushed further and further from the top-level decisions that hone generalist policy adviser skills. The result is that career staff today may be less able to perform top-level synthesis and certainly are less likely to be called on to do it than in the past. This places the bulk of the policy synthesis on the OMB political executives. Does this shift from OMB careerists to political executives mean a decline in competence? A NAPA panel in a report on the 1988–89 presidential transition argued that "the rapid turnover which characterizes political appointees has . . . contributed to the decline of expertise in [OMB] decisionmaking."[25] There is no question that such was the case in the Miller OMB. The Stockman period is less certain. But even here, generalist policy adviser depth was less than in the past. The clear implication that can be drawn is that OMB's overall policy adviser skills were more variable than in the past, when careerists provided stability. Furthermore, the top policy adviser effort appears much less likely to benefit from the institutional wisdom that historically had been a key aspect of the budget office. The changes that were intensified in the Reagan era have weakened the institutional presidency. An incoming president may not be able to find the institutional knowledge and generalist policy adviser capabilities that marked the budget office before it became more politicized in the Nixon administration.

In summing up OMB after eight years of the Reagan era, four deleterious developments in OMB should be stressed. First, institutional memory and neutral competence suffered. Both appear to have declined and been pushed well down in the organization, with far less likelihood of use at the top. Second, the great loss of competence in OMB has not been technical capacity but rather the broad skills of the generalist career civil servant. Third, institutional commitment and credibility in the Reagan years reached their lowest level since the budget office came to the EOP a half century ago. Fourth, as an interviewee with long experience in both executive branch and congressional policy analysis suggested, "OMB's success in recruiting good entry level people reflects, at least in part, an increasingly out-of-date public image so that when the perception in the professional and academic communities catches up with reality, the recruiting task is likely to become much more difficult."

The interviewee pointed out in comparison that congressional agencies such as GAO were experiencing the opposite impact, as images of their competence have grown in the last decade and a half.[26]

POLITICS, POLICY, AND THE DECLINE
OF THE INSTITUTIONAL PRESIDENCY

A number of presidential scholars, at least before Iran-Contra, believed that the Reagan era was producing a stronger presidency, one that afforded maximum White House control. These scholars, however, were unclear at times whether that control was over political standing, policy formulation, implementation, or some combination of the three. Reagan, it was argued, did it "right" in gaining a level of control at the top, unmatched in recent administrations. He was successful in creating a much more politicized presidency *and* in making policy breakthroughs rivaled only by Franklin Roosevelt and Lyndon Johnson in the last half century. But the scholars ignored or downplayed the questions of control and purpose, quality of governance, and the efficacy of policy. Control can be an end in itself in *political* terms, but it is only a means in *policy* terms. And nothing is worse than effective bad policies.

British political scientist David Mervin, writing after the Iran-Contra scandal, observed: "Recent events have made us aware of some of the hazards of Reagan's style, yet that should not blind us to its strengths or to the president's earlier achievements. The Iran debacle may, in any case be partly explained by a sharp decline in the quality of Reagan's senior staff in his second term and by the effects of advancing years on the president himself. Looked at in the long term, and taking account of his presidency as a whole, we may expect Reagan to be rated ultimately as one of the most successful modern presidents."[27] Brookings political scientist Terry Moe's analysis of Reagan's first term focused on the increasing centralization and politicization of the presidency as an institutional trend, on the central role of the Reagan administration in these developments, and on what Moe believed were misplaced criticisms by those who attack the trend in calling for more professionalism. Moe holds that this trend toward White House centralization and politicization is systemic, driven by the nature of the American institutions and by the resources, incentives, and constraints of the presidency. Increasing centralization and politicization are inevitable, with a consequent decline in the use of career professionals. Reagan's contribution, however, has been especially important, argued Moe: "Reagan did much more than continue a historical trend. . . . [H]e built a set of administrative arrangements that by past standards prove coherent, well integrated, and eminently workable. . . . [F]uture presidents . . . will have every reason to learn from and build upon the Reagan example in seeking to enhance their own institutional capacities for leadership. This places Reagan in a pivotal historical position, and could well establish him as the most administratively influential president of the modern period."[28] Reagan's tight control yielded short-run political gains at the cost of disastrous long-term policies.

Although the critics of greater centralization and politicization are a diverse lot, Moe saw their work as grounded in the academic traditions of public administration, with its "blind" adherence to the career professional. The "public administration" epithet was used broadly to include public policy analysts and others who appear to favor more professionalism at the top and see presidents as part of the problem, failing in Moe's opinion to recognize that the system, not a president, is the real cause. Moe argued that this "naive" group thought the big problem was organizational, not political, so that what are fundamentally political problems were approached with nonpolitical solutions. Moe's basic thesis is: "There is also good reason to believe that the president's short-term time perspective discourages investment in competence-building institutions, to his own disadvantage. But this is less than half the story. It ignores the potential contributions of politicization and centralization to responsiveness, innovation, and other components of presidential leadership. It ignores the demonstrated compatibility with presidential incentives—a crucial property that is the Achilles' heel of standard reform proposals. . . . It ignores the necessary trade-offs that presidents are forced to make in seeking a working balance between responsiveness and organizational competence."[29] What presidents want, Moe asserts, is not neutral competence but "responsive" competence, because strengthening the former may simply increase the bureaucracy's power to obstruct, while the latter meets the president's political needs and the demands to which he must respond. The president can seek some candidates for staff appointments primarily for responsiveness, where such factors as loyalty and ideology dominate; and other candidates primarily for organizational competence, where professionalism, substantive expertise and administrative experience are most important. Moe's warning is useful in stressing that critics of politicization often ignore its positive aspects or fail to appreciate the difficult trade-offs demanded when a president tries to balance the needs of executive leadership with those of organizational competence. The Reagan administration's main contribution has been to push this balance even more toward overresponsiveness to the president. If no one at the top of an administration sees the need for organizational competence or for penetrating policy analysis or if the president and his inner circle all believe the careerists are tainted, blind loyalty and ideological adherence will dominate.

The danger of overresponsiveness to the president is that the question of "control for what purpose" is seldom asked. Winning is everything. No concern is expressed about effective governance, policy effectiveness, or the desirability of policy goals. Control becomes an end in itself. Professionalization, institutional memory, and solid analysis are made subordinate to the political responsiveness of the staff. My argument is not for analysts to be on top. However, an even graver mistake than always listening to the experts is *never* heeding them. The search is for a balance, and the overriding lesson of the Reagan administration is that it was hopelessly out of balance, with maximum political responsiveness and minimum organizational and analytic competence. The Reagan management style was a formula for political triumph and policy disaster when driven by Reagan's charisma and politics of unreality. It was also a formula for destroying the capacity of White House analytic staffs to serve the institutional presidency.

HOLLOW, INCOMPETENT GOVERNMENT

Reagan-era cutbacks in career staff occurred even though demands on the domestic agencies were rising significantly. Despite increasing demand for its services, the Social Security Administration (SSA) declined from 80,000 to 63,000 staff members. After findings of long delays in service, "tens of thousands of poor people who are aged, disabled or blind [being] mistakenly deprived of their Supplemental Security Income payments because of staff shortages," and 51 percent of an SSA staff sample characterizing their morale as poor or extremely poor, President Bush stopped a further OMB proposed cutback to 58,000.[30] In discussing a reduced FDA staff, Dr. Samuel Thier, president of the Institutes of Medicine in the National Academy of Sciences said "[FDA] is a demoralized group, being asked to do too much with too few resources."[31] While laws require FDA to review new drug applications within six months, the average review now takes 31 months. Between 1980 and 1988, the number of drug and food inspections declined from nearly 33,000 to slightly under 20,000 — a drop of almost 40 percent.

A critical federal agency function is oversight to determine whether laws are being carried out as mandated by Congress, how well laws are being implemented and/or managed, and whether specific illegal acts such as fraud are occurring. The failure of the executive branch to fulfill fundamental oversight responsibilities can undermine government credibility and result in costs far in excess of the personnel outlays needed for effective oversight performance. For example, Secretary of Energy James Watkins in announcing on December 1, 1989, that the Rocky Flats nuclear weapons plant was to be closed indefinitely said that the plant had been "mismanaged by [his] own department," and pointed out "the screw-up was in management, not the plant."[32] HUD is another case in point. An independent audit performed by the accounting firm Price Waterhouse for the GAO found that HUD's Federal Housing Administration (FHA) had suffered a record loss of $4.2 billion, as compared with the earlier reported figure of $858 million, determined by an internal FHA audit; and Comptroller General Charles Bowsher pointed out that the Price Waterhouse audit offered considerable evidence that FHA did not properly oversee the private lenders who gained control over loans under the Reagan deregulation efforts.[33] One reason is that HUD had cut more than 4,000 persons from its payrolls, including many who monitored HUD (FHA) projects.[34] Because of inadequate staff the Forest Service has been unable to monitor properly private timber logging on public lands, and illegal logging is estimated to cost the federal government over $100 million a year in stolen marketable lumber.[35] According to a majority report of the Senate Federal Services Subcommittee of the Governmental Affairs Committee, the Department of Energy (DOE) has over 100,000 contract employees, compared with 16,000 civil servants, with the former helping perform "virtually all [of the agency's] basic functions."[36] As the report pointed out, DOE had become quite restricted in terms of the monitoring needed to determine potential conflicts of interest, both generally and specifically in terms of the firms that supply the DOE contract employees.

Nowhere do the costs of hollow incompetent government become so apparent as in the S&L scandal. President Carter and Congress share blame with President Reagan. The Deregulatory and Monetary Control Act of 1980 removed interest rate restrictions on the S&Ls and raised Federal Savings and Loan Insurance Corporation coverage from $40,000 to $100,000 per individual depositor account. The Garn–St. Germain Depository Institutions Decontrol Act of 1982 allowed S&Ls to invest deposits much more broadly than in the traditional loans for housing (e.g., in so-called junk bonds) and lowered the already low 4 percent ratio of net worth to deposits to a "minuscule" (to quote Paul Zane Pilzer) 3 percent.[37] The stage was set for disaster. However, two more critical elements made the S&L setting particularly explosive. First was the cutback in executive branch oversight which reflected both budget tightness and the Reagan view that deregulation meant no government control. Second, Congress turned its back on declining executive branch monitoring and pressed hard in a number of cases against executive branch attempts at controlling the S&Ls.[38] Pilzer observed: "What virtually guaranteed that this sort of reform [e.g., the Garn–St. Germain Act] would lead to disorder was that Congress and the Reagan administration neglected to accompany it with any sort of increase in government supervision. Indeed, oversight actually declined. In 1982, as the restraints came down, the FHLBB [Federal Home Loan Bank Board] conducted 2,796 field examinations of thrift institutions. That was 12 percent fewer than the year before and almost 20 percent under the 1979 level. . . . The first weakness was a critical lack of trained examiners and supervisors . . . which was a direct result of Reagan-era deregulation. According to the Reagan administration, deregulation meant not just fewer regulations, but fewer regulators as well."³⁹ Congress joined the Reagan administration in attacking the regulators who tried to stem some of the worst excesses of an industry that was "on a deregulatory high."⁴⁰

The paradox of deregulation is that implementing it successfully generally demands the substitution of one form of government control — greater capacity to determine that the rules of the game (e.g., the market) are not being subverted — for the command-and-control approach of crafting strict government rules to cover as many specific cases as possible. Both forms of control require monitoring, but deregulation generally requires even greater monitoring. The need is likely to be for *fewer total* monitors but *more* high-powered ones. The overriding point is that both greater regulation and less regulation (deregulation is a misnomer if it is meant to imply lack of any government regulation) demand an *adequate cadre of competent monitors*. And in the case of the federal government that demand falls first upon the executive branch agencies charged by law with implementing and managing the policy. Neither the Reagan administration nor Congress understood this organizational imperative. This lack of understanding has brought and will continue to bring astronomical costs that threaten the nation's economic viability and social fabric.

In their long review of Reagan and the federal bureaucracy, Peter Benda and Charles Levine concluded:

> Reagan has damaged, perhaps irreparably, two vitally important institutions that will be needed to address future problems effectively: OMB, and the senior ranks of the career civil service. . . . [By] screening, placing, and directing political apointees in the upper levels of executive branch agencies and in some places encouraging (or at least tolerating) contentious relations between its appointees and career officials, the administration has succeeded in driving many of the latter into retirement. This development may deprive the next administration, and perhaps future administrations as well, of a very valuable resource and make the task of governing all the more difficult. . . .
>
> More generally, we would argue that a principal failing of the Reagan administration lay in its apparent inability or unwillingness . . . to take a serious look at the problem of the long-term erosion of the capacity of the federal workforce — a dubious legacy that the next administration will surely have to face.⁴¹

Striking at the highest-level career managers can be particularly destructive, since experienced managers may be difficult to replace. There are a number of unanswered questions. Were the people who retired at the top the best and the brightest, who had a number of productive years left? What about the next level? Generally, the expectation is that the most competent would have the greater number of alternative offers to leave the federal government. No one knows across the federal work force how serious the damage was. But it is clear that the Reagan administration diminished the most critical of resources — competent people. How hollow and inept the executive branch is, as the result of the Reagan era, can only be answered over a number of years.

Reagan's attack on the executive branch's capacity to carry out the law of the land and to meet overriding domestic policy needs was evident almost from the outset, and critics, including the author, warned of probable harm.[42] The nation had ample warnings of the potential destructiveness of the Reagan administration to effective executive branch governance and of the costly consequences. No one foresaw the extent of the financial costs, as in the case of the S&L scandal, or of the human suffering as in the HUD case, in which federal cutbacks and gross mismanagement contributed significantly to rising homelessness. No one perceived Reagan's tremendous charismatic power or its impact on Congress and the public.

The consequences of hollow, incompetent federal governance were badly underestimated because Congress and much of the American press turned their backs on clear failures to execute the law of the land. At the same time the folly of federal personnel cuts — pennywise, pound-foolish grossly understated the relationship that was more like pennywise, hundreds of pounds foolish — was painfully obvious to those who would take a hard, analytic look. How long will it take Americans to understand both that the federal government not only is, but must be, a crucial factor in the nation's economic and social viability and concommitantly that federal government "on the cheap" can be a formula for disaster? An article in the September 12, 1982, *Seattle Post-Intelligencer* ended: "My great fear is that the federal government will actually become as inefficient and ineffective as its critics claim it now is. The federal agencies may no longer be able to carry out the law of the land. I'm not sure many people understand what a really inept and inefficient government is like. I don't think they will like it at all. But such a federal government may be one of Ronald Reagan's lasting legacies."[43] Government is part both of the problem and of the solution.

Not since the structural changes of the New Deal that established the EOP has a president succeeded as Reagan has in making such basic shifts in both the internal White House policy process and the relationships between the White House and agency political executives. Nor has any president so threatened the underlying executive branch capacity to generate sound, timely, relevant expert policy information and analysis by shunning hard-edged analytic and evaluative efforts and relying on ideological certainties. It was the first anti-analytic presidency since the start of the analytic revolution. By 1989 the Reagan administration had materially damaged the executive branch information and analytic infrastructure, thereby undercutting the longstanding federal capacity to produce the policy information and analysis needed for Congress, states, localities, and ultimately the public, to make decisions fundamental to American democracy. The Reagan administration, with its cutbacks in federal staff, its negative view of the federal domestic government generally, and its career civil servants specifically, along with its mismanagement, also greatly weakened the capacity of the executive branch to execute its legislative mandates. By 1989 it was appropriate to speak of a hollow, incompetent federal government in the domestic policy arena.

6
Presidential Role, Style, and Competence

Did giants walk the Washington corridors of power in the early postwar years? When we set George Marshall, Dean Acheson, or Robert Lovett against Edwin Meese, Casper Weinberger, Donald Regan, that earlier period seems particularly strong. Postwar American economic and geopolitical dominance reached an ideal point that made for a reasonable match between problems and resources. A policy such as the Marshall Plan could be formulated and implemented with a high expectation of success. That these early postwar leaders would stride so successfully through the problems of today without the reasonable match between problems and resources is most unlikely. But they did combine integrity, loyalty, commitment, and competence in ways that now seem highly praiseworthy. Walter Isaacson and Evan Thomas quoted Henry Kissinger: "My generation doesn't produce people in the selfless tradition of a McCloy. We're too nervous and ambitious!"[1]

Isaacson and Thomas's *The Wise Men* makes an invidious comparison between the old "Establishment" symbolized by the six men featured in the book and the new "Professional Elite" (their term) represented at its worst by Zbigniew Brzezinski, President Carter's national security adviser. My problem is not with their belief that these men of the earlier period were better public servants, offered better policy advice, and made better policy than their successors, but with how Isaacson and Thomas misleadingly lump together a number of variables. Consider this statement about the Establishment, which had been blamed for the Cold War because of the policies of the Truman years:

> The pendulum has swung partway back; the policies of Acheson and Lovett may have been flawed, but they were at least consistent; the men who made them may have been narrow-sighted, but they were a good deal more selfless and disciplined than their modern counterparts. . . .
> Curiously, the small group of amateurs who revolved in and out of

the State Department in the 1940s managed to get far more accomplished than the legions of full-time professionals who now inhabit the downtown think tanks and office warrens of Foggy Bottom, Capitol Hill and the West Wing. Perhaps that is because the older generation was primarily concerned with serving their president and country, while the newer seems inordinately preoccupied with serving themselves.[2]

Labeling the Wise Men as amateurs compared with the new Professional Elite is wrong. The six Wise Men served long apprenticeships in the federal government prior to taking on critical tasks after World War II. Bohlen and Kennan were career foreign service officers. The other four had extensive service in the Roosevelt government as political appointees up to the under-secretary level. The six men were not only foreign policy experts, but they had extensive experience with the foreign policy process within the government. The amateur versus professional contrast presented by the authors is most misleading if it is intended to imply anything about the preparation for positions high in the foreign-policy decisionmaking process. The six Wise Men were better prepared for their tasks at the top than were Brzezinski and Kissinger, who knew foreign policy substance but had little or no exposure to the foreign-policy process itself. The Wise Men were competent policy generalists capable of providing sound policy advice.

Contrast Averell Harriman with Kissinger and Brzezinski, all of whom served presidents in national security advisory positions. Few individuals had either the desire to be at the top or the capacity to promote himself as did Harriman. He wanted to be at the center of action and saw the position of secretary of state as capping his long, distinguished career. But this strong personal ambition was bounded by a sense of loyalty and a set of rules of the game that guided his behavior in his national security advisory role to President Truman. Harriman followed institutional rather than personal dictates by scrupulously protecting the status and responsibilities of Secretary of State Dean Acheson, his strong rival. Such integrity can hardly be attributed to Kissinger or Brzezinski. Isaacson and Thomas saw Brzezinski as shamelessly ambitious and unprincipled in undercutting Secretary of State Vance and badly misserving the president and the country, including a case where "Brzezinski flat-out lied . . . to the president" about a secret channel of communication to Iran.[3] Isaacson and Thomas are not unaware of the shortcomings of the six Establishment figures. It was a white, waspish, elitist group of males who at times were arrogant and condescending and possibly anti-Semitic. The Establishment drew people mainly from the right backgrounds and the right schools, but on occasion did let in poor people who worked their ways up the "right" way. However, the Establishment did serve both as a screening device for entry and as a mechanism for limiting behavior. The newer breed of competent policy advisers such as Kissinger probably had more technical skills than did those of the old Establishment, but the six Wise Men were the kind of policy adviser generalists needed in future administrations. Isaacson and Thomas confused matters when they created an ill-defined category labeled the "New Professional Elite," to which they attribute a general lack of integrity, loyalty, and commitment. My purpose is not to exonerate the new professionals, including the policy analysts, but to point out that those who have recently operated at the level of Acheson, Harriman, and Lovett were not professional policy analysts but outsiders who well may have been highly ideological and often lacked both substantive and organizational process knowledge in the policy areas where they would be making the key decisions. The mark of these people, particularly in the Reagan administration, has been to ignore expert policy advice and to proceed, following their ideological predilections.

CHIEF POLITICAL OFFICER, STRATEGIST, AND MANAGER

A number of recent presidential scholars have argued that the president is not the chief manager of the executive branch. Stephen Hess says the president is the chief political officer; Arnold notes that "a contemporary president would be ill-advised to assume that his role regarding the executive branch is managerial."[4] A president should not become too entangled in management, but the fact remains that the president must be the chief manager of the executive branch. "[T]he president is a chief [political], and he is not merely an executive [manager]. But he is the chief executive."[5] Both responsibilities of chief and executive go with the job. *That the president must be chief manager is not a normative proposition, but results pari passu because politics, policy, and management are inseparable in the policy equation.* To assert that the president is the chief manager of the executive branch is not an argument for increasing White House control through more politicization and centralization, with the president's top staff expected to run the government from the West Wing. To be an effective domestic policy manager, a president should reject strengthening the White House at the expense of the agencies and instead seek a balance between a strong White House and strong agencies.

To say that the president is the chief manager of the executive branch is not to deny the other key domestic policy functions of chief political officer and chief strategist. Indeed, all are closely interrelated. Consider the president's role as chief strategist. The development of broad objectives — the president's vision for the nation — is the first crucial step. It is an essential element of effective political leadership. The second stage is careful analysis that determines the internal consistency of the broad goals and the feasibility of their implementation. These broad objectives should undergo rigorous testing and may be modified and refined. It is not enough to ask where one wants to go; the next step is to determine how to get there. Only through hard analytic effort can presidential objectives be hammered into a reliable directional guide and a realistic starting road map be developed. The third stage of strategy is the logical extension of the second. As time passes, circumstances change. No one has a sure course. The initial strategy is certain to need tactical revision over time. And in cases where the environmental changes are dramatic, fundamental rethinking about the broad objectives may be required.

A realistic strategic plan alone is not enough. The fourth task is sustained political leadership that must build and maintain support for the strategy. The president needs the usual political skills of influence and persuasion, the capacity to "see" or sense political issues in other issues (e.g., this policy will cost support in the South), and an appreciation of the times that politicking is necessary.[6] The exercise of strategic political leadership is particularly demanding because the president must make the necessary political adjustments to gain and sustain support over a considerable period. These adjustments pose the political leader's most difficult task — to decide where no further tradeoffs can be made without undercutting the basic thrust of the strategy. It is the ultimate demand made on the strategist, requiring the political wisdom to find the right balance. This task is difficult because the point of balance is not fixed — indeed not even knowable — at the beginning of the political search process but rather must be found within that process. Bernard Asbell, describing a two-year legislative effort by then Senator Edmund Muskie that resulted in enacting a new Clean Air Act, observed that "Muskie himself is satisfied that the new law has located itself at that magical point of political balance: The boldest feasible act in the public interest that takes into account the relative political strengths and conflicting demands for justice of all contenders."[7] Finding that balance point yielding the "boldest feasible act" is the ultimate test of the political courage and wisdom of the strategic leader. Finally, there is the need to manage the policy. The president may delegate that task to an agency and do no more than have the effort monitored by White House staff. But that is a big managerial decision — the kind that only the president can make. It may be helpful to think of politics as first, policy second, and management third, but that is misleading if it implies that the three are separable.

PRESIDENTS AND ORGANIZATIONAL COMPETENCE

Sound EOP analytic structure and strong agencies are highly interrelated in terms of effective presidential governance and ultimately of desirable societal outcomes. On the one hand, the White House needs to develop a strong analytic structure that supports both policy formulation and the monitoring of the implementation of presidential policies. On the other hand, the actual implementation must be carried out by the agencies. Implementation can be monitored within the EOP analytic structure but not executed from it. To weaken agencies in order to gain political control strikes at the heart of the organizational capacity needed for strong presidential governance. Sound information and analysis are not intrinsically valuable but they acquire value through use in decisionmaking and management — that is, in the policymaking process. *Sound policy analysis without underlying organizational capacity and competence to implement formulated policies is of limited value, except to indicate the basic organizational deficiencies that block effective policies.* The anti-bureaucratic, anti-government presidents did not appreciate this organizational truth and thereby diminished the value of sound information and analysis by undercutting agency capacity to manage implementation and operations. This is why the Eisenhower presidency is so critical. The big difference between Eisenhower and the anti-bureaucratic, anti-government presidents is organizational competence. Eisenhower was the master of large-scale organizational processes, of obtaining well-critiqued, well-thought-through policy alternatives, and of choosing cabinet and staff based on their particular skills and their blend of skills. Later presidents often lacked in-depth experience with large-scale public organizations. They did not understand the intricate processes of these large institutions and had little appreciation of fitting the person with the specialized demands of the job, a debilitating flaw. Presidential organizational mastery has been the missing link in the presidential policy equation. Its absence has contributed materially to both inept presidential governance and deleterious policy outcomes.

Eisenhower: The Organizational Virtuoso

Few presidents stepped down with so little esteem as an effective leader as did Dwight Eisenhower. A poll shortly after he left office put him close to the bottom in presidential ratings. Recent polls rank him ninth from the top, and his biographer Stephen Ambrose speculated that Eisenhower will be ranked just below Washington, Jefferson, Jackson, Lincoln, Wilson, and Franklin Roosevelt.[8] When he left office Eisenhower was seen as a do-nothing president who played golf and did what he was told by his staff. Nothing could have been further from the truth. Consider the case of Secretary of State John Foster Dulles, who was viewed as the man making foreign policy. Clearly there was a peer policy adviser relationship between Dulles and Eisenhower, with the two in constant contact, even when Dulles was overseas. However, the direction of the relationship was the opposite of what people thought at the time. What stands out is Eisenhower's ability to lead strong cabinet members, adroitly balancing his control and their autonomy. This was a classic case of hidden-hand leadership masterfully executed by the man who had spent almost his entire career as a military manager, culminating in leadership of all Allied forces in Europe. A "hidden hand," given Watergate and Iran-Contra, may not be what the United States wants or needs. The key point, however, is not style but the recognition that has emerged from the recent reassessment of Eisenhower as to how critical his organizational competence was to his successful performance. And it is in the area of performance, not image and rhetoric, that history now gives such high marks to Eisenhower. What did he do right? These summary statements indicate his organizational competence:

- Eisenhower had the interpersonal skills and confidence to be a good judge of people, to lead without appearing to do so, to choose persons who compensated for his own personal weaknesses, to put together a strong team of persons, and to work comfortably with outstanding individuals.
- He had sufficiently deep knowledge and understanding of the workings of formal and informal institutional structures, processes and behavior and of the value of institutional routine to permit him to use the available organizations in pursuing his objectives.
- He was a pragmatic man of broad vision who subjected his most fundamental objectives to the reality testing of internal consistency and implementation feasibility.
- He understood the importance of sound information and analysis in support of policymaking and used his White House staff adroitly.
- He recognized the critical role of the strong executive agencies in policy management and kept White House staffs from undercutting agency authority and autonomy.

Eisenhower had the capacity to choose good people and use them effectively. "[He] wanted competent, proven administrators, men who thought big and acted big. Completely free of any need to boost his own ego, or to prove his decisiveness or leadership, he wanted to 'build up' the men who worked with him."[9] He not only picked good people, but he could assess each person's strengths and weaknesses and combine individuals to increase their strengths and minimize their weaknesses. Such a capacity requires a leader to have both deep introspection in knowing his own deficiencies and a good eye for talent in others. Eisenhower perceived the need for strong government not just at the center, but in the agencies, for the exercise of effective presidential governance. Also becoming clear is that Eisenhower was an astute politician, using his claim of being above politics to operate effectively in the partisan political arena.[10] He had the capacity to balance effectively the inseparable, but competing, tasks of chief political officer, strategist, and manager. What distinguishes Eisenhower from more recent American presidents is his command of the machine and the organizational competence of his government. He was the last elected president to use his cabinet effectively. Some members of the cabinet, such as Dulles, were personal policy advisers, but the first qualification of a cabinet officer was to be able to run his or her agency. Cabinet members were expected to do this day-to-day job, just as Eisenhower's generals in World War II had been. That was to change dramatically under Kennedy.

The claim that Eisenhower let subordinates dominate him could not have been further from the truth; Eisenhower operated with such consummate organizational skill that his domination was not known. He could be "good ol' Ike" to the public while running the White House with a hidden iron fist. Eisenhower was criticized because he was not an activist president, and this factor was central in the interpretation of Eisenhower until the recent round of reevaluations. Robert A. Divine in his revisionist work on Eisenhower makes this point:

> Nearly all of Eisenhower's foreign policy achievements were negative in nature. He ended the Korean War, he refused to intervene militarily in Indochina, he refrained from involving the United States in the Suez crisis, he avoided war with China over Quemoy and Matsu, he resisted the temptation to force a showdown over Berlin, he stopped exploding nuclear weapons in the atmosphere. *A generation of historians and political scientists, bred in the progressive tradition, have applied an activist standard to Ike's negative record and have found it wanting.* Yet in the aftermath of Vietnam, it can be argued that a president who avoids hasty military action and refrains from extensive involvement in the internal affairs of other nations deserves praise rather than scorn.[11]

Anti-Bureaucratic, Anti-Government Leaders

The anti-bureaucratic, anti-government style of presidential leadership that attacks the government itself, including the permanent career staffs, did not spring full-blown but emerged over time. The period of almost three decades that began with Roosevelt and ended with Eisenhower was the first phase of the modern presidency and can be labeled the "progovernment, probureaucracy era." Presidents of that period (1) saw a pressing need for federal government action and more generally viewed the federal government as a positive force, (2) were generally comfortable with the federal bureaucracy and did not have major reservations about working with career civil servants, and (3) adhered to the principle of strong agencies. If this era was being analyzed in depth rather than captured broadly, it could be shown that each president complained of the bureaucracy, if not of government itself. Such sentiments did not bring Presidents Roosevelt, Truman, or Eisenhower to the view that emerged with Kennedy. Eisenhower had extremely strong views about the foreign policy bureaucracy and would have been quite willing to cut domestic programs drastically. But more than any other president, he understood large-scale organizations and the critical place of orderly procedures and high staff morale. The second era of the modern presidency that began with Kennedy had a characteristic anti-bureaucratic perspective. Restricting ourselves to elected presidents, this era has two clear parts with Kennedy and Lyndon Johnson still being pro-government. Both conceived of government as a positive force held back by the dead hand of bureaucracy. Nixon, Carter, and Reagan, in contrast, were anti-government in rhetoric and campaigned on an anti-government theme. But neither Nixon nor Carter had the consistency of Ronald Reagan, or his capacity to appear as outside government even while heading it.

John F. Kennedy — based in part on faulty analysis of Eisenhower — immediately started in a new direction by casting aside not only the "bureaucrats" but his own cabinet appointees, to rely on his little circle of generalists. Garry Wills says, "In his 1963 book on Kennedy, Hugh Sidey celebrated the escape from Eisenhower: 'John Kennedy, it is clear, recaptures all the power and more which Dwight Eisenhower ladled out to his Cabinet officers. In fact, Kennedy in the first week nearly put the Cabinet on the shelf as far as being a force in policy matters, and he rarely bothered to dust it off.' . . . In order to get the country 'moving again . . . ' crisis teams would have to save the bureaucracy from itself, take over its duties, force it to join the successful operation of the outsiders. Henry Fairlie rightly called this a vision of "guerrilla government."[12] The Kennedy changes, hailed at the time as a sign of strength and daring leadership, were more a sign that neither Kennedy nor his inner circle had a deep understanding of institutional governance. What was not understood was that being the "best and the brightest" in analytic or academic terms did not qualify an individual for all tasks in government, particularly those tasks in which organizational knowledge and skills loomed large. The incoming people, who waged a guerrilla war in the name of the president, seldom had the combination of organizational knowledge and skills necessary to battle successfully. They tended to combine a lack of knowledge about "the enemy" and its organizational structures and procedures with both arrogance about their own abilities and a gross underestimation of the abilities and knowledge of the permanent civil servants. Kennedy both undermined the legitimacy and reduced the effectiveness of the permanent government. His was a full, frontal attack on the presidency and on institutional commitment. The institution, as embodied in the permanent staff and their procedures, was the enemy. Kennedy and his generalists did not recognize that orderly, routinized government has its place. Professional civil servants offer a store of knowledge and experience that can be used effectively by political appointees. Drawing on the regular personnel and procedures of government potentially can make government action more effective. Such a statement does not imply that political appointees should sit back and let career staff alone run things or only inquire meekly how something is to be done. There is a need for political appointees to find the civil servants with whom they can work. That may require some effort, but the payoff can be extremely high. The valid argument made by Hugh Heclo in *A Government of Strangers* is that incoming political appointees should view civil servants as neither innocent nor guilty but as potential resources that require some inspection to determine if and how they are to be utilized.[13] Just as not all civil servants are intelligent, cooperative, and innocent of harboring partisan views, so not all of them are stupid, intransigent, or closet enemies. Nearly thirty years of presidencies in which the latter combination was assumed surely has proved the dangers of such an approach.

In this oversimplified but sweeping discussion, differences are too sharp between Eisenhower and his successors. Detailed analysis would indicate more overlap, with a degree of organizational mastery exhibited by the more recent leaders. But such detail would only soften the differences. No president since Eisenhower can be labeled an organization-man leader, both understanding and able to cope with the large-scale organizational behavior in the executive branch. The new leadership style that has emerged mitigates against the kinds of organizational behavior that so strengthened the Eisenhower government.

Historical revisionism has its dangers, too. Recognizing Eisenhower as a superb organizational president can lead us to rate him too highly overall. Even strong revisionist Divine underscored that Eisenhower's major foreign policy accomplishments were negative. Kennedy deserves downgrading after what appears to be a clear overrating because of his style, but there well may be an overreaction. Robert Levine has pointed out that Kennedy's record may not be plus, minus, or zero but unassessable in that there was just not enough time in his brief presidency. Erwin Hargrove and Michael Nelson see both Eisenhower and Kennedy as successes — the former as a president of consolidation, the latter as a president of preparation, exerting legislative leadership in dramatizing issues for which he lacked the votes to pass, thereby setting the stage for LBJ.[14] If they are right, Kennedy may not have greatly marred his own record with his organizational ineptitude, since presidents of preparation rely mainly on policy formulation and presentational skills. They do not need to have strong organizational skills because they do not progress to the implementation stage. However, the much-praised Kennedy approach that was anti-bureaucratic and appeared activist (at least in rhetoric) probably was a key factor in hamstringing later presidents who had to manage major legislated programs — Johnson and Nixon, for example.

The assessments lead to two key points. First, care must be taken to evaluate presidents in the historical setting in which they operate. Second, the critical issue posed to each president is how to balance the competing, interrelated roles of chief political officer, strategist, and manager in the particular environment he faces. An analogy that comes to mind is the one used to describe the mix of federal, state, and local government inputs as a marble cake rather than a layer cake. Perhaps better is the artist's mixing of colors to yield a particular shade of red, which appears as a single color; the proportions that produced it are not discernible. Other proportions yield a single but different shade. So it is with the president's palette of politician, strategist, and manager. If we accept Hargrove and Nelson's thesis that the political environment at that time blocked the passing of the legislative program of Lyndon Johnson, then Kennedy had an effective mix mainly of politics and strategy. A corollary of the first point is that presidents need to be careful in using a predecessor's successful mix in a quite different environment.

PRESIDENTIAL GOVERNANCE APPROACHES

Each new president inherits the legacy of the existing permanent government. How will he decide to use it? Eisenhower reshaped it to fit his needs and manipulated staff, structure, and process within the bureaucratic rules inherent in large-scale organizations. His approach produced both a strong EOP and strong agencies run by secretaries who were expected to manage them. Eisenhower understood that the first and foremost task of his political appointees was to manage their organizations so that major presidential and agency policy decisions could be well implemented. A secretary who mastered his agency became a better adviser, but advice was not the cabinet members' main responsibility to the president. The cabinet was not a decisionmaking body but a source of advice, and several strong secretaries were influential. Eisenhower observed that "you must get courageous men, men of strong views, and let them debate and argue with each other" and sought such confrontations in the NSC, but made final decisions himself without seeking a unanimous judgment.[15]

Finally, Eisenhower recognized the interrelationship of institutions and information and with his knowledge of institutional process used it to produce sound information and analysis. He used staff information and analysis in a structure and process that forced decisions to undergo wide and hard scrutiny; he perceived the need for an orderly process that institutionalized multiple advocacy. Eisenhower's formal procedures supported the "rigorous staff work and systematic institutional back-up for policymaking [that] is persistently lacking in modern presidencies, as is the teamwork that is an informal offshoot of this procedure."[16]

Because it seeks to bring together the key organizations in the executive branch, Eisenhower's governance approach can be labeled "institutional integration." Two other governance approaches, sometimes in combination, have been used by the anti-bureaucratic, anti-government leaders: domination and takeover, and image building. The first in its purest form is exemplified in the Nixon administration in the operation of the Kissinger NSC staff effort. Nixon's goal was to freeze cabinet members out of the White House advisory structure. More broadly, Nixon wanted the cabinet members under full control of the White House. He tried to cut them off as principal spokesmen for the administration and as the administration's link to interest groups, and to control their functions as department managers. President Johnson, whom I consider the greatest social-program president of the postwar years and perhaps in American history (Roosevelt is the only real challenger), practiced a particular version of domination and takeover — "brute force" — in which his brightness, stamina, determination, toughness, meanness, and constant hard work kept him on top of the government. By bullying, intimidating, and wearing people down with brute force, Johnson got his way where others would fail. At his best President Johnson pushed through a level of social legislation unmatched in American history — civil rights, voting rights, Medicare, Medicaid, educational aid to the disadvantaged, and through his creation of the new OEO, help to the poor and disadvantaged in a number of other areas, particularly in community action. In that brief period from mid-1964 until Vietnam became Johnson's obsession, America truly started a war on poverty. The dark side of Johnson's brute force shackled that war for a war that permanently scarred the nation when Johnson turned his energy and will on Vietnam.

Reagan was the foremost practitioner of governance by image building. Kennedy, however, discovered its usefulness; and Kennedy's style led to a new politics that aimed to leap over established institutions, including the political parties and focus directly on the atomized electorate through mass communication.[17] The image was of youth and unfulfilled promise. It helped Lyndon Johnson sell the Great Society as a memorial to the assassinated president to whose image he repeatedly paid tribute. Ironically, the Johnson programs have been the ones people saw as going wrong and tarnishing the American dream. "It may indeed be a special irony of Kennedy's image that it has profited from his inability to achieve some of the prime objectives of his presidency for that failure has allowed Kennedy to escape responsibility for the problems that followed his death."[18] The Kennedy image of youthful unfulfilled promises re-emerged as central in the selling of America's oldest president, who also had a special appeal to youth. Here again the assassination motif has been prominent, validating for Reagan the same kind of heroic image that Kennedy sought so hard to establish before his death. The Reagan administration reached a level of proficiency in image building far beyond anything done before. For a major part of the Reagan presidency, image was dominant. The Baker-Darman team focused on protecting their charismatic product.

The governance approaches of the anti-bureaucratic, anti-government presidents mitigate against strong cabinet officers and may impede the development of sound policy information and analysis. Dominance-and-takeover, by definition, seeks maximum cabinet control by the White House. Johnson and Nixon, with quite different presidential styles, came to similar outcomes in creating relatively weak agencies. The need for dominance, however, does not necessarily rule out a strong institutional analytic capacity. At least in the foreign policy arena, sound information and strong policy analysis and strategic thinking were central concerns, even though the Nixon style may have warped the analytic process by cutting out multiple advocacy. The obsession with secrecy and the weakening of the departments meant both that the agencies lacked implementation capacity and that they had less bureaucratic need to give institutional support to policies that had been dictated from above without significant agency involvement in policy formulation. The Nixon-Kissinger grand scheme that yielded relatively sound information and analysis for White House foreign policymaking pari passu undercut its usefulness by lessening the commitment and capacity of the agencies to implement successfully the president's policies. President Johnson was also oriented toward information and policy analysis, but larger than life, his style so often overwhelmed analytic or organizational concerns. Dominance was the bedrock of Johnson's presidential style.

Perhaps because they lacked the style or the skills, the presidents between Kennedy and Reagan were not image-driven leaders. Kennedy was not anti-analytic — brightness and quick, penetrating analysis were marks of his administration. The problem was Kennedy's relative organizational ignorance. Reagan went the next step, as image became the dominant motif of his presidency, driving out analytic and organizational concerns. In Reagan, a charismatic leader who must be protected, dominance-and-takeover melded with the image control operation.

This discussion of governance approaches can be sharpened by posing four questions. First, how explicitly do institutional integration and dominance-and-takeover differ, since both involve gaining presidential control? In answering the question, let us assume in both approaches that control is sought in order to insure that presidential policies are implemented to reflect the president's objectives — that is, control is aimed at policy performance. The main difference is that with institutional integration, the leader plays by the bureaucratic rules, accepts organizational limits and demands, and tries to use the bureaucratic rules and mores to his or her advantage. With a dominance-and-takeover style, leaders try to squelch the elements of the institutional structure and process they do not like. Institutional integration involves a much deeper understanding of organizational procedures and behavior — for example, recognizing that autonomy and control are the two central elements of realistic delegation of authority and responsibility in large-scale organizations in both the private and the public sectors. On the one hand, subordinate managers — cabinet and subcabinet members in the case of the presidency — need sufficient autonomy to make their own decisions and hence be accountable for them. Reasonable discretion is an essential element in developing clear lines of responsibility. Control is the opposite side of realistic delegation, where the top imposes its will. The leader must seek a delicate balance. Too little White House control threatens the carrying out of the president's will by agencies lacking the commitment to do so; too much White House control threatens the agencies' managerial capacity, which is needed to implement the president's policies. Thus, political leaders have two paramount tasks. The first is the classic political charge to provide long-term objectives and to motivate those below to seek them. The second is to seek balance between innate conflicts such as that between control and autonomy. Such steering is both less dramatic and less visible than motivational leadership. Yet finding and keeping the delicate balances may be the most difficult leadership trick. While autonomy and control are in conflict in all larger institutions, a president also needs to balance the innate clash between the organizational and political dimensions.

The second question, which to some extent addresses the balance issue, is whether Eisenhower would have mastered the executive branch today. Would he currently be able to bring off both a competent White House staff that provided credible information and analysis and well-managed agencies where secretaries operated with reasonable levels of autonomy? There is no reason to doubt that the answer is an unequivocal "yes." The executive branch is not unmanageable in its underlying structure, despite the dramatic increase in policy complexity. At the same time, strong presidential management neither leaps over the structural barriers imposed by the Constitution nor makes complex, conflicting problems solvable. A president does not need to be the organizational virtuoso Eisenhower was to manage the executive branch, but he or she does need deep organizational understanding gained in part from experience.

One of the most interesting aspects of the assessments at the end of the Reagan presidency was that President Reagan, in contrast to the beleaguered Carter, was on top of the job with little effort or strain. David Broder quoted Stuart Eizenstat and Secretary of Defense Richard Cheney, then a member of Congress and earlier President Ford's second chief-of-staff, respectively, as follows: "What has been written off only eight years ago as an impossible job, destined to crush any mortal, has been turned around. It now appears that a mortal can handle the job and be successful" and "the job isn't bigger than the man. Maybe it was luck, but the problems Nixon, Ford, and Carter encountered and could not survive, he [President Reagan] has withstood."[19] It was not just luck; it was a charismatic president adroitly packaged to create the image of being on top of the job, when in truth most of the time Reagan was detached from any role but carefully crafted television bits that made the nightly national news shows. Managing the image was a challenging task for Baker and Darman, but the strain on Reagan was minimal. In contrast, an Eisenhower-like president would not necessarily appear on top of the job in the sense of effortlessness, and like Nixon, Ford, and Carter, might not survive as he or she engaged in the difficult and time-consuming task of exerting organizational mastery. But this Eisenhower-like president could actually be on top of the job in managing the executive branch, as opposed to just appearing to be in control.

Third, could an organization master win the presidency? Why not? Eisenhower hardly seems a less likely winner than Nixon or Carter or Bush. Eisenhower was the master of masking managerial competence in an avuncular style, and his occasionally tortured syntax surely was no worse than that of President Bush. Far less clear is that a candidate with both political and organizational skills can be found.

Finally, would organizational mastery take too much time away from the exercise of political mastery or demand presidential or EOP behavior that would be counterproductive to gaining political mastery? No obvious answer emerges. Exercising both the high-level political and the organizational mastery that is usually required to manage effectively may be too demanding. However, here the various institutional factors including the analytic structure and process become critical. A strong institutional analytic structure can provide the information and analysis needed to manage in ways that reduce the president's day-to-day involvement. For example, the president and his staff can receive information and analysis that will facilitate monitoring agency efforts, including those to implement the president's decisions without the kind of White House staff interference that has consumed too much presidential and staff time and weakened the agencies as well. Sound policy information and analysis including evaluative data do not automatically bring a good balance between politics and organization, or between White House control and agency autonomy. However, without such information and analysis, it is hard to see on what basis a president will manage if his objective is better policy performance.

These critical balances cannot be worked out unless a president, in addition to being political, possesses organizational competence. Organizational incompetence in varying degrees marked the elected presidents from Kennedy through Reagan. Even though Nixon and Johnson were not lacking in organizational competence, White House control was sought at the expense of agency autonomy, with most limited insight into the costs of that imbalance. Presidential governance style has been deeply flawed since the Eisenhower years. It reached its lowest point in the Reagan administration, where the style involved ignoring and disdaining both sound information and analysis and fundamental organizational principles. At the same time, organizational mastery alone is not sufficient for effective presidential governance and, as a means, can be as useful in doing evil as in doing good. But even when high organizational mastery is available for fulfilling desirable policy objectives, it is not enough by itself. First, political mastery or dire need will be required to mobilize political support for a policy. Second, organizational mastery does not necessarily provide solutions to difficult policy problems. Organizational knowledge does not tell which educational approach will produce high learning rates (neither, necessarily, will policy analysis) but only that some approaches may be more or less feasible. Third, organizational mastery does not necessarily afford the ability to make major decisions. Eisenhower and Clement Attlee, the only two organizational virtuosos who headed postwar American and British governments, are cases in point. Eisenhower was an extraordinary decisionmaker, willing and able to make a critical decision; Attlee was not. Faced with major problems such as the 1947 convertibility and the 1949 devaluation crises, Attlee appears to have panicked. But no British or American postwar leader, not even Eisenhower, measured up to Attlee as an implementer.[20] Despite these caveats, organizational mastery has been the pivotal missing ingredient in the presidencies since Eisenhower.

7

Institutional Fixes

The writings of the post-Watergate reformers, which include those of organizations such as the National Academy of Public Administration (*A Presidency for the 1980s*) and the President's Commission for a National Agenda for the Eighties (*The Electoral and Democratic Process in the Eighties*) and individuals such as Ben W. Heineman and Curtis A. Hessler (*Memorandum for the President*), converge in prescribing less power for White House staffs and more for the cabinet.[1] The following are representative of the post-Watergate thinking:

- •EOP staff (a) is too large, (b) has too few experienced career personnel, (c) is too White House control-oriented, (d) is too oriented to short-run crisis management, and (e) lacks capacity to focus on longer-range strategic issues.
- •The EOP structure (a) lacks clarity in roles and responsibilities both within its own operations and between the EOP and the agencies, (b) lacks coherence and consistency in policy and program development and coordination of policies and programs, and (c) creates an adversarial relationship between the EOP and the agencies.[2]

Perhaps embedded in the shortcomings, but not made explicit by most post-Watergate reformers, are the weaknesses in the EOP structure, staffing, and process that fail to yield sound information and analysis either to support presidential decisionmaking or to monitor agency performance.

The overriding problem seen by the reformers is how to check staff power. They argue that White House policy staffs should be coordinators, facilitators, process managers, and honest brokers, not key advocates, and certainly not policymakers. The problem is that honest brokering and advocacy are difficult to mix and balance. The NSC apparatus illustrates the *inherent conflict* in the honest broker and the policy adviser-advocate roles that cannot be bounded by rules because no one is wise enough to set out rules ex ante. Reformers today agree that the Kissinger and Brzezinski approaches were unbalanced toward advocacy and White House decisionmaking but generally would argue that the national security adviser is an important source of advice and is the policy adviser on national security affairs most likely to have the president's perspective. The issue is one of balance—a most delicate balance that cannot be captured fully by structure, functional designations, or rules. It must be managed over time by the president.

The President's Commission for a National Agenda for the 1980s argued that secretaries should again have major policy formulation roles; the NAPA panel claimed that "a president can most effectively keep his own staff functioning legitimately—as staff, and not as executives—if he develops a close, confidential relationship with top appointees in the departments and agencies."[3] Walter Mondale, writing as senator in 1975, underscored the critical congressional connection, pointing out the damage done by elevating White House staff, who are neither confirmed by the Senate nor forced to testify before Congress, over those individuals whom he labeled as the "only truly accountable Executive Branch officials, the cabinet officers and the executive agency heads," and then argued that "the more relevant and helpful the cabinet department officers are to future presidents, the better the executive branch will be able to relate to the Congress."[4] That is, Congress cannot be adequately informed of major decisions made by White House staff members who are protected from testimony by executive privilege. Congress is thus deprived of critical information, and the fundamental constitutional relationship among the president, the executive branch, and Congress is threatened.

Heineman and Hessler took the next crucial step—the managerial connection—to argue that if secretaries are to be held accountable by the president, they should have a reasonable degree of autonomy and full authority to appoint their top subordinates.[5] The post-Watergate reformers want to shift the White House–agency balance back toward a more powerful cabinet of the days of Truman and Eisenhower, seeking to reestablish cabinet members as the principal policy advisers to the president, as strong managers, or as both. However, elevating cabinet members to the status of top policy advisers where they help the president decide on issues beyond the mandate of their own departments has a high price. First, to do a good job as a generalist policy adviser is time-consuming. Second, cabinet members face a conflict of interest on crosscutting issues that affect their own departments. A White House policy adviser well may have a comparative advantage in representing the president's legitimate interests on issues ranging across several departments. Third, managing a major agency is a full-time task. A strong case can be made for a cabinet secretary as top manager and as a main policy adviser on his agency. The next step of White House policy adviser general-ist across departments is a shakier proposition, however.

Finally, the post-Watergate reformers recommend a longer White House time perspective. Heineman and Hessler call for a "strategic presidency"; the NAPA panel and the President's Commission propose a long-term policy analysis staff.[6] John Hart points out that the NAPA panel writes that "the *Executive Office of the President* needs institutionalized arrangements for longer-term policy research and analysis," not saying "*the president needs.*"[7] Whether this is purposeful, with a subtle focus on the presidency, or inad-vertent, Hart's point is well taken. By definition the presidency needs a longer-run view. So does a president, but he may not want it and may well question the reformers' distinction between the president and the presidency, which is central to reformers' arguments against politicization and deinstitutionaliza-tion.[8] That is the basic dilemma.

The post-Watergate reformers wrote mainly in the period before the start of the Reagan presidency with an eye toward influencing incoming presidents in 1977 and thereafter. Not only did Carter and Reagan not heed the institu-tional advice, but they took action that went in the opposite direction. In President Reagan's two terms there was such striking movement away from the reform proposals that we now need to consider the *Tower Commission Report*, which addressed the national security institutional structure and pro-cess after the Iran-Contra scandal. The commission's three members, John Tower (chair), Edmund Muskie, and Brent Scowcroft — who among them have served as senators, secretary of state, and national security adviser — would not appear to lack an understanding of politics and presidential real-ity, as might people with backgrounds in academic public administration or policy analysis.

The Tower Commission noted that there is no magic formula for an op-timum NSC structure and process, that the need is for flexibility, not rigidity, and that the danger is that overprescription can destroy the system or make it ineffective. The key actor is the president, who has a special responsibility for the NSC's effective performance and should provide explicit guidance as to how the key actors will relate to each other, what procedures they should follow, and what is expected of each. Most critically, if the president's ad-visers fail to perform as he wants, he is the only one who can intervene. The commission goes on to underscore that two NSC principals (the secretaries of defense and state) participate in a unique capacity. They gain their seats because of their official status as agency heads, but they serve the president strictly as generalist policy advisers. The president alone decides on policy. The NSC principals who are secretaries receive the president's decisions as agency heads charged with the responsibility of implementing the president's decisions accurately and effectively.

Both a president and a departmental secretary need to understand that bureaucratic resistance from career staffs, whether civilian or uniformed, is part and parcel of large-scale public institutions. Sometimes it is justified, blocking foolish decisions; other times, not. Bureaucratic resistance is almost always important in the executive branch equation of governance, but so are career staff expertise and institutional memory. Using the good and mitigating the bad is the heart of effective presidential governance. Presidents need organizational mastery to play the institutional game, not only to control the bureaucracy and cabinet members but to manage the process effectively. The search is for a continuing balance between White House control and agency autonomy. The Tower Commission observed:

> The policy innovation and creativity of the president encounters a natural resistance from the executing departments. While the resistance is a source of frustration to every president, it is inherent in the design of government. It is up to the politically appointed agency heads to ensure that the president's goals, designs, and policies are brought to bear on the permanent structure. Circumventing the departments, perhaps by using the national security adviser or the NSC staff to execute policy, robs the president of the experience and capacity resident in the departments. . . .
>
> This tension between the president and the executive departments is worked out through the national security process. . . . It is through this process that the nation obtains both the best of the creativity of the president and the learning and expertise of the national security departments and agencies.
>
> This process is extremely important to the president. . . . Process will not always produce brilliant ideas, but history suggests it can at least prevent bad ideas from becoming presidential policy.[9]

The Tower Commission tried to sort out the various institutional roles, starting with the national security adviser, who should be primarily responsible for managing the NSC process on a daily basis. The adviser, as honest broker, is charged with seeing that the president receives a full range of options from the key participants, but he should also be an important policy adviser-advocate. The commission, however, admonished that the national security adviser "should present his own views, but he must at the same time represent the views of others fully and faithfully to the president." The national security adviser should keep a low profile, not competing with the secretary of state or the secretary of defense as the "articulator of public policy," and "'a passion for anonymity' is perhaps too strong a term, [but] the national security adviser should generally operate offstage."[10] Both the national security adviser and the NSC principals, the Tower Commission argued, ought to have direct access to the president but no one should use this access to circumvent the system. The Tower Commission opted for a small, competent NSC staff, experienced in the making of national security policy. The commission lamented the NSC staff's lack of institutional memory and suggested some alternatives, including a small permanent executive secretariat, noting that any options to reduce the loss of institutional memory would not help unless each succeeding president subscribed to them. While arguing the legitimacy of policy advocacy by the national security adviser, the commission opted for a much more limited role for several good reasons. First, in order to implement presidential programs successfully, the agency heads must be masters in their own houses. Second, a limited national security adviser role is easier to manage. That is, relatively powerful national security advisers, even if they are not supposed to take over from the secretaries, are likely to operate in gray areas, where they may encroach on secretaries. Even if they do not, stopping just at the imaginary power line limit, secretaries may feel threatened. For example, President Ford had a smaller management task with William Seidman and the EPB than President Carter did with Stuart Eizenstat and the DPS. The issue comes down to the interpersonal relationships among central actors — the president, the national security adviser, the state and defense secretaries, and perhaps the chief-of-staff — with the president by his action (or inaction) driving the system. The critical presidential behavior includes both his choices for the critical positions and his structuring of the NSC process, including the institutional power grants to the other key actors. But a president is not locked in; he can on his own or with congressional concurrence change both the actors and the power configuration. Ultimately, it is not the static structure and staffing pattern or the stated power configuration that is determinant, but the dynamics of presidential management. At the same time, structure and staffing are critical variables in the presidential performance equation, particularly at the top where a president has his maximum control over appointments.

STRUCTURING AND STAFFING THE EOP

Structure, as used here, applies to people and units assigned on an organization chart along with their functions, the resources that a unit has to carry out its functions, and the process lines of communication and control that connect organizational boxes. It is viewed as both static and impersonal — the organization chart on the wall, the table of organization and equipment. Staffing has a static aspect, too, flowing from structure, with the specification of functions, staff size, ascribed status in the unit, and job descriptions, including statements about relevant training, skills, and experience. Staffing also has the more dynamic implications of personal competence, commitment, and integrity — that is, people in action. An organizational chart that shows only formal titles — for example, the unnamed national security adviser — and job descriptions, can be somewhat illuminating by indicating status (reports directly to the president) and functions (coordinates the national security process). Put names in the boxes, and the chart is more illuminating. But the question of dynamic interaction remains. Consider the Carter chief-of-staff experience, where not having such a role at the top has been viewed as a fundamental error. Would Carter have named anyone but Hamilton Jordan? Would Jordan have behaved differently because of the official title? Without the title, Jordan's status would have allowed him to act as the chief-of-staff. There is no structure for all presidents; nor is there an ideal type staff person to fit any president's needs. The right structure must be tailor-made when a president takes the job, to fit his individual needs. Reformers' "suits" are, by definition, off-the-rack, but that does not mean no wise outside advice can be proffered.

The analysis of structure rests on the basic normative assumption that each president ought to be responsible (accountable) to the Congress, and ultimately to the nation, for developing and maintaining a strong institutional policymaking structure in the executive branch that should provide:

- A sitting president with sound policy information and analysis to support (a) policy formulation and decisions and (b) the White House monitoring of the federal agencies' implementation and management of policies and programs, particularly the implementation of the president's main policy initiatives.
- The federal executive agencies with sound policy information and analysis to support policy formulation and decisions, policy implementation, and operational management and with sufficient organizational autonomy and capacity to manage the implementation and operation of agency programs.
- The Congress and the public with the sound policy information and analysis needed to support the careful scrutiny of federal programs.
- Future presidents with the legacy of a viable institutional information and analytic structure at the start of their administration.

A number of points must be stressed about the basic normative assumption that underlies much of the discussion that follows. First, the assumption rests on the foundation of the causal model and is therefore policy-outcome oriented. Second, in order to simplify the presentation, political information and analysis are not treated explicitly in the normative proposition. Presidential political mastery and political standing are clearly key factors in the presidential success equation for positive policy and program performance. Third, the normative proposition moves to murky constitutional issues concerning the relationship of the president to the agencies and Congress and ultimately to the people. The thrust of Hart's *The Presidential Branch* is that the United States has experienced the emergence of a fourth branch—the "presidential branch" (which Hart equates with the EOP)—separate from the three traditional branches and not necessarily compatible with them. Hart argues that (1) presidential staff constitutionally is simply an extension of the president without its own separate identity and with the "mere existence of a staff . . . [in no way] contrary to the spirit of the Constitution;" (2) the presidential branch disturbs and frustrates the relationships among the president, the rest of the executive branch, and the Congress, for example, by reducing a presidents's dependence on the agencies for information and analysis; and (3) the presidential branch makes Congress' ties with executive agencies less potent than they once were.[11] Point 2 describes the current setting; points 1 and 3 merit further discussion. Whether the EOP in its present institutional form, with its extreme centralization and politicization, or the use of that institution by recent presidents is contrary to the Constitution can be left to constitutional scholars. However, the spirit of the Constitution is being violated; both the basic checks and balances and the accountability of the president to the people are undercut when a president sabotages the information flow. GAO—the congressional unit with the biggest role in congressional evaluation activities—sees executing credible evaluations as a fundamental executive branch function, arguing that the evaluative information shortage is "really everyone's concern, because good information is . . . the responsibility of government to the people of the country."[12] If so, how is sound information to be obtained as a basis for congressional oversight, if not supplied by the executive branch? While Congress appropriately has its own analytic capacity, creating a full-scale evaluative effort to develop primary data appears to go too far. Evaluations are too expensive and too intrusive for both departmental and congressional staffs to engage in large-scale evaluations of the same policy and program areas. The current system of making the departments responsible for evaluating their own policies and programs, but having Congress mandate specific evaluations, is not without problems. The most basic problem is what Congress should do if departments perform poorly, since limiting the flow of expert policy information threatens the basic oversight function of Congress. Should Congress make the mandates more explicit? Should it cut funds (and if so, which funds)? Or should Congress itself take over the evaluative function, at least in part? There is no sure course of action. The availability of sound policy information, including evaluative data on executive branch performance, is a bridge between the president, the Congress, and the people. In the era of expert information, the failure of the executive branch to produce credible, relevant, timely policy information raises grave constitutional issues.

Table 7.1 presents ten guiding propositions for structuring and staffing the

Table 7.1 Organizational Propositions to Guide Structuring and Staffing
the EOP Institutional Analytic Structure

1. Strategy should dominate the design of organizational structure and processes.

2. Sound policy information and analysis and strong executive branch management
   are essential for effective presidential governance.

3. Inadequate EOP structure and staffing almost certainly will produce inept presidential governance; however, sound EOP structure and staffing alone will not
   yield competent presidential governance.

4. Top-level White House policy advisers with both technical and general analytic
   experience and skills and the specific function of bringing analytic results to the
   president should serve as the critical institutional linkage point between the president and the institutional analytic structure.

5. EOP analytic units are likely to have a major impact on presidential policies only
   if the president (a) recognizes the importance of sound policy information and
   analysis in the policy process, (b) gives the analytic units and their top analysts
   high White House status and major analytic responsibilities, and (c) provides the
   analytic units sufficient high-level positions to develop a viable analytic staff.

6. A mixture of technically qualified political appointees and career staff is needed
   in EOP policy units to provide the president and his top policy advisers with the
   institutional knowledge needed to make sound policy decisions.

7. In light of the fallibility of available analytic tools and techniques, the combination of a managed distribution of analytic resources aimed at a fair level of competition among analytic units and the use of simple, straightforward analytic techniques, wherever possible, is the best means of producing sound expert policy
   information and analysis.

8. White House policy units should be primarily brokers, consumers, and trans-
   lators of in-depth agency analyses and evaluations. Policy advice and analysis,
   including policy-political synthesis, strategic thinking, process management, and
   the monitoring of the agencies' policy implementation and management efforts,
   should be the primary EOP policy unit functions, not implementing or managing
   programs and policies not necessary for White House internal operations.

9. Department and agency heads should be major policy advisers to the president
   on their agency's specific programs and policies, and the *only* officials other than
   the president articulating such policies and programs.

10. Department and agency heads should have the managerial autonomy to appoint
    their top subordinates.

EOP institutional analytic structure, including the organizational relationships between the White House and the agencies. Basically, the ten propositions are static. They treat structure in terms of stated responsibilities and
indicated skills and experience requirements, but they do not consider competence. For example, an analytic position could require a doctorate in economics and five years of relevant experience — on-paper credentials. The importance of these requirements should not be underplayed; they can lay a

solid foundation for effective institutional analytic performance. Static requirements can only go so far, however. A president may not be interested in or capable of using them.

Proposition 1 derives from the work of Alfred Chandler and others on corporate strategy. It sets forth the notion that structure is a *means* of getting the organization, whether a business or a government, where it desires to go (that is, its objectives) and so should mesh with—be dominated by—those objectives.[13] Another major figure in the field of strategy-structure, Kenneth Andrews, writes: "[T]he chief determinant of organizational structure and processes . . . should be the strategy of the firm, not the history of the company, its position in its industry, the specialized background of its executives, the principles of organization as developed in textbooks, the recommendations of consultants, or the conviction that one form of organization is intrinsically better than another."[14] You need to know where you want to go, and when, before you buy a ticket. Reorganization in government has often been a disaster for a number of reasons, one of the most important of which is using structure, which is a means to accomplish another means—control. A means becomes an end. This means-end fallacy is most likely at the outset of a presidency or when a new agency head takes over and reorganizes to show the power of the new people. But the question remains, "control for what purpose?" If the real answer is to make a show of power, the reorganization has no underlying strategy. The first rule of restructuring must be that a well-thought-through strategy, which addresses a president's objectives, underlies the change process.

Proposition 2 sets forth the fundamental concept that strong management demands timely, relevant, sound information and analysis, and such information and analysis gain value from the capacity of operating agencies to employ it. Both the EOP and the agencies need to be strong. As Renate Mayntz observed in her overview of the West German federal government: "A strong chancellor does not employ ministers who are weak in their own sphere."[15] Proposition 2, in combination with the last three propositions, stresses the necessary balance between White House control and agency autonomy, recognizing that information and analysis are the critical link between the two.

Proposition 3 states that although bad organization almost certainly makes for poor institutional performance, good organization does not necessarily lead to strong institutional performance. As President Eisenhower said, "Organization cannot make a genius of an incompetent; even less can it, of itself, make the decisions which are required to trigger the necessary action. On the other hand, disorganization can scarcely fail to result in inefficiency and can easily lead to disaster."[16] Developing a sound organization on paper with boxes and functions that support overall organizational strategy, but with no names, is the equivalent of policy formulation. Putting in the names, working out the kinks, and fixing the flaws involve implementation. If that phase is successful, continuing success still demands astute management. Even then, organization is but one of the tools (means) of presidential governance. Political ineptitude, deleterious environmental factors, and the like can still result in policy failure.

Proposition 3 carries with it another critical implication. Neither staff size nor specific statements about functions, procedures, and process, nor any other static effect to configure organizational boxes pari passu will bring effective or efficient institutional behavior. A good example is staff size. Almost all recent critics bemoan the bloated EOP staff. However, Hart, who traced the development of presidential staff from 1789, has made the point that some post-Watergate reformers failed to appreciate that the problem of overreaching presidential staffs had occurred in earlier presidencies where the staff had been small.[17] He points out that specifying functions will not do the job either: "Such recommendations present problems because of the hazy, almost indefinable line between the 'acceptable' textbook role of senior presidential aides — policy advice, policy coordination, and what writers now call *process management* — and the 'unacceptable' role of interfering with the work of departments and agencies."[18] It is illuminating to note that the line is indefinable in static terms; it can be defined in dynamic terms by a president, but it will demand adjustments. Keeping White House staff on tap, not on top, requires both clarifying what is desired and then enforcing it.

Proposition 4 expresses the need for a person or persons at the top with appropriate technical and generalist skills and experience and the functional designation to link the president and his top staff to the institutional analytic process — to bring together policy and politics at the top. The top policy analyst may not be a principal political actor (although here, he or she will be more engaged in the political arena than lesser analysts will be), but the top policy adviser generalist will be. It is the most demanding staff position in government. Proposition 5 underscores the centrality of the president in the analytic equation. If a president wants sound policy information analysis and is willing to pay the bureaucratic price for obtaining it, he has a good chance of securing it. Both propositions 4 and 5 underscore the importance of high status and appropriate responsibilities as the institutional base for the effective use of policy analysis in the presidential policymaking process.

Proposition 6 concerns the lack of institutional memory problem, which most outside critics see as a major White House weakness. The need is not simply for apolitical people who remember the past. It is for career professionals who have a deep knowledge of politics and policy but who are able to serve presidents of different political persuasions. The argument for career staff at the top is not a call for a pristine budget staff returned to old BOB staff dominance. OMB needs a layer of political executives at the top to handle policy issues that present partisan political problems. However, the decline of the careerists has gone too far, leading Hugh Heclo to lament: "I must admit that if, forced to choose, I would rather see the Executive Office of the President bureaucratized with civil servants than by the customary layers of governmentally inexperienced short-timers. I say this because most of the real world pressures in the presidency constantly converge to drive out longer-term institutional perspectives. But we should not have to choose between a government of tyros or of mandarins."[19] This lamentation is almost uniformly echoed by the post-Watergate reformers.

Proposition 7 first sets forth the critical need for fair competition among rival policy advisers. If analytic tools and techniques were far more accurate and powerful, doing analysis without competition behind closed doors would not fit with democratic principles, but it could be highly effective. Bureaucracy often tries to minimize competition, to have tables of organization and clear functional lines that emphasize cooperation. But the organizational neatness that makes for order in the life of the bureaucrat can render the organization complacent or arrogant toward criticism and questioning. Too much cooperation within can be deadening. The threat of scrutiny and challenge should be present, both from within and without. The basic point in organizational terms is that the distribution of resources among policy adviser advocates should be controlled (regulated, limited) so that the potential for a fair fight remains. Here is a classic example of the dictum that no specification of structure and staffing at one point will ensure the desired outcome over time. There is no substitute for competent management of the institutional process by a president and his delegated managers.

The second part of proposition 7 rests on the premise that the overuse of esoteric methods has led to both abuse and mistrust of policy analysis. In general simpler approaches are preferable. The combination or relatively straightforward analytic and research techniques and bureaucratic-political knowledge and judgment will often yield valuable information and recommendations for policymaking. In part this view reflects the notion that analytic and research information should be scrutinized by nontechnicians. The more straightforward the techniques, the less likely that wrongheaded analysis and research will slip through under the cover of "high-powered" methodology. Furthermore, such approaches, which can be understood at least at the conceptual level by nontechnicians, appear to be the ones most likely to benefit significantly from inputs of bureaucratic and political wisdom. They are most likely to lead policy analysts to ask the right question, which is the most difficult — but not the most esoteric — of the analytic tasks. In the short term they are also likely to (1) increase capability in the analytic-decision system so that more complex approaches can be employed, if needed, and (2) restore confidence in the use of scientific techniques.

Proposition 7 recognizes some hard truths about policy analysis — the fallibility of the tools and techniques, the overuse of esoteric methods and jargon, and the political and bureaucratic blinders so prevalent among policy analysts, particularly those who overestimate the power of the tools or who see themselves as nonpartisan, objective scientists in government. These tendencies constitute the current structure of policy analysis as we know it today. It is the task of the manager of the institutional analytic structure to maximize the good features and minimize the bad ones. Structure and process (e.g., analytic competition) are major means of accomplishing this task.

Proposition 8 describes the policy units' functions in the EOP. With the exception of OMB, these units' main products should be policy advice, policy analyses, strategic plans, policy-political syntheses, process management, and the monitoring of agency programs. Process management for the president should be a major ongoing task, as long as the White House policy advisers serve mainly as honest brokers. The monitoring of agencies' efforts to implement and manage presidential programs and policies is a fundamental element of White House process management that is considered separately to highlight its importance. A competent EOP monitor should have the knowledge and experience to distinguish among expected organizational difficulties that always plague large-scale implementations, poor implementation because of agency ineptitude, and bureaucratic footdragging intended to undercut the president's policy. Process management and monitoring can take the analysts too far into the agencies' rightful domain, but to some extent they are bounded by propositions 9 and 10. Other institutional factors can also limit the policy unit, such as a clear statement of mission that emphasizes the objective of improving the policy information and analytic base for presidential decisionmaking.

Proposition 8 makes clear that the agencies are the primary producers of information and in-depth analyses and evaluations. Consumption, brokering and translation of information, policy analysis, and research are what the EOP policy units should be doing. Specifying needed technical skills and experience in the White House policy units can also be important for building institutional constraints. Appropriate backgrounds raise the likelihood of reasonable interpretations of policy analyses and monitoring reports from the agencies. White House staff with experience in the development and execution of major policy analyses, evaluations, and monitoring efforts should appreciate agency difficulties. Staffs should be "lean and mean." The former speaks to size alone; the latter, to skills and experience. The institutional need is for a core of policy analysts who have the skills and experience to interact on a collegial basis with the agency analytic and monitoring staff.

In *Memorandum for the President*, Heineman and Hessler also spell out four EOP functions — advice, process management, strategic thinking, and delegated decisionmaking. The latter is a relatively low-level activity to save the president's time, such as deciding on routine program and budget details that are below the view of the department secretaries or deputy secretaries. No one would argue against OMB decisions on budget details within boundaries set by the president. The problem is that rules cannot pinpoint an exact stopping point just before OMB begins to usurp presidential prerogatives or at least appears to do so in the eyes of the departments.

Proposition 8 also addresses the broad issue of the demarcation line between the White House Staff and the departments and agencies. It relates to the final two propositions. White House policy units should not engage in implementing or managing federal programs for which the agencies have responsibility; they should restrict themselves to monitoring agency efforts. There are gray areas, however. When EOP monitoring indicates that an agency is doing a poor job of implementing a high-priority presidential program, what is the next step? If the implementation problems flow from difficulties that an agency has not been able to overcome, the next step may be to rethink the implementation strategy, not to send in White House troops. However, if the agency does not appear to be making a good effort, the strong temptation is to have a White House staff person become more involved. But much depends on what had transpired before. Did the agency secretary know what the president wanted? President Eisenhower's second Special Assistant for National Security Affairs, Dillon Anderson, pointed out that the president "invited a lot of give and take" from cabinet representatives before making a decision, but after having participated in the decision, the department "damn well knew what it was and there'd be no fuzzing up as to what the president's decision had been."[20] If the department was subverting Eisenhower's decision, the secretary answered to the president, not his staff person. The beauty of clean lines of responsibility is that they provide both a base of action and a focus of praise or blame.

Proposition 8 recognizes the delegated decisionmaking function where budget preparation is OMB's operational responsibility. Other analytic staffs, however, have no such operational responsibilities. Budget preparation is best viewed as a form of process management so complex and detailed that the task of making lower-level budget decisions needs to be delegated to budget staff members. Regulation review, even elevated as it was under President Reagan, was still a process in which OIRA made delegated decisions that the agencies were expected to implement, and OIRA staff then engaged in monitoring responsibilities. Proposition 8 does not envision an EOP policy staff going operational to carry out such activities as covert tasks that are beyond necessary White House operations.

Along with proposition 8, propositions 9 and 10 speak mainly to the need for greater agency autonomy so as to restore a better balance with White House control. Here again the structure under President Eisenhower is exemplary. There were clear, direct institutional lines from the president to his secretaries, not blurred by White House staff. Fred I. Greenstein has written of Eisenhower's "skill and subtlety in delegating power" and observed in reference to John Foster Dulles: "Eisenhower stayed in charge, but he did not try to do everything himself. He was gifted at conveying general policies to his subordinates and then allowing them much leeway for specifics."[21] At issue is the fundamental leadership challenge of the realistic delegation of responsibility so that subordinates – in this case both White House staff and departmental secretaries – have a reasonable chance of accomplishing the objectives for which they bear responsibility. Who could be in favor of unrealistic delegation or a less-than-reasonable chance for a subordinate to reach stated goals? Indeed, it seems elementary until we delve below the surface to ask what the conditions for setting of realistic lines of responsibility and delegation are. Superiors want a reasonable level of control, which means restrictions on subordinates. The dilemma is that subordinate managers can be left so few resources or so little discretion that the chance of reaching assigned goals may be all but foreclosed. This balance is at the heart of the question of responsibility delegation. Delegated responsibility, if it is to work, must be a two-way street.

Proposition 9 indicates that department and agency heads should be major advisers to the president on their own programs and policies. It does not call for them either to be the only policy advisers on their programs or to be generalist policy advisers on overall federal programs and policies. Nor does proposition 9 rule out department and agency heads as generalist policy advisers. There are dangers in both roles. If secretaries are not generalist policy advisers, White House staff can overstep boundaries. But generalist policy advice takes time away from managing a department. Eisenhower used his cabinet as a sounding board for formulating policy with generalist participation encouraged. Attorney General Herbert Brownell said that he did not like to speak on policy issues concerning other departments but noted that "I think . . . one reason he [Eisenhower] liked Foster Dulles and George Humphrey . . . [was that] they freely commented on other departments' operations."[22] Here again, there is an artful balancing issue that finally goes beyond the structure to a president's style and competence.

Ten is such a tempting number when setting out propositions, luring one toward portentous pronouncements about organizational commandments. But the ten propositions are not written in stone and under the best of circumstances are but guides, to be factored into the equation along with political considerations, presidential idiosyncrasies, and various "objective" circumstances, such as the state of the economy, international tensions, and so on.

Staffing Knowledge, Skills, and Size

Table 7.2 indicates the broad range of knowledge and skills needed in a White House policy unit staff if it is to have the technical and generalist capacity to improve the president's base of decisionmaking. At this point it is useful

Table 7.2 Staffing Knowledge and Skills in a White House Policy Unit

1. Integration capacity—the ability to synthesize across policies and between policy and politics.

2. Strategic thinking—the ability to develop broad (macro) objectives, to analyze these objectives and the underlying assumptions as to consistency with other stated objectives and as to feasibility of implementation, and to refine and integrate these objectives.

3. Process management leadership—the ability to manage for the president (or his inner-circle designee) policy formulation or problem resolution in the executive branch.

4. Policy analysis and quantitative techniques—a mastery of the various policy analysis approaches and techniques and statistical techniques used by peer analysts inside and outside the government.

5. Substantive (policy area) knowledge—an in-depth understanding of particular policy areas, including relevant scholarly work, program and policy information, and analyses.

6. Political knowledge—an in-depth understanding of the political process, including the politics of particular substantive areas as manifested in the EOP, Congress, and federal agencies.

7. Organizational knowledge—an in-depth understanding of the organizational structure and bureaucratic politics of the agencies responsible for particular substantive areas.

8. Monitoring—the capacity to engage in efforts to ascertain how well policies and programs in the analyst's policy area are being implemented or managed.

---

to cast these requirements in part in terms of competence. For example, the discussion of policy analytic techniques goes beyond training or experience with approaches and techniques to call for "mastery." If it is expected that one individual—the top policy adviser generalist—will have a high level of mastery across all listed technique and knowledge areas, then the job description had best read "Wanted: Superman, Wonder Woman, or modern-day Thomas Jefferson." Not expecting to find any such people, the question becomes how much knowledge or skill in each of the areas must top generalist policy advisers have in order to carry out a policy-political synthesis. The question may be cast as a concern with what policy advisers know (their command of an area), how well they understand what they do not know (their knowledge and skill deficiencies), and how well they are able to compensate for their deficiencies.

The last five areas of skills and experience (4–8) represent technique or mastery of knowledge and differ significantly from process management leadership, integration capacity, and strategic thinking. Process management demands general leadership skills along with analytic knowledge and experience. The dimensions and difficulties of process management leadership depend at least in part on whether the policy staff member is cast as honest broker, advocate, or both. Integration capacity is the unique policy-politics quality—the skill needed to bring everything together. On the one hand, those who cannot integrate across policies or between policy and politics obviously will not succeed as generalist policy advisers, no matter how great their mastery in the five techniques and knowledge areas. On the other hand, weaknesses in necessary skills and experience may not hold back the individual with synthesizing capacity as long as he or she knows how to draw on others' skills and experience. Strategic thinking is also a scarce talent needed by the policy unit at least to the extent of giving attention to the longer-run aspects of domestic policies. An EOP policy unit must balance skills and knowledge with specialist and generalist traits. As compared to a strong assistant secretary-level agency analytic unit or the CBO, the balance should have fewer hard-edged analytic types and more persons with generalist policy adviser skills and orientation. As is clear from Table 7.2, the demand is for people who combine specialist skills and knowledge (e.g., an education specialist) with a generalist's orientation.

Where are these generalists to be found? Experience is a key factor. Policy analysts can hardly avoid political and organizational reality in an agency, congressional, or EOP analytic office. At the same time, the strong analytic offices have tended to bring together people of similar training and orientation so that the policy analysts with their tools and techniques do not necessarily work closely with political or organization analysts. Moreover, the strong analytic offices will foster professional norms that stress objectivity and mitigate against politically oriented approaches. Thus, the orientation of the hard-edged professional policy analysts, who so value rigorous quantitative approaches and academic acceptability, works against acquiring the knowledge and the orientation needed by the policy generalist.

Certain kinds of policy experience can contribute significantly to the development of generalists. John W. Ellwood's findings from a CBO study offer interesting evidence. Ellwood compares CBO staffs with the staffs of the Senate and House Budget Committees. Basically, Ellwood was looking at units within the three expert staffs, which are much more likely than other units to have a substantial percentage of Ph.D.'s. Ellwood found that the three groups were similar on most characteristics at the time they took their positions; however, big differences emerged when there were job changes: "Although the numbers are small, I would argue that the real differences between the staffs show up in their career pattern. All three organizations tend to hire technical experts. . . . But service on the budget committees appears to modify the career pattern of a large portion of the professional staff. Thus, while 87 percent of the CBO staff came from a non-political career and returned to a non-political job after leaving the Office, only 48 percent of Senate Budget Committee . . . staff and 19 percent of the House Budget

Committee . . . staff followed this pattern."[23] Why are Senate and House Budget Committee staffs more likely to go into politically oriented positions after serving on these committees? It could be that there is a distinct difference between the CBO staff members and the Budget Committee staff members that does not show up in Ellwood's data. That undetected difference could be either a predisposition of the Budget Committees' staffs toward becoming more political or it could be less technical capability in Budget Committee staff members in terms of the dominant professional norms. We can only speculate as to whether the "political" experience in the Senate and Budget Committees made staff members more likely to go into politically oriented jobs than their CBO counterparts.

At the same time, experienced policy adviser generalists themselves will probably have the capacity to spot others with such potential, whether the potential candidates come from a more technical background such as CBO or a more political one such as the budget committee staffs. One interviewee with extensive congressional experience told me he could tell in the first ten minutes of an interview for a broad policy position whether the candidate had the breadth of vision, political sensitivities, and interpersonal skills that were likely to make him or her capable of doing policy-political integration. He said that some people, whose past experience had been in a technical environment where the main payoff was for rigorous research and analysis, could still be good generalists. The key point is that we know what is needed and that competent policy adviser generalists both by talking to others whose judgment they respect and by interviewing the candidates can raise the probability of finding potentially sound policy generalists.

Whatever the causal relationship, however, breadth of experiences in the past seems the best indicator of the capacity to be a policy adviser generalist, except, of course, a proven track record. This breadth of experience may come from training in different areas, from different kinds of jobs (e.g., one emphasizing analysis, another politics), or both. Such people are more likely to break out of the narrow confines of a single profession and have the "double vision" needed by the good generalist policy adviser. Unfortunately, no institutional setting alone necessarily leads to the development of competent policy generalists. The need remains to search in a variety of places for the policy adviser virtuosos.

White House domestic policy units can be relatively small for two reasons. First, extensive analysis within the federal government should be carried out by the agencies that will implement and manage the programs. Second, external think tanks, such as Rand, Brookings, the American Enterprise Institute, the Urban Institute, and the Heritage Foundation, reduce the needed size of both White House and agency domestic policy units.[24] The policy research and analysis of the think tanks make it possible for executive branch domestic policy offices to engage in less internal research and policy analysis and still develop sound policy prescriptions. At the same time, the external analytic products are more ideologically driven than earlier, so competent internal staffs, even if legitimately smaller than previously, are still needed to determine the president's or agencies' needs. These needs are not necessarily the same as those of the think tanks. Even if outside policy prescriptions fulfill internal executive branch requirements when policies are being formulated, competent internal analysts are still needed to adjust and correct these policies.

The growth of the think tanks since the early 1960s has yielded much relevant external domestic policy analysis and research and generally has produced an adequate supply of competent journeyman analysts for executive branch domestic policy offices. Such offices now can be "lean and mean," avoiding some of the more deleterious aspects of large, entrenched bureaucracy. At the same time the demand for competence on the smaller staff is likely to be even more severe. There will tend to be a somewhat smaller need for highly technical skills, which are in adequate supply, and a greater need for generalist policy advisers, who blend both technical and synthesizing capabilities and are in short supply. The abundance of policy ideas places a high premium on domestic-policy unit competence to sort through the ideas to find reasonable ones that fit the president's or the agencies' needs. Someone else may do the preliminary homework, but presidential or agency policy staff must determine quality and relevance and integrate the analysis into the policy process.

8

Effective Presidential Governance

Presidential governance must translate into the executive branch capacity to develop, package, sell, implement, and manage sound programs and policies. Presidents should be held accountable for making their best efforts to bring about desired final outcomes. In particular, presidents must be held fully accountable for the effectiveness of their governance. Effective presidential governance and the factors that precede it in the causal model have been the center of discussion because poor performance in these areas in the last three decades has visibly harmed the nation, bringing economic decline and greater inequality. A president who cannot cope adequately with the factors preceding presidential governance greatly decreases the chances that he will perform effectively and that the nation will achieve the desired outcomes. And getting the machinery of government factors wrong tends to reduce the likelihood of presidential effectiveness more than getting these factors right increases it. The general competence of a president's top policy advisers, the soundness of the EOP institutional analytic process, and the status and competence of his policy analysts are not only key indicators of how he is doing, but also the governance factors over which he has the greatest control. Effective presidential governance remains the pivotal factor in the presidential policy performance equation.

THE PRESIDENT AND INSTITUTIONAL FIXES

Increasing the federal government's institutional capacity to generate sound, credible expert policy information and analysis and to implement and manage policy is a necessary condition for the policy changes needed to combat America's economic and social problems. Big institutional problems demand big structural changes. Major institutional changes alter individual and organizational status and power, creating expected and unexpected risks. First, the major institutional change could be in the wrong direction. Second, it could start right but then go seriously wrong. Third, even a positive institutional reform that clearly reaches its intended objectives can leave bureaucratic wounds.

Why then risk major institutional change? Because not changing or making only incremental changes can be more dangerous. Difficult tradeoffs will be needed at the time of the change and over time as changes unfold. This is critical—the implementation period for a major structural change is likely to be an extended one. The new structure should be amenable to error correction. There is, however, an ever present danger of changes in the new structure that drive it back to the old structure with only superficial differences. No task of political leadership is more demanding than guiding the implementation process for major structural change, making necessary modifications, but preventing those that attack the underlying integrity of the new structure. Keeping the focus on the critical elements of a major structural change over time amid the swirl of competing demands—staying the course—demands both great political and organizational skill and much time.

If a new president wants to restructure the EOP to have more sound expert policy information and analysis for White House policy formulation and stronger agency managerial capacity, it is difficult but possible. First, there are no major constitutional, legislative, or executive branch hurdles. President Reagan carried through major EOP changes such as making both the national security and domestic policy advisers report to Counselor-to-the-President Edwin Meese. Since key staff will not be in place, the usually bloody battles over the particular status and turf that belong to specific individuals will be unnecessary. Though some prospective national security advisers may decide not to accept the position because they cannot be secretary of state in the White House, they almost certainly would be the wrong people for the job anyway. Moreover, a newly elected president can begin immediately in the transition period to think about the right people for the jobs—e.g., secretaries with strong management skills. Although other implementation obstacles may be too difficult to overcome, the importance of not having to surmount the usual troublesome status and turf barriers erected by potential losers, such as when major changes occur in established agency fiefdoms, cannot be overstressed.

Second, much is known about building an EOP policymaking structure that will yield sound information and analysis and greater agency management capacity. Although no detailed blueprint for the ideal EOP structure is proposed, the ten organizational propositions for the EOP and the eight skill and knowledge requirements for policy units set out the broad dimensions of a viable EOP policymaking structure:

•The top generalist policy advisers should have as a major function linking the president with the EOP analytic structure, and they need analytic
competence to perform the job effectively.

•Policy units need to be smaller and more competent, with strong analytic, strategic, and monitoring skills.

•Policy units should have policy analysts in the top leadership of the
unit and career staff in major positions.

•Policy unit staff members ought to be brokers, consumers, and trans-
lators of in-depth agency policy analyses and evaluations performed
outside the EOP.

•Analytic competition should be institutionalized, with strong policy
units in the White House and in the agencies interacting in presidential
policy formulation.

•Agency heads should be the chief spokespersons for their departments,
and major presidential policy advisers for their agencies' programs.
They should have authority to appoint all political executives, and they
should have agency resources sufficient to undertake successfully the
implementation and management of mandated policies (the last element of sufficient agency resources goes beyond EOP structure per se
but is central to it).

The six features of a sound EOP contain no surprises; they flow straight
from the normative and organizational propositions and the skill and knowledge requirements developed in the last chapter. A few points must be emphasized, however. First, a president's efforts to configure the EOP in line
with these six dimensions force some needed steps, such as placing policy
analysts and career staff in key positions in policy units and allowing agency
heads to choose their political executives. Second, a small staff is desirable,
but competence is more important. Having more people with the capacity
to do technical jobs correctly is critical, and having enough of them to perform these tasks can help keep staff under control. Counting heads is not
enough. Roles, functions, and skills must be spelled out. Third, the tasks of
implementing and managing the EOP loom large.

IMPLEMENTING AND MANAGING
A MAJOR REORGANIZATION OF THE EOP

A big implementation problem in the transition period is time pressure, unless the president-elect already has developed a good game plan for restructuring. There is no inherent reason a game plan cannot be finished before
election day; however, the all-out-to-win-the-election pressures militate against
it. Even formulating such a plan early in the transition period should not

be difficult. For example, giving department and agency heads power to appoint subordinates requires that the president-elect "just say yes." Reorganization may seem less important than choosing the cabinet and the top White House staff. Also complicating the problem is the long period for investigating and confirming cabinet and subcabinet members. In the EOP only the OMB director, among the critical early actors, requires Senate confirmation and is likely to be hurried through to put the key White House people in place. Although the deputy director of the OMB and others in the EOP such as the three members of the CEA, must be confirmed by the Senate, none necessarily have key roles. Under almost any circumstances, future White House staff, who can be off and running early in the transition period, have an inherent head start, even if their cabinet rivals have close ties to the president or their own power base.

The problem at the top among key White House aides and cabinet secretaries, however, may be far less important than the absence of subcabinet appointees. Judith Havemann reported in early April 1989 that the administration had nominated but 50 of 750 subcabinet positions and that the *lone* Bush appointees in Transportation, Agriculture, Health and Human Services, Interior, Labor, Energy, and the EPA were the agency heads. After seven months Havemann reported a Democratic Study Group claim that for approximately 40 percent of the top 394 executive positions President Bush had failed to nominate anyone.[1] Career civil servants can keep the agencies running at operating level (Social Security checks are written, Corps of Engineers' projects continue); however, important decisions or activities either shift to lower level White House staff, are decided or undertaken by holdovers from the last administration, or get postponed. The slower White House nomination and Senate confirmation process that leaves critical agency subcabinet positions unfilled may be the greatest continuing threat to shifting power back to the agencies and to orderly governance in the early part of a new administration.

After implementation of a major structural change is completed, the task of managing it lies ahead. Assume a new president has put in place a new White House structure that fosters analytic competition, places more reliance on career staff, makes such key actors as the top domestic policy adviser mainly honest brokers, and gives the departments and agencies more autonomy to implement and manage programs. That is, the structural reorganization has moved successfully through the implementation state to the operational one. Big management problems, however, remain, as the power players engage in skirmishes to regain lost power or to solidify their new standing. Operational process management is a continuing presidential task. Three critical management questions arise: First, can the president and his process management delegatees keep the new structure balanced? Second, will the departments get out of control? Third, will effective White House policy management either be so time-consuming as to threaten the needed political effort to uphold the president's standing, or will it demand presidential behavior that is not compatible with high political standing? Effective process management requires adroit moves to keep a reasonable competitive balance between analytic advocates and between White House staff and agency political executives. There are likely to be winners and losers. Does this mean an important input must be lost because of a weak advocate? If not, should the president fire the weak advocate (or "promote" him out of the key position as private-sector firms sometimes do), or weaken the winners? Such balancing to keep a strong multiple-advocacy process is difficult. The second question focuses more sharply on the key White House control/agency autonomy balance that has been at the center of declining executive branch managerial capacity. The White House fears that agency political leaders will be thwarted by permanent staffs who are trying actively to subvert White House plans or passively waiting out the president by not volunteering necessary information and analysis. Worse yet, wily "bureaucrats" may coopt the political executives, turning them and the agency from presidential objectives to agency objectives, which may conflict with those of the president. These contingencies press presidents toward seeing the value of using White House staff to keep the agency heads in line, of putting presidential loyalists in key subcabinet positions (and hence not giving the cabinet member or agency head appointment power), or of both. The third question asks if the president and his key staff can exert both political and organizational mastery and more specifically if the exercise of organizational mastery, either in the time demanded or in the specific actions required, will undercut the high presidential political standing that is the first prerequisite of effective presidential governance.

Cutting across all three management questions is the issue of bureaucratic resistance. Bureaucratic pathology is a reality, not simply a myth created by organizationally inept presidents. Permanent staff members not only have a tendency to dig in and protect the status quo, but they are also strong opponents with in-depth knowledge of the tricky bureaucratic terrain. They have a store of tactics from earlier battles. At the same time, many career civil servants see their primary responsibility as serving their politically appointed leaders. By definition, however, permanent staff members are followers, not leaders. Bureaucracies must be well managed. A president has three options in countering bureaucratic resistance. First, he can try to run the agencies out of the White House. That strategy is feasible on budget issues and in some cases if the goal is to have the agency do nothing or at least as little as possible (the early Reagan strategy). Active agency domestic policy execution, however, can almost never be managed from the White House. Second, the president can try to control the agency by placing loyalists in key subcabinet positions. This strategy, also used by Reagan, can work in both the budget issues and the do-little-or-nothing cases. It might work with active policies, since the subcabinet is ostensibly in charge. This strategy, however, is almost always undertaken on the premise that the bureaucrats are the enemy and often that the secretary is not to be trusted fully. That view makes success difficult. The third strategy is to choose loyal secretaries with proven managerial skills and give them the autonomy to lead the agency. A possible acceptable variation, although it is more difficult to do, is a top management team with a politically experienced secretary as the "outside" person and a proven manager as the number two "inside" person. Success here is far from assured, even if the president picks a competent manager. But at least there are a number of good guidelines for assessing the career staff to determine if they are both competent and committed and for developing analytic staffs that can overcome the bureaucrats' "buried" information tactics. Managing a large-scale public organization is never easy. It is an unavoidable truth each president must face. And ultimately much rests upon the president's own organizational mastery, including picking the right secretary or team.

The question of both political and organizational mastery is particularly vexing because Eisenhower is the last successful example. The difficulties today are greater than they were three decades ago. The federal government is larger and operates in more policy areas. The number of key institutional players has increased materially. The political arena appears to be almost totally transformed, with television, political action committees, and political consultants and handlers placing increasingly greater premiums on continuous campaigning and the artful management of the president's image. Furthermore, increased policy complexity also makes successful presidential policy performance more difficult. In a harsh criticism of his first weeks in office, the *Economist* complained that President Bush still appeared to be on the campaign trail: "In place of ideas and thoughts for the future, he offered sound-bites and issues of the day [during the campaign]. He has taken this winning strategy into office with him, heedless of the gulf between campaigning and governing (or, as one wag puts it, stagecraft and statescraft)."[2] For an ordinary president without charisma or an extraordinary, mobilizing event, however, the need to be seen as on top of the job — and in Bush's case be his own man, not a Reagan clone, and yet be as tough — may demand far more stagecraft than statescraft early in the administration.

These management questions again underscore the limits of institutional restructuring in its static dimensions. That is, putting the right organizational boxes, interrelationships, processes, functions (including job specifications), and responsibilities on paper is a first step toward an effective presidential institutional structure, but it is only one step. At the same time no task is under greater direct presidential control than the institutional structuring of the EOP. The president can specify White House staff status, functions, desired skills and experience, responsibilities, and the intended relationships with the agency political executives. The exceptions are reorganizations that require congressional approval, but presidential flexibility at this point permits major EOP restructuring without having to go to Congress. John Tower notwithstanding, much the same can be said of the next step of staffing the key White House and agency political executive positions, despite the need for Senate confirmation. *Not getting the EOP structure and staffing right and keeping it viable is always mainly the president's fault — a failure to manage effectively either the implementation of needed EOP structural and staffing changes or the continuing operation of his executive office.*

TOWARD EFFECTIVE PRESIDENTIAL GOVERNANCE

Exogenous factors such as skyrocketing OPEC prices can make a president look bad on the inflation front, but plummeting oil prices make a great inflation fighter. Moreover, such events that are mainly or fully outside a president's control generally dominate desired societal outcomes. At the same time a president's capacity to govern will have an impact at the margin on how the nation responds to powerful exogenous factors. This is why the book has centered on White House structure and staffing. Reforming these key institutional building blocks for effective presidential governance, however, presents two frustrations. First, if organizational mastery is the missing link of effective presidential governance, a president with strong organizational skills can cut the Gordian knot of seemingly insurmountable institutional problems that have overwhelmed presidents since Eisenhower. Second, the emerging political climate makes selecting and electing a presidential candidate who has superior organizational skills more difficult and can complicate that president's exercise of organizational mastery. Both problems are ultimately political in nature.

Organizational Mastery: The Missing Link

Set the ten organizational propositions to guide restructuring and the EOP policymaking process before a president with deep organizational knowledge and experience in managing large-scale public institutions, and he or she likely will find them unobjectionable but hardly wondrous breakthroughs. Although elaborating on the propositions may prove useful in helping a president think through structural and staffing issues, the last thing to expect from presidents with organizational mastery is that they would follow any outsider's structural game plan slavishly. That is one reason why no specific EOP structure has been set out, only some critical guidelines. Even if two presidents had roughly similar levels of organizational mastery and both agreed generally with the ten restructuring guides, they would not be expected to arrive at the same structural configuration, since that would depend on their particular individual styles and competence. For example, the two presidents would not have the same organizational strengths and weaknesses and so would use different approaches in trying to maximize their organizational strengths and minimize their weaknesses. Much also would depend on the particular competences of their top aides. Even more important would be the particular circumstances – the internal and external environments – under which each president had to operate.

A president with organizational mastery would probably immediately reject the blindness of the superrealists and be appalled at Carter and Reagan's structural and staffing efforts. This president would not so fear the dreaded bureaucrats that the only avenue that appeared open would be takeover and control. Nor would the president have the misguided arrogance to underestimate the capacity of the career staff to protect status, turf, and their interpretation of institutional objectives. A president with organizational mastery, knowing various bureaucratic strategies and ploys, would use this knowledge to craft an organizational strategy aimed at containing the career staffs' weaknesses but still utilizing their strengths. Finally, and most critical of all, he would know both that a mere handful of appointments would shape the EOP analytic structure and the executive branch managerial process (mainly the top White House staff and the department and agency heads) and what knowledge, skills, and experience these key appointees must have if there is to be both a strong EOP analytic and monitoring capacity and strong agencies with the institutional autonomy and the individual competencies to implement and manage programs effectively.

In the opposite case, where a newly elected president has little understanding of complex organizational processes, the situation may be nearly hopeless. Organizational wisdom is seldom amenable to quick study. Learning it on-the-job is hazardous for a president and for the nation. The problem is that a president-elect without organizational skills will not appreciate the value of an organizational strategy and reject it out-of-hand or not have the time to master it. Today a presidency starts at the latest on the day after the election in November. By January 20, critical organizational decisions will have been made and, most importantly, the top positions will have been announced. The difficulties pertain much more to the White House control-agency autonomy balance than to building analytic strength. Competent analytic staffs have been assembled without a president's having deep organizational knowledge. What demands such organizational knowledge is how to develop and use the analytic product most effectively. Developing a strong EOP institutional analytic structure is a first step and a necessary one for effective governance. But it needs to be blended with sound agency analytic staffs and strong agency managerial capacity to implement the president's policies. This next step, which integrates White House and agency analysis and management has been the critical missing factor needed for effective presidential governance. This integration is the crucial test of a president's organizational wisdom.

Two more comments on organizational mastery are essential. First, effective presidential governance does not demand an organizational virtuoso of the caliber of Dwight Eisenhower. President Ford appeared to be establishing a better control-autonomy balance and might have emerged as a strong organizational president if he had been re-elected in 1976.[3] There is some middle ground between organizational ignorance and virtuosity. In this middle area reorganization guidelines for structuring and staffing the EOP have their greatest potential value for strengthening presidential governance. Synthesizing the missing ingredients for presidents with a degree of organizational mastery and some sense of organizational strategy can help. Second, and closely related, organizational mastery itself ultimately becomes a political issue. Presidential candidates offer a combination of skills, values, and styles, and citizens must vote on those combinations as packaged in each candidate. A loyal Democrat who sees the importance of organizational mastery may pick a candidate in a Democratic primary because of that person's superior organizational capabilities but not vote Republican even if the Republican candidate outshone the Democratic one on the organizational dimension. A candidate with the "right" values from a voter's perspective should dominate an organizational virtuoso with the "wrong" values. The deeper issue is how the political system can produce candidates with the organizational competence to move the federal government toward those desired values.

Political Climate

Political climate involves such variables as how presidential candidates are chosen, how the candidates communicate with the public and are covered by the media, and how presidents are assessed. It is an amorphous concept, but it cannot be avoided; political climate is one of the factors — perhaps the most critical one — affecting, first, whether an organizationally oriented president will be chosen and, second, how difficult it will be for a president with such institutional skills to exert organizational mastery. The current political climate, as compared with that climate in the early postwar years, lessens the chances of an organizationally competent president being elected, *and* it raises the level of organizational skills needed to exercise effective presidential governance. Consider the six presidents since Eisenhower, from Kennedy through Reagan. The only one who seemed to have real organizational competence — Gerald Ford — was the only one not elected. Others may have had considerable organizational knowledge. We can speculate whether Nixon's paranoia and Johnson's bigger-than-life, brute-force personality overwhelmed potential organizational skills. But whatever their organizational wisdom was, it did not translate into mastery. No president in this group had as little large-scale organizational background as did Kennedy, and so his organizational ignorance, even if surrounded by the best and the brightest, was hardly surprising. More discouraging is that Carter and Reagan had been governors, which would seem to be a better training ground for acquiring organizational wisdom than would Congress.

Which political climate changes since the Eisenhower presidency make for both the greater difficulty of electing organizationally capable presidents and the higher demands on their organizational skills after they have been elected? First, the United States is the only country in the world to allow voters, rather than small groups of party leaders, to determine candidates for chief executive. As James MacGregor Burns argues: "[No] polity on earth [has] put such civic demands on its citizens as [does] the American. . . . It is above all the decline of party in the United States that has made the citizen's task so overpowering."[4] Since political parties no longer are the mediating institution between presidential candidates and the people, they do not serve the critical function of putting before the voters the major issues facing the nation.[5] Second, television now dominates all other media. Not only has television come to dominate presidential campaigns, but it may be shaping the thinking of the American public about how to assess a president, his policies, and his performance. In *Amusing Ourselves to Death*, Neil Postman launched an all-out polemical attack against televison: "The result of . . . [the television age] is that Americans are the best entertained and quite likely the least well-informed people in the Western world. . . . [Americans] are deprived of authentic information. . . . [W]e are losing our sense of what it means to be well informed."[6] Third, short television commercials have become the weapon of choice in presidential campaigns. Television contributed to the lack of emphasis on substantive issues and the negativeness of the Bush-Dukakis presidential campaign. Jack W. Germond and Jules Witcover argued that Bush ran the "most mean-spirited and negative campaign in modern-day American political history" and appealed to the lowest common denominator in the electorate in focusing on such questions as flag burning and Dukakis' veto of a bill requiring the pledge of allegiance, to the exclusion of truly serious issues facing the nation.[7] Television — where image dominates words — is the perfect vehicle for the politics of unreality. Fourth, the media lack the capacity and the incentives to replace the political parties. Thomas E. Patterson has pointed out that the press is in the news business (profits as bottom line), not the political, business so its agenda bears little relationship to the parties. He observed: "Alone among democracies, the United States is willing to turn the task [of presenting the presidential candidates] over to an institution, the press, that was designed for different purposes and lacks the incentives to do the job properly. In a basic sense, the present system of electing presidents is constitutionally flawed."[8] News coverage, which had never focused much on candidates' competence to master large-scale institutions, in stressing personality and in emphasizing a fast start as opposed to a reasoned one, has moved further from major presidential issues. Lewis Wolfson centers on the critical point that news media persons do not analyze institutional governance: "They fail to set out independently to explain government's operation. They don't analyze political processes and institutional relationships behind 'the news' . . . They are not inherently interested in what's involved in . . . administering a program. . . . Lou Cannon says they are not 'management minded.'"[9] Austin Ranney's more scholarly work contrasts sharply with Postman's polemical tone and style, but not in message. Ranney's starting point is also the dominance of television. Competence is a key issue, since broad generalists dominate among media persons, who probably majored in English, speech, drama, or journalism. Few of them majored in economics, political science, or history.[10] Ranney argues that television newspeople think of politics mainly as a game that is played by the individual politician for personal gain. Reporters stress the strategy and tactics of winning, and the progress of the race. They often have little interest in policy issues and none in how candidates will select and organize analytic and advisory staffs to serve the presidency. Such issues as presidential candidates' views on organization and the machinery of government and how they would run the government if elected are issues often outside the competence of the media people—not thought of at all, not appreciated, or else viewed as too esoteric or mundane to be newsworthy.

The four-year marathon that stretches from the first Wednesday after election day to the next presidential election has misshaped the presidential selection process. The intense pressures yield the "right" person for the task at hand—winning the presidency. A useful analogy is to parliamentary question time in Britain, where the prime minister and other ministers are subjected to harsh, often embarrassing questions on the floor of the House of Commons. It can be high drama worthy of front pages and prime-time television, but as Geoffrey Smith and Nelson W. Polsby argue "[parliamentary question time] is the modern equivalent of the medieval tournament. . . . [A] flash of wit is worth an hour of administrative wisdom."[11] Yet, question time performance is all-important to a prime minister and ministers, as a perpetual test of their political "manhood" (Prime Minister Thatcher, in these terms is the toughest of the lot). Fail, and a career can be destroyed. The problem is that the intensity of parliamentary question time misshapes the perspective of both ministers and the high civil servant mandarins who attend them, by focusing on snappy debate, not on ministry mission, and in so doing is a major cause of British governance problems. Interestingly, the West German government after World War II adopted question time in its parliamentary body, but the questions are usually answered by civil servants and are not a threat to ministers' political standing. The U.S. electoral process also errs in exerting great pressure for finding presidential candidates with the debating and presentational skills that look good on the campaign trail and especially on television. At question in both countries are two kinds of competence — winning and governance — with the latter getting almost no reinforcement in the British parliamentary and in the U.S. presidential election processes. To complicate matters even more, winning and governing have become inseparably bound together. Robert Denton, who sees Ronald Reagan as the first true television president, labels the Reagan years the "primetime presidency," and argues that governing today means "controlling the videos in the evening news" so that television is "the primary tool and battleground for governing the nation."[12] In the Reagan era, news management skills became more important than organizational management competence. The former most often came down to getting the right presidential image on prime-time television news because the picture that conjured up the image of strong leadership dominated television news commentators' words, which might have belied it. What CBS White House correspondent Leslie Stahl thought was a highly critical attack on President Reagan is fascinating. Stahl used positive video images from the White House while saying that Reagan's actions contradicted his claims. Reagan's White House news managers, rather than being upset by Stahl's effort, as she had anticipated, were pleased because they understood that the positive picture overwhelmed the negative words. Ironically, this is made more vivid in a memorable Bill Moyers television special shown November 22, 1989 on PBS that shows Stahl with consternation on her face telling of her bewilderment at the turn of events and a smug Michael Deaver pointing out that the positive Reagan image drowned out Stahl's harsh comments.[13] Such considerations move us to what may be the ultimate crisis of the presidency — the final responsibility for preserving democracy is on the backs of the citizen voters.

With all the difficulties created by the long primary period and the media, individual citizens remain responsible for obtaining the information needed to make wise presidential choices. The Founding Fathers understood the need both for competence among leaders *and* for an informed citizenry with the capacity to judge leadership competence. What they could not foresee was the increasing complexity of U.S. policymaking, which now places far greater demands on a president and on citizens than in the past. The fundamental assumption of American democracy, that the electorate can choose wisely, is at risk. The electorate must find presidential candidates with the generalist and specialist skills and experience needed to lead the United States toward better performance if the nation is to have prosperity and freedom. People can debate endlessly on the limits of government — on what the federal government or all governments, including state and local governments, ought to be doing for citizens. The capacity issue, however, requires no agreement on what government ought to be doing. At some point the people decide on the tasks that governments will undertake. Defense, managing the economy, basic income protection, and justice, for example, are continuing missions of the federal government and of lesser governments. Once these missions are decided, people of quite different political persuasions can agree generally that the government should do what it is charged with doing, both efficiently and effectively. Beyond promise is performance. And central to performance is capacity. Government must be competent if democracy is to survive. A hollow, incompetent federal executive branch in this era of complexity fundamentally threatens the nation's economic, social and political viability. And it does so increasingly as the United States ceases to be the world's economic hegemony and becomes one of several world economic power centers. Somehow the U.S. voter must come to grips with the hard fact that government is *both problem and solution* or run the risk of material economic and social decline.

Herein lies the U.S. democratic dilemma. Although the Founding Fathers both restricted the definition of a voter and put constraints on direct democracy, no mediating institutions, such as political parties or the press, were placed between the people and the election of the president. Constitutionally speaking, the people had the basic responsibility for demanding that presidential candidates present themselves honestly, set out their positions on major national issues, and generally demonstrate their ability to be president. The political parties acquired this mediating role between the people and the president, with party leaders choosing the candidates as late as 1968 (recall then Vice-President Hubert Humphrey, who won no primaries in that year). After that, the mediating role fell to the media, leading Thomas Patterson to argue: "The real flaw in the modern presidential campaign is that it asks its three principals — the voters, the candidates, and the news media — to exercise responsibilities they cannot exercise competently. . . . The greatest flaw in the modern system of electing presidents, however, is its dependence on the news media."[14] Although the news media that acquired the mediating job by default has neither the incentives nor the capacity to fulfill that role adequately for the great bulk of the nation's citizens (voters), no substitute is in sight.[15]

The people have the responsibility either to find an adequate mediating mechanism between themselves and presidential candidates or to do the job themselves. That is the heart of the problem. And it is made so difficult because, as Jean Bathke Elshtain points out, "no handy criteria exist to allow either the voter or the political analyst to separate real from symbolic or rhetorical issues."[16] Newspaper columnists or academic panelists may have lamented that in 1988 the candidates did not tackle the most critical issues facing the country, but that is a value judgment. Elshtain argues that voters and candidates are "co-constructors" of issues, that voters are not crudely manipulated by candidates; that "concern and anxiety about crime, morality, and patriotism" were real (not candidate-created) issues in 1988; and that these issues can be justifiably deemed as important or more important than issues such as double deficits or hollow government.[17] Her argument cuts to the heart of democratic theory. Democracy, after all, does not require that the people choose wisely.

U.S. democracy, as conceived by the Founding Fathers, does demand that citizens expend the effort to be well-informed. They assumed that wise choice rests on a basis of sound information. Today, being an informed electorate is more of a task than when Washington, Jefferson, and Madison led the nation. The Founding Fathers did not dwell on macroeconomic policy or on analytic and managerial capacity. But they did understand both the need for competence among leaders and for sound public knowledge as the base for assessing such competence. As Madison wrote W. T. Barry on August 4, 1822, "A popular Government without popular information or the means of acquiring it, is a Prologue to a Farce or Tragedy."[18]

Notes

CHAPTER 1. EXPERT INFORMATION,
THE ANALYTIC REVOLUTION, AND
PRESIDENTIAL GOVERNANCE

1. Richard E. Neustadt, *Presidential Power* (New York: John Wiley & Sons, 1980), p. 243.

2. Elliot Richardson, *The Creative Balance* (New York: Holt, Rinehart & Winston, 1976), p. 105.

3. Frank Fischer, "Policy Expertise and the 'New Class': A Critique of the Neoconservative Thesis," in Frank Fischer and John Forester (eds.), *Confronting Values in Policy Analysis* (Beverly Hills, Calif.: Sage Publications, 1987), pp. 120–121.

4. Bradley H. Patterson, Jr., *The Ring of Power: The White House Staff and Its Expanding Role in Government* (New York: Basic Books, 1988), p. 107.

5. Laurence E. Lynn, Jr., "Policy Analysis in Bureaucracy: How New? How Effective?" *Journal of Policy Analysis and Management* (Summer 1989):374–375. This issue also contains articles tracing the history of analytic offices at the State Department and the Department of Interior.

6. Giandomenico Majone, *Evidence, Argument and Persuasion in the Policy Process* (New Haven, Conn.: Yale University Press, 1989), p. 21.

7. Other EOP units at the end of the Reagan administration were the Office of the U.S. Trade Representative, the Council on Environmental Quality, the Office of Science and Technology Policy, and the Office of Administration. For a good general treatment of the EOP, see John Hart, *The Presidential Branch* (Elmsford, N.Y.: Pergamon, 1987). The exact composition of the EOP changes over time, and Hart includes (pp. 236–238) a table showing roughly forty units that at one time or another inhabited the EOP between 1939 and 1986.

8. To be sure, the EOP structure to some extent has a life of its own based on prior history and the general demands that would confront any president. Still, a president has much discretion, particularly in terms of policy. For a good statement of EOP continuity, see Samuel Kernell, "The Evolution of the White House Staff," in John E. Chubb and Paul E. Peterson (eds.), *Can the Government Govern?* (Washington, D.C.: Brookings, 1989), pp. 185–237; and Samuel Kernell and Samuel Popkin (eds.),

Chief-of-Staff: Twenty-Five Years of Managing the Presidency (Berkeley: University of California Press, 1986).

9. For discussions of special analytic problems and issues in Congress, see William H. Robinson, "Policy Analysis for Congress: Lengthening the Time Horizon," *Journal of Policy Analysis and Management* (Winter 1989):1–9; and Carol H. Weiss, "Congressional Committees as Users of Analysis," *Journal of Policy Analysis and Management* (Summer 1989):428.

10. Peter J. May, "Policy Analysis: Present, Past and Future," a paper presented at the annual meetings of the American Political Science Association, September 4–8, 1988, pp. 8–10. In the case of Congress, I have not used the GAO figures, since accountants still predominate in that organization.

11. Arnold J. Meltsner, *Policy Analysts in Bureaucracy* (Berkeley: University of California Press, 1986), pp. 295 and 299.

12. For general treatments of the limits of policy analysis and the need to take account of organizational and political factors, see Alexander L. George, *Presidential Decisionmaking in Foreign Policy: The Effective Use of Information and Advice* (Boulder, Colo: Westview Press, 1980); Charles E. Lindblom, *The Policy-Making Process*, 2d ed. (Englewood Cliffs, N.J.: Prentice-Hall, 1980); Majone, *Evidence, Argument and Persuasion in the Policy Process*; and Herbert A. Simon, *Administrative Behavior: A Study of the Decision-making Processes in Administrative Organizations*, 3d ed. (New York: Free Press, 1976).

13. *The Tower Commission* (New York: Time/Bantam Books, 1987), p. 90.

14. Terry M. Moe, "The Politics of Bureaucratic Structure," in Chubb and Peterson, *Can the Government Govern?* pp. 267 and 329.

15. For an extended discussion of these points, see Walter Williams, *Government by Agency: Lessons from the Social Program Grants-in-Experience* (Orlando, Fla.: Academic Press, 1980); and Walter Williams, *Washington, Westminster and Whitehall* (New York: Cambridge University Press, 1988).

16. Irving L. Janis, *Crucial Decisions: Leadership in Policymaking and Crisis Management* (New York: Free Press, 1989), p. 20.

17. Ibid., pp. 134–135, emphasis in the original. Janis treats extensively the issue of the relationship between the soundness of the analytic process and decision outcomes. See particularly "Are the Main Assumptions about Process and Outcome Warranted?" (pp. 119–135). He finds the available evidence "not definitive" but argued that there is "a sufficient empirical base" for regarding the relationship as plausible.

18. Terry M. Moe, "The Politicized Presidency," in John E. Chubb and Paul E. Peterson (eds.), *The New Direction in American Politics* (Washington, D.C.: Brookings, 1985), p. 239.

19. Paul C. Light, *The President's Agenda: Domestic Policy Choice from Kennedy to Carter* (Baltimore: Johns Hopkins University Press, 1982), pp. 228–230. Light's book is particularly strong on the competence argument. Also see Paul J. Quirk, "Presidential Competence," in Michael Nelson (ed.), *The Presidency and the Political System*, 2d ed. (Washington, D.C.: CQ Press, 1988), pp. 161–183.

20. I.M. Destler, "National Security II: The Rise of the Assistant (1961–1982)," in Hugh Heclo and Lester M. Salamon (eds.), *The Illusion of Presidential Government* (Boulder, Colo.: Westview Press, 1981), pp. 279–280 and 282.

21. Terrel H. Bell, *The Thirteenth Man: A Reagan Cabinet Memoir* (New York: Free Press, 1988), p. 2.

22. David Stockman, *The Triumph of Politics* (New York: Harper and Row, 1986), pp. 80 and 341.

23. *Report of the Congressional Committees Investigating the Iran-Contra Affair* (Washington, D.C.: Government Printing Office, 1987), p. 22.

24. *The Tower Commission Report*, p. 79.

25. "Program Evaluation Issues," *Transition Series* (Washington, D.C.: General Accounting Office, GAO/OCG-89-9TR, November 1988), pp. 1 and 8.

26. Ibid., pp. 24–25.

27. Two books, Benjamin Friedman's *Day of Reckoning* and the Urban Institute's *Challenge to Leadership*, provide a strong, mainly negative case against the Reagan administration. Harvard's Friedman in *Day of Reckoning* offers almost unrelenting criticism of the Reagan economic policies and makes the most convincing argument to date for a relative decline in the U.S. standard of living and a fall from super economic power status over time. Stanford's Michael Boskin, who later was chosen as George Bush's Chair of the Council of Economic Advisers, has provided the best positive view of Reagan economic policy although he too is quite critical at times. See Benjamin M. Friedman, *Day of Reckoning* (New York: Random House, 1988); Isabel V. Sawhill (ed.), *Challenge to Leadership: Economic and Social Issues for the Next Decade* (Washington, D.C.: Urban Institute Press, 1988); and Michael J. Boskin, *Reagan and the Economy: The Successes, Failures, and Unfinished Agenda* (San Francisco: ICS Press, 1987).

28. Isabel V. Sawhill, "Reaganomics in Retrospect," in John L. Palmer (ed.), *Perspectives on the Reagan Years* (Washington, D.C.: Urban Institute Press, 1986), p. 115.

29. *Background Material and Data on Programs within the Jurisdiction of the Committee on Ways and Means* (U.S. House of Representatives) (Washington, D.C.: U.S. General Printing Office, March 15, 1989), p. 945.

30. Ibid., p. 995.

31. *The 1989 Joint Economic Committee Report*, U.S. Congress, April 1989, pp. 67–68.

32. *Economist*, January 28, 1989, p. 27.

33. "The Budget Deficit," *Transition Series* (Washington, D.C.: U.S. General Accounting Office, GAO/OCG-89-ITR, November 1988), pp. 7 and 10.

34. *New York Times*, December 22, 1989.

35. *Seattle Post-Intelligencer*, December 24, 1989.

36. See *1989 Joint Economic Committee Report*, pp. 22–23.

37. *New York Times*, January 23, 1989.

38. For a good general discussion of the claims made of harm from the budget deficit and the embarrassment of failed predictions, see Jonathan Rauch, "Is the Deficit Really Bad?" *Atlantic Monthly* (February 1989):36–42.

39. *Economist*, January 21, 1989, p. 13.

40. All statistics are taken from *New York Times*, December 12, 1989.

41. Mark L. Goldstein, "Hollow Government," *Government Executive* (October 1989):14. The personnel numbers are from the U.S. Office of Personnel Management.

42. Quoted in ibid., p. 13, emphasis added.

43. For a good account of the craft of policy analysis, see David L. Weimer and Aidan R. Vining, *Policy Analysis: Concepts and Practice* (Englewood Cliffs, N.J.: Prentice-Hall, 1989). How policy analysis is practiced in the executive branch is treated in Meltsner, *Policy Analysts in Bureaucracy*; Laurence E. Lynn, Jr., and David de F. Whitman, *The President as Policymaker: Jimmy Carter and Welfare Reform* (Philadelphia: Temple University Press, 1981); and Walter Williams, *Social Policy, Research and Analysis: The Experience in the Federal Social Agencies* (New York: Elsevier, 1971).

44. Moe, "The Politicized Presidency"; and John Hart, *The Presidential Branch* (Elmsford, N.Y.: Pergamon, 1987).

45. Light, *The President's Agenda*, pp. 225 and 231.

46. Fred. I. Greenstein, *The Hidden-Hand Presidency: Eisenhower as Leader* (New York: Basic Books, 1982), p. 245.

47. Ibid., pp. 246–247.

48. The presidential scholar Erwin Hargrove in his latest book on the presidency written with Michael Nelson sets out a similar list of presidential skills: "The four [presidential leadership] capacities are *strategic skill*, which includes the ability to formulate coherent policy goals that match the historical situation and to develop strategies for their attainment that are based on the political resources that are available or can be developed; *skill at presenting oneself and one's ideas to the public* through rhetoric and drama; *the tactical capacity* to construct coalitions of power holders to secure agreement on particular questions; and *skill in managing authority* for policy formulation and administration." Hargrove and Nelson's first skill combines strategic and analytic capacities. Their next two are the equivalent of political mastery; their final skill matches organizational mastery. They, too, stress the latter in pointing out that administrative leadership requires experience and knowledge about how large-scale organizations work, how to combine staff advisers and agency operators, and how to delegate authority for implementation while retaining control. Erwin L. Hargrove and Michael Nelson, *Presidents, Politics, and Policy* (New York: Knopf, 1984), pp. 87–89, emphasis in the original.

49. Bert A. Rockman, *The Leadership Question: The Presidency and the American System* (New York: Praeger, 1984), p. 14.

50. For extended treatments of the parliamentary/party approaches see Charles M. Hardin, *Presidential Power and Accountability: Toward a New Constitution* (Chicago: University of Chicago Press, 1974); James L. Sundquist, *Constitutional Reform and Effective Government* (Washington, D.C.: Brookings, 1986); James MacGregor Burns, *The Power to Lead* (New York: Simon and Schuster, 1984); and Theodore J. Lowi, *The Personal President: Power Invested, Power Unfulfilled* (Ithaca, N.Y.: Cornell University Press, 1985).

51. See Williams, *Washington, Westminster and Whitehall*.

52. Lowi, *The Personal President*, pp. 57, 115, 151, 156, and 208; and Hart, *The Presidential Branch*, pp. 3–4 and 214–219.

53. Hart, *The Presidential Branch*, pp. 296 and 213.

CHAPTER 2. THE PRESIDENT'S POLICY ADVISERS AND POLICY ANALYSIS

1. Alice M. Rivlin, "A Public Policy Paradox," *Journal of Policy Analysis and Management* 4, 1 (1984):18.

2. *New York Times*, December 12, 1984.

3. Robert H. Nelson, "The Economics Profession and the Making of Public Policy," *Journal of Economic Literature* (March 1987):66–67. For a detailed account of Heller's views in his own words, see Erwin C. Hargrove and Samuel A. Morley (eds.), *The President and the Council of Economic Advisers: Interviews with CEA Chairman* (Boulder, Colo.: Westview Press, 1984), pp. 163–215.

4. Walter Isaacson and Evan Thomas, *The Wise Men: Six Friends and the World They Made* (New York: Simon and Schuster, 1986), p. 656.

5. Ibid., pp. 722 and 732.

6. A number of writers have pointed out the cognitive limits to policy analysis. See Alexander L. George, *Presidential Decisionmaking in Foreign Policy: The Effective Use of Information and Advice* (Boulder, Colo.: Westview, 1980); Charles E. Lindblom, *The Policymaking Process*, 2d ed. (Englewood Cliffs, N.J.: Prentice-Hall, 1980); and Herbert A. Simon, *Administrative Behavior: A Study of Decisionmaking Processes in Administrative Organizations*, 3d ed. (New York: Free Press, 1976).

7. Yehezkel Dror, "Think Tanks," in Carol H. Weiss and Allen H. Barton (eds.), *Making Bureaucracies Work* (Beverly Hills, Calif.: Sage Publications, 1980), p. 139.

8. Hugh Heclo, "Issue Networks and the Executive Establishment," in Anthony King (ed.), *The New American Political System* (New Haven, Conn.: Yale University Press, 1979), pp. 12–13.

9. Sir Alex Cairncross, "Economics in Theory and Practice," *American Economics Association Papers and Proceedings* (May 1985):6.

10. Henry J. Aaron, *Politics and the Professors* (Washington, D.C.: Brookings, 1978), p. 159.

11. Rivlin, "A Public Policy Paradox," p. 20.

12. Nelson, "The Economics Profession and the Making of Policy," p. 59.

13. Peter J. May, "Policy Analysis: Past, Present, and Future," paper delivered at the American Political Science Association Annual Meeting, Washington, D.C., September 1–4, 1988, p. 1.

14. Ben W. Heineman, Jr., "Marrying Politics and Policy," in Lester M. Salamon and Michael S. Lund (eds.), *The Reagan Presidency and Governing of America* (Washington, D.C.: Urban Institute Press, 1984), p. 169.

15. Ben W. Heineman, Jr., and Curtis A. Hessler, *Memorandum for the President: A Strategic Approach to Domestic Affairs in the 1980s* (New York: Random House, 1980), p. 35, emphasis in the original.

16. Stephen Hess, *Organizing the Presidency*, 2d ed. (Washington, D.C.: Brookings, 1988), p. 175.

17. John Hart, *The Presidential Branch* (Elmsford, N.Y.: Pergamon, 1987), pp. 194 and 197.

18. Paul H. O'Neill, a presentation to OMB staff, The Center for Excellence in Government, Washington, D.C., September 6, 1988, p. 1.

19. Ibid., p. 2.

20. Richard Nelson, *The Moon and the Ghetto* (New York: Norton, 1977), p. 23.

21. For extended discussions of the number of lawyers in the United States and their orientation, see Jethro K. Lieberman, *The Litigious Society* (New York: Basic Books, 1981); and Marshall E. Dimock, *Law and Dynamic Administration* (New York: Praeger, 1980). The latter observed (p. 43): "There is by far a higher percentage of lawyers to the total population in the United States than in any other country." A December 12, 1983, *New York Times* column by Peter Megaree Brown reported that "U.S. lawyers now number more than 600,000 — one lawyer for every 388 people. . . . Two-thirds of all lawyers in the world are in the United States."

22. Dimock, *Law and Dynamic Administration*, pp. 40–41.

23. Peter L. Szanton, "Public Policy, Public Good, and the Law," P-4928 (Washington, D.C.: Rand Corporation, December 1972), pp. 6 and 12.

24. *Legal Times*, November 14, 1983, emphasis in the original.

25. Ibid.

CHAPTER 3. DOMESTIC POLICY ANALYSIS
IN THE EXECUTIVE BRANCH, 1964-1980

1. For a good brief account of domestic policy advisers in the postwar years up to the creation of the Domestic Council, see Erwin C. Hargrove and Michael Nelson, *Presidents, Politics, and Policy* (New York: Knopf, 1984), pp. 176-181. Califano and his tiny staff, whom I observed during my tenure at the Office of Economic Opportunity, were at times extremely powerful when Johnson disengaged from domestic policy as Vietnam became a major war. Domestic policy cabinet secretaries waited outside Califano's office for an appointment. But it was an individual filling of a power vacuum. Much more can be gleaned from the Nixon and Carter operations in terms of structural and staffing concerns.

2. A summary of the two surveys is presented in K. E. Marvin and A. M. Rouse, "The Status of PPB in Federal Agencies: A Comparative Perspective," in *The Analysis and Evaluation of Public Expenditures: The PPB System* (Washington, D.C.: Joint Economic Committee, U.S. Congress, 1969), vol. 3, pp. 803-817 (the quote above is on page 814); and Edwin L. Harper, Fred A. Kramer, and Andrew M. Rouse, "Implementation and Use of PPB in Sixteen Federal Agencies," *Public Administration Review* (November/December 1969):623-632.

3. For a discussion of the manpower program delegation, see Walter Williams, *Social Policy Research and Analysis: The Experience in the Federal Social Agencies* (New York: Elsevier, 1971), pp. 36-52.

4. William Gorham, "Getting into the Action," *Policy Sciences* 1 (1970):170.

5. Joon Chien Doh, *The Planning-Programming-Budgeting System in Three Federal Agencies* (New York: Praeger, 1971), p. 114.

6. See Robert H. Nelson, "The Office of Policy Analysis in the Department of the Interior," *Journal of Policy Analysis and Management* (Summer 1989):395-410, especially pp. 397-399.

7. Doh, *The Planning-Programming-Budgeting System in Three Federal Agencies*, pp. 119-121. The National Aeronautics and Space Agency (not a success) was the third agency.

8. Arnold J. Meltsner, *Policy Analysts in Bureaucracy* (Berkeley: University of California Press, 1976), p. 220.

9. Raymond J. Waldmann, "The Domestic Council: Innovation in Presidential Government," *Public Administration Review* (May/June 1976):266.

10. Thomas E. Cronin, *The State of the Presidency* (Boston: Little, Brown & Co., 1976), p. 127.

11. Ibid., p. 89.

12. Hugh Heclo, "OMB and the Presidency—the Problems of 'Neutral Competence,'" *Public Interest* (Winter 1976):89.

13. *The Executive Presidency: Federal Management for the 1990s*, A Report by an Academy Panel for the 1988-89 Presidential Transition (Washington, D.C.: National Academy of Public Administration, September 1988), p. 38.

14. Heclo, "OMB and the Presidency," p. 89.

15. *Watergate: Its Implications for Responsible Government* (Washington, D.C.: National Academy of Public Administration, March 1974), p. 43.

16. Alexander L. George, "The Case for Multiple Advocacy in Making Foreign Policy," *American Political Science Review* (September 1972):753. See also I. M. Destler, *Presidents, Bureaucrats and Foreign Policy: The Politics of Organizational Reform* (Princeton, N.J.: Princeton University Press, 1972), p. 126.

17. Roger Porter, *Presidential Decision Making: The Economic Policy Board* (New York: Cambridge University Press, 1980), p. 45.

18. Ibid., pp. 185–186.

19. Alexander L. George, *Presidential Decisionmaking in Foreign Policy: The Effective Use of Information and Advice* (Boulder, Colo.: Westview Press, 1980), p. 170.

20. For a good brief case against multiple advocacy, see Paul C. Light, *The President's Agenda: Domestic Policy Choice from Kennedy to Carter* (Baltimore: Johns Hopkins University Press, 1982), pp. 199–201.

21. Porter, *Presidential Decision Making*, p. 198.

22. Ibid., p. 201.

23. Ibid., p. 173.

24. Erwin Hargrove, *Jimmy Carter as President: Leadership and the Politics of the Public Good* (Baton Rouge: Louisiana State University Press, 1988). Hargrove offers a much more positive view of Carter, but he found Carter weakest in domestic policy. See also Light, *The President's Agenda*; and Colin Campbell, *Governments under Stress: Political Executives and Key Bureaucrats in Washington, London, and Ottawa* (Toronto: Toronto University Press, 1983).

25. Betty Glad, *Jimmy Carter: In Search of the Great White House* (New York: Norton, 1980), p. 476.

26. Laurence E. Lynn, Jr., and David de F. Whitman, *The President as Policymaker: Jimmy Carter and Welfare Reform* (Philadelphia: Temple University Press, 1981), pp. 272–273. Joseph Califano wrote: "Carter was bent on mastering every detail. . . . [H]e was, as an HEW staffer remarked after one of my welfare reform briefings, the highest paid assistant secretary for planning that ever put a reform proposal together." Joseph A. Califano, Jr., *Governing America* (New York: Simon and Schuster, 1981), pp. 402–403. While Califano is hardly a neutral observer, he writes what others kept telling me privately.

27. Carter's intelligence is a recurrent theme. Haynes Johnson, *In the Absence of Power: Governing America* (New York: Viking, 1980), pp. 218 and 256; and Glad, *Jimmy Carter*, p. 500.

28. Erwin C. Hargrove, "The Uses and Limits of Skill in Presidential Leadership: The Case of Jimmy Carter," a paper prepared for the International Society of Political Psychology, Toronto, Canada, June 1984, p. 6.

29. Peri E. Arnold, *Making the Managerial Presidency: Comprehensive Reorganization Planning 1905–1980* (Princeton, N.J.: Princeton University Press, 1986), p. 336.

30. Quoted in Joel Havemann, "The Cabinet Band—Trying to Follow Carter's Baton," *National Journal*, July 16, 1977, p. 1108.

31. For a discussion of CPRS, see Walter Williams, *Washington, Westminster and Whitehall* (New York: Cambridge University Press, 1988), pp. 72–76, 161–162.

32. Light, "White House Domestic Policy Staff Plays an Important Role in Formulating Legislation"; and Dom Bonafede, "Stuart Eizenstat—Carter's Right-Hand Man," *National Journal*, June 9, 1979. These articles offer extended descriptions of DPS operations including sketches of individual staff members.

33. Ben W. Heineman, Jr., and Curtis A. Hessler, *Memorandum for the President* (New York: Random House, 1980), p. 208, emphasis added. Also see Campbell, *Governments under Stress*, pp. 32 and 123.

34. Giandomenico Majone, *Evidence, Argument, and Persuasion in the Policy Process* (New Haven, Conn.: Yale University Press, 1989), p. 19.

35. Peter J. May, "Policy Analysis: Past, Present, and Future," a paper presented

at the 1988 annual meetings of the American Political Science Association, Washington, D.C., September 1-4, 1988.

36. See Peter J. May, "Politics and Policy Analysis," *Political Science Quarterly* (Spring 1986):109-125.

37. Henry J. Aaron, "Politics and the Professors Revisited," *American Economic Review* (May 1989):13.

38. Robert W. Komer, *Bureaucracy at War: U.S. Performance in the Vietnam Conflict* (Boulder, Colo.: Westview Press, 1986), p. 165.

39. Alain C. Enthoven and D. Wayne Smith, *How Much Is Enough?* (New York: Harper Colophon Books, 1971), p. 307.

CHAPTER 4. THE REAGAN ERA: FIRST TERM

1. See Clifford Geertz, *The Interpretation of Cultures* (New York: Basic Books, 1973), especially the chapter entitled "Ideology as a Cultural System" pp. 193-233; and Fred I. Greenstein, "Reagan and the Lore of the Modern Presidency: What Have We Learned?" in Fred I. Greenstein (ed.), *The Reagan Presidency: An Early Assessment* (Baltimore: Johns Hopkins University Press, 1983), pp. 171-172.

2. This type of polling began during the Roosevelt years but no approval poll was conducted within a year of FDR's death in 1945. The approval and rating information are drawn from a *New York Times*/CBS poll of 1,533 adults conducted January 12–15, 1989 and a *Washington Post* poll of 1,006 adults conducted during January 11-15. See *New York Times*, January 18, 1989 and *Washington Post National Weekly Edition*, January 23-29, 1989.

3. Such domination did not shield Reagan against significant fluctuations in his approval ratings. For example, he fell from a 1981 high of 68 percent in early May after he recovered from the assassination attempt and appeared before Congress on April 28 to a low of 41 percent approval in mid-1982 during the worst postwar recession. See Greenstein, "Reagan and the Lore of the Modern Presidency: What Have We Learned?" pp. 174-176; and James Ceaser, "The Reagan Presidency and American Public Opinion," in Charles O. Jones (ed.), *The Reagan Legacy: Promises and Performance* (Chatham, N.J.: Chatham House, 1988). Ceaser provides a detailed account of the ups and downs of President Reagan's approval ratings in the period 1981-1987.

4. Ann Ruth Willner, *The Spellbinders: Charismatic Political Leadership* (New Haven, Conn.: Yale University Press, 1984), pp. 33-41.

5. Ibid., p. 39.

6. Ibid., p. 6.

7. *Seattle Times*, January 24, 1988.

8. Werner Stark, *The Sociology of Knowledge* (Boston: Routledge & Paul, 1958), p. 48.

9. David Calleo, *Beyond American Hegemony: The Future of the Western Alliance* (New York: Basic Books, 1987), pp. 219-220.

10. David A. Stockman, *The Triumph of Politics* (New York: Harper & Row, 1986), pp. 377 and 380, emphasis added.

11. Gary Wills, *Reagan's America: Innocents at Home* (New York: Doubleday, 1987), p. 386, my emphasis. *Reagan's America* is the best treatment of Reagan's lack of attachment to reality and his belief in a mythical America. Also, see Michael Rogin, *Ronald Reagan, the Movie and Other Episodes in Political Demonology* (Berkeley, Calif.: University of California Press, 1987), pp. 1-43.

12. Ann Reilly Dowd, "What Managers Can Learn from Manager Reagan," *Fortune*, September 15, 1986, p. 38.

13. See Stockman, *The Triumph of Politics*, pp. 229–235.

14. Wills, *Reagan's America*, p. 321.

15. Bert A. Rockman, "An Imprint but Not a Revolution," in B. B. Kymlicka and Jean V. Matthews (eds.), *The Reagan Revolution?* (Chicago: Dorsey Press, 1988), p. 203.

16. Martin Anderson, *Revolution* (San Diego: Harcourt Brace Jovanovich, 1988), pp. 288–289.

17. Ibid., p. 290.

18. Eleanor Chelimsky, "Budget Cuts, Data and Evaluation," *Society* (March/April 1985):73.

19. "Program Evaluation Issues," *Transition Series* (Washington, D.C.: General Accounting Office, GAO/OCG-89-8TR, November 1988), pp. 1 and 7.

20. *New York Times*, October 30, 1989. All quotes and data in this paragraph are from this article.

21. The data in these paragraphs are from *R & D Funding: The Department of Education in Perspective* (Washington, D.C.: General Accounting Office, GAO/PEMD-88-18FS, May 1988), pp. 6 and 10.

22. All data and the quote are from "Program Evaluation Issues," pp. 9–11.

23. Ibid., p. 8.

24. *Education Information: Changes in Funds and Priorities Have Affected Production and Quality* (Washington, D.C.: General Accounting Office, GAO/PEMD-88-4, November 1987), pp. 21 and 76.

25. Ibid., p. 30.

26. *HCFA Research: Agency Practices and Other Factors Threaten Quality of Mandated Studies* (Washington, D.C.: General Accounting Office, GAO/PEMD-88-9, June 1988), pp. 74–76.

27. *Weapons Testing: Quality of DOD Operational Testing and Reporting* (Washington, D.C.: General Accounting Office, GAO/PEMD-88-32BR, July 1988), p. 1.

28. Ibid., pp. 17, 19, 22, and 31.

29. Ibid., p. 31.

30. Peter May, "Policy Analysis: Past, Present and Future," a paper presented at the 1988 meeting of the American Political Science Association, Washington, D.C., September 1–4, 1988, pp. 8 and 10.

31. James L. Sundquist, "But the System Still Won," in Lester M. Salamon and Michael S. Lund (eds.), *The Reagan Presidency and the Governing of America* (Washington, D.C.: Urban Institute Press, 1984), p. 295.

32. Chester A. Newland, "The Reagan Presidency: Limited Government and Political Administration," *Public Administration Review* (January/February 1983):5.

33. Joseph G. Peschek, *Policy Planning Organizations: Elite Agendas and America's Rightward Movement* (Philadelphia: Temple University Press, 1987), p. 158.; and Charles H. Heatherly (ed.), *Mandate for Leadership: Policy Management in a Conservative Administration* (Washington, D.C.: Heritage Foundation), 1981.

34. Dick Kirschten, "Reagan's Cabinet Councils May Have Less Influence Than Meets the Eye," *National Journal*, November 28, 1981, p. 1246.

35. Dick Kirschten, "His NSC Days May Be Numbered but Allen Is One for Bouncing Back," *National Journal*, November 28, 1981, p. 2115.

36. Ronald Brownstein and Dick Kirschten, "Cabinet Power," *National Journal*, June 28, 1986, p. 1589.

37. Hedrick Smith, *The Power Game: How Washington Works* (New York: Random House, 1988), p. 312.

38. Lou Cannon, *Reagan* (New York: Putnam, 1982), p. 381.

39. Janet Mayer and Doyle McManus, *Landslide: The Unmaking of the President 1984-1988* (Boston: Houghton Mifflin, 1988), p. 324.

40. See Richard P. Nathan, *The Administrative Presidency* (New York: John Wiley & Sons, 1983).

41. Quoted in Smith, *The Power Game,* pp. 302-303.

42. Chester A. Newland, "Executive Office Policy Apparatus: Enforcing the Reagan Agenda," in Salamon and Lund, *The Reagan Presidency and the Governing of America*, p. 153. For a more extended treatment of the cabinet councils, see ibid., pp. 153-161. For the positive view of the Reagan staff person most associated with the council concept, see Anderson, *Revolution*, pp. 228-229. A more neutral presentation of the councils is presented in Peter M. Benda and Charles H. Levine, "Reagan and the Bureaucracy: The Bequest, the Promise, and the Legacy," in Jones, *The Reagan Legacy*, pp. 108-112.

43. Stockman, *The Triumph of Politics*, p. 1.

44. Ibid., p. 99.

45. Hugh Heclo, "Executive Budget Making," in Gregory B. Mills and John L. Palmer (eds.), *Federal Budget Policy in the 1980s* (Washington, D.C.: Urban Institute Press, 1984), p. 263.

46. Stockman, *The Triumph of Politics*, p. 83.

47. Ibid., pp. 80 and 91.

48. Ibid., pp. 108-109, 173, and 353.

49. Heclo, "Executive Budget Making," p. 279.

50. Stockman, *The Triumph of Politics*, p. 341, emphasis added.

51. Ibid., p. 37.

52. Ibid., p. 91.

53. I am much oversimplifying since the legislation will not go into effect until the start of a new fiscal year, and whether funds in that year will decline depends on funds in the pipeline. But such issues need not concern us here.

54. Anderson, *Revolution*, p. 227; Stephen Hess, *Organizing the Presidency*, 2d ed. (Washington, D.C.: Brookings, 1988), p. 154.

55. See Smith, *The Power Game*, p. 305; and Michael Rogin, *Ronald Reagan, the Movie and Other Episodes in Political Demonology* (Berkeley: University of California Press, 1987), pp. 1-43.

56. Bob Woodward, *Veil: The Secret Wars of the CIA 1981-1987* (New York: Simon and Schuster, 1987), p. 336. Also see Mayer and McManus, *Landslide*, p. 32.

57. See Alexander L. George, "The Case for Multiple Advocacy in Making Foreign Policy," *American Political Science Review* (September 1972):751-785; and I. M. Destler, *Presidents, Bureaucrats and Foreign Policy: The Politics of Organizational Reform* (Princeton, N.J.: Princeton University Press, 1972).

58. Ann Reilly Dowd, "What Managers Can Learn from Manager Reagan," *Fortune*, September 15, 1986, p. 33.

59. Terrel H. Bell, *The Thirteenth Man: A Reagan Cabinet Memoir* (New York: Free Press, 1988). One insider told me Bell's book is to be read with caution since he was not the hero he portrays, especially in standing up to David Stockman, but this aspect of *The Thirteenth Man* is not important to the account that follows.

60. See ibid., pp. 39 and 52-56.

61. Quoted in Bell, *The Thirteenth Man*, pp. 123-124.

62. Ibid., pp. 158-159 and 161.

CHAPTER 5. THE REAGAN LEGACY

1. For a good summary, see the "Executive Summary," *Report of the Congressional Committees Investigating the Iran-contra Affair with Supplemental, Minority, and Additional Views* (Washington, D.C.: Government Printing Office, 1987), pp. 3–22 (hereafter cited as *Report*). The best popular treatment is found in Jane Mayer and Doyle McManus, *Landslide* (Boston: Houghton Mifflin, 1988).

2. James W. Ceaser, "The Reagan Presidency and American Public Opinion," in Charles O. Jones (ed.), *The Reagan Legacy: Promise and Performance* (Chatham, N.J.: Chatham House, 1988), pp. 197–198.

3. Quoted in Mayer and McManus, *Landslide*, p. 315.

4. *New York Times*, January 12, 1987.

5. Mayer and McManus, *Landslide*, pp. 173–175.

6. *Report*, p. 13.

7. Hedrick Smith, *The Power Game: How Washington Works* (New York: Random House, 1988), p. 326.

8. Donald T. Regan, *For the Record: From Wall Street to Washington* (San Diego: Harcourt Brace Jovanovich, 1988), p. 285.

9. A 33 percent rate applies to a portion of income, but that rate need not concern us here.

10. Smith, *The Power Game,* pp. 498 and 507.

11. *The Executive Presidency: Federal Management for the 1990s,* A Report by an Academy Panel for the 1988–89 Presidential Transition (Washington, D.C.: National Academy of Public Administration, September 1988), p. 38, italics in the original.

12. Chester A. Newland, "Executive Office Policy Apparatus: Enforcing the Reagan Agenda," in Salamon and Lund, *The Reagan Presidency and the Governing of America*, p. 167.

13. Bruce E. Johnson, "From Analyst to Negotiator: The OMB's New Role," *Journal of Policy Analysis and Management* 3, 4 (1984):512.

14. Lawrence J. Haas, "What OMB Hath Wrought," *National Journal*, September 3, 1988, p. 2191.

15. Ibid.

16. Ibid.

17. Frank Fischer, "Policy Expertise and the 'New Class': A Critique of the Neoconservative Thesis," in Frank Fischer and John Forester (eds.), *Confronting Values in Policy Analysis* (Beverly Hills, Calif.: Sage Publications, 1987), pp. 116, 119, emphasis in the original.

18. See Fischer and Forester, *Confronting Values in Policy Analysis.*

19. Quoted in *Presidential Management of Rulemaking in Regulatory Agencies*, Report by a Panel of the National Academy of Public Administration (Washington, D.C.: National Academy of Public Administration, 1987), p. 26.

20. Ibid., p. 37.

21. Ibid., p. 38.

22. See Eugene Bardach and Robert A. Kagan, *Going by the Book: The Problem of Regulatory Unreasonableness* (Philadelphia: Temple University Press, 1982).

23. "Surviving at the EPA: Gary Dietrich," Kennedy School of Government Case Program, C16-84-592 (Cambridge, Mass.: Kennedy School of Government, 1984), p. 2.

24. Ibid., p. 6.

25. *The Executive Presidency: Federal Management for the 1990s*, p. 38.

26. Benda and Levine report others have reached similar conclusions: "In the view

of some long-term observers of the agency, [the marked increase in the numbers and influence of political appointees at the expense of the career staff] has seriously compromised OMB's reputation for political neutrality and its institutional capacity." Peter M. Benda and Charles H. Levine, "Reagan and the Bureaucracy: The Bequest, the Promise, and the Legacy," in Jones, *The Reagan Legacy*, p. 138.

27. David Mervin, "The Competence of Ronald Reagan," *Parliamentary Affairs,* (April 1987):216.

28. Terry M. Moe, "The Political Presidency," in Chubb and Peterson, *New Directions in American Politics*, p. 271.

29. Ibid., p. 268.

30. *New York Times*, December 15, 1989.

31. *New York Times*, December 4, 1989. The data in the rest of this paragraph are taken from this article.

32. Quoted in *Seattle Times*, December 2, 1989.

33. Ibid.

34. Mark L. Goldstein, "Hollow Government," *Government Executive* (October 1989):16.

35. Ibid., pp. 16–17.

36. *New York Times*, November 6, 1989.

37. The account of the S&L scandal relies heavily on Paul Zane Pilzer with Robert Deitz, *Other People's Money: The Inside Story of the S&L Mess* (New York: Simon and Schuster, 1989), pp. 69–79 (the quote is from p. 73).

38. For example, Jim Wright, both as (Democrat) majority leader and as Speaker of the House, was particularly active. See ibid., pp. 192–199.

39. Ibid., pp. 77 and 151.

40. Ibid., p. 81.

41. Benda and Levine, "Reagan and the Bureaucracy," pp. 138–139.

42. For early highly critical assessments of the Reagan administration see Dick Kirschten, "Inferior Departments," *National Journal*, June 27, 1981, p. 1170; Walter Williams, "Reagan and the Machinery of Government Issue: The First Six Months," Institute for Public Policy and Management, Public Policy Paper No. 14, August 1981; Walter Williams, "Reagan: The First Two Years," Institute for Public Policy and Management, Public Policy Paper No. 18, January 1983; and Murray Comarow, "The War on Civil Servants," *Bureaucrat* (Winter 1981–1982):8–9.

43. *Seattle Post-Intelligencer*, September 12, 1982.

CHAPTER 6. PRESIDENTIAL ROLE,
STYLE, AND COMPETENCE

1. Quoted in Walter Isaacson and Evan Thomas, *The Wise Men: Six Friends and the World They Made* (New York: Simon and Schuster, 1986), p. 740.

2. Ibid., pp. 736 and 739–740.

3. Ibid., p. 727.

4. Stephen Hess, *Organizing the Presidency*, 2d ed. (Washington, D.C.: Brookings, 1988); Peri E. Arnold, *Making the Managerial Presidency: Comprehensive Reorganization Planning 1905–1980* (Princeton, N.J.: Princeton University Press, 1986), p. 364.

5. Bert A. Rockman, "The Style and Organization of the Reagan Presidency," in Charles O. Jones (ed.), *The Reagan Legacy: Promise and Performance* (Chatham, N.J.: Chatham House, 1988), p. 28.

6. See Kellerman, who uses such terms as "interpersonal competence" and "political intellect." Barbara Kellerman, *The Political Presidency* (New York: Oxford University Press, 1978), pp. 42 and 159.

7. Bernard Asbell, *The Senate Nobody Knows* (New York: Doubleday, 1978), p. 452.

8. Stephen E. Ambrose, *Eisenhower: The President* (New York: Simon and Schuster, 1984), p. 627. For the recent historiography on Eisenhower, see ibid. (Ambrose gives the most complete treatment); Fred I. Greenstein, *The Hidden-Hand Presidency: Eisenhower as Leader* (New York: Basic Books, 1982); and Robert A. Divine, *Eisenhower and the Cold War* (New York: Oxford University Press, 1981). For a brief but useful critique of the Eisenhower literature starting with the early books that derided his presidency, see Anthony James Joes, "Eisenhower Revisionism: The Tide Comes In," *Presidential Studies Quarterly* (Summer 1985):561-571. As Joes writes, "The contrast between the Childs [1958]-Hughes [1963] view of Eisenhower . . . and that of Greenstein and Divine . . . is so arresting as to amount not to a revision of the former by the latter but to its repudiation." Ibid., p. 569.

9. Ambrose, *Eisenhower*, p. 20.

10. Henderson is particularly good on this point. See Philip G. Henderson, *Managing the Presidency: The Eisenhower Legacy—From Kennedy to Reagan* (Boulder, Colo: Westview Press, 1988), pp. 21-23.

11. Robert A. Divine, *Eisenhower and the Cold War* (New York: Oxford University Press, 1981), p. 154, my emphasis.

12. Gary Wills, *The Kennedy Imprisonment* (New York: Atlantic–Little, Brown, 1981), pp. 167 and 170.

13. Hugh Heclo, *A Government of Strangers* (Washington, D.C.: Brookings, 1977), pp. 191-194 and 215-217.

14. Erwin Hargrove and Michael Nelson, *Presidents, Politics, and Policy* (New York: Knopf, 1984), p. 76. Of the five modern presidents from Roosevelt through Nixon (Carter and Reagan are not rated because not enough time has passed), Johnson and Nixon are adjudged failures. Roosevelt is also a success, another "president of achievement."

15. Quoted in Philip G. Henderson, "Advice and Decision: The Eisenhower National Security Council Reappraised," in R. Gordon Hoxie and others, *The Presidency and National Security Policy* (New York: Center for the Study of the Presidency, 1984), p. 162. The Eisenhower statement was made in a 1967 Columbia Oral History Interview.

16. Greenstein, *The Hidden-Hand Presidency*, p. 247.

17. Thomas Brown, *JFK: History of an Image* (Bloomington: Indiana University Press, 1988), pp. 4-5 and 14.

18. Ibid., p. 45.

19. Quoted in *Washington Post National Weekly Edition*, January 16-22, 1989.

20. See Walter Williams, *Washington, Westminster and Whitehall* (New York: Cambridge University Press, 1988), p. 97.

CHAPTER 7. INSTITUTIONAL FIXES

1. Hart provides the best available summary and critique of the writings of the post-Watergate reformers and is drawn on heavily in this section. See particularly his chapter entitled "Post-Watergate Perspectives on the Presidential Staff," in John Hart, *The Presidential Branch* (Elmsford, N.Y.: Pergamon, 1987), pp. 176-213. *A*

CHAPTER 8. EFFECTIVE PRESIDENTIAL GOVERNANCE

1. *Washington Post National Weekly Edition,* April 3-9, 1989, and September 4-10, 1989.

2. *Economist,* March 11, 1989, p. 25.

3. The Ford presidency has not been considered other than in the discussion of the Economic Policy Board, mainly because so little has been written about it. For a useful, relatively brief account that suggests Ford's organizational skills, see R. Gordon Hoxie, "Staffing the Ford and Carter Presidencies," in Bradley D. Nash and others (eds.), *Organizing and Staffing the Presidency* (New York: Center for the Study of the Presidency, vol. 3, no. 1, 1980): pp. 44-55.

4. James MacGregor Burns, *The Power to Lead* (New York: Simon and Schuster, 1984), pp. 160-161.

5. See Michael Nelson (ed.), *The Elections of 1988* (Washington, D.C.: CQ Press, 1989), particularly Paul J. Quirk, "The Election," pp. 63-92, and Thomas E. Patterson, "The Press and Its Missed Assignment," pp. 93-109.

6. Neil Postman, *Amusing Ourselves to Death: Public Disclosure in the Age of Show Business* (New York: Viking, 1985), pp. 106-108.

7. Jack W. Germond and Jules Witcover, *Whose Broad Stripes and Bright Stars: The Trivial Pursuit of the Presidency 1988* (New York: Warner Books, 1989), pp. 413 and 458-460.

8. Patterson, "The Press and Its Missed Assignment," pp. 107-108.

9. Lewis W. Wolfson, *The Untapped Power of the Press: Explaining Government to the People* (New York: Praeger, 1985), pp. 28-29.

10. Austin Ranney, *Channels of Power: The Impact of Television on American Politics* (New York: Basic Books, 1983), p. 50.

11. Geoffrey Smith and Nelson W. Polsby, *British Government and its Discontents* (New York: Basic Books, 1981), p. 126.

12. Robert E. Denton, Jr., *The Primetime Presidency of Ronald Reagan: The Era of the Television Presidency* (New York: Praeger, 1988), pp. xii, 71, and 91.

13. Ibid., p. 70.

14. Patterson, "The Press and Its Missed Assignment," pp. 93-94.

15. The capacity statement refers to most of the nation's newspapers, the big three television networks, the popular news magazines and so on, not a few great newspapers and specialized publications such as the *National Journal.*

16. Jean Bathke Elshtain, "Issues and Themes in the 1988 Campaign," in Nelson, *The Elections of 1988,* p. 117.

17. Ibid., pp. 117-122.

18. Gaillard Hunt (ed.), *The Writings of James Madison* (New York: G. P. Putnam's Sons, 1910), vol. 9, p. 103.

List of Abbreviations

AEI	American Enterprise Institute
AIDS	acquired immune deficiency syndrome
BOB	Bureau of the Budget
CBA	cost-benefit analysis
CBO	Congressional Budget Office
CEA	Council of Economic Advisers
CPRS	Central Policy Review Staff
CRS	Congressional Research Service
DOD	Department of Defense
DOE	Department of Energy
DOT&E	Director of Operational Test and Evaluation
DPS	Domestic Policy Staff
ED	Department of Education
EOP	Executive Office of the President
EPA	Environmental Protection Agency
EPB	Economic Policy Board
FDA	Food and Drug Administration
FHA	Federal Housing Administration
GAO	General Accounting Office
GNP	gross national product
HCFA	Health Care Financing Administration
HEW	Health, Education, and Welfare
HHS	Health and Human Services
HUD	Housing and Urban Development
ICS	Institute for Contemporary Studies
NAPA	National Academy of Public Administration
NSC	National Security Council
OASPE	Office of the Assistant Secretary for Planning and Evaluation

OEO	Office of Economic Opportunity
OIRA	Office of Information and Regulatory Affairs
OMB	Office of Management and Budget
OPD	Office of Policy Development
OPEC	Organization of Petroleum Exporting Countries
OTA	Office of Technology Assessment
PPBS	Planning, Programming, Budgeting System
PR&E	Planning, Research, and Evaluation
R&D	research and development
RCRA	Resource Conservation and Recovery Act
RPP&E	Research, Plans, Programs, and Evaluation
S&L	savings and loan
SDI	Strategic Defense Initiative
SSA	Social Security Administration

Index